Chasing the Dream

Chasing the Dream

A Mid-life Quest for Fame and Fortune
on the Pro Golf Circuit

HARRY HURT III

AVON BOOKS  NEW YORK

AVON BOOKS
A division of
The Hearst Corporation
1350 Avenue of the Americas
New York, New York 10019

Copyright © 1997 by Harry Hurt III
Interior design by Kellan Peck
Visit our website at **http://AvonBooks.com**
ISBN: 0-380-97307-3

Library of Congress Cataloging in Publication Data:
Hurt, Harry.
    Chasing the dream / by Harry Hurt III.
        p.   cm.
    1. Golf—United States.   I. Title
GV981.H87   1997   97-2386
796.352'0973—dc21   CIP

First Avon Books Printing: June 1997

AVON TRADEMARK REG. U.S. PAT. OFF. AND IN OTHER COUNTRIES, MARCA REGISTRADA, HECHO EN U.S.A.

Printed in the U.S.A.

FIRST EDITION

QPM   10   9   8   7   6   5   4   3   2   1

To my wife and my brother,
and my father, in memoriam

Contents

_____

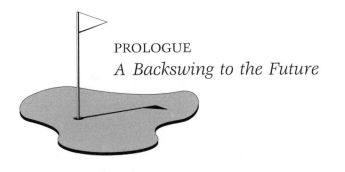

PROLOGUE

A Backswing to the Future

I really don't feel much different today from the way I felt when I was eighteen. All a guy needs to keep going in tournament golf is good health, the same ambition he had when he was younger, and maybe two or three putts that fall at the right time.

—LEE TREVINO, at age forty,
to Herbert Warren Wind

barcelona Neck cranes from the rich green fields at the far eastern end of Long Island where both America and American golf were born. The poet Walt Whitman once observed that Long Island resembles a whale with a bulbed nose diving toward Manhattan and a forked tail kicking out into the Atlantic Ocean. On the map as in metaphor, Barcelona Neck appears to be only a briny barnacle clinging to the inside edge of the lower tail fin that forms the island's south fork. But ever since the first white settlers arrived,

Barcelona Neck has been a site where storied conquests begin. The brownish, wind-battered bluffs that rim Barcelona Neck's ragged coastline along Peconic Bay inspired ship captains to name the place after the famous cliffside city on the Spanish Main. It was originally known, however, as Russell's Neck in honor of the family that staked claim to the land and adjacent waterways in the mid-1700s. Long before the nearby town of Sag Harbor grew to prominence as a capital of the whaling trade, one of the sheltered inlets overseen by the Russells served as the principal port for the local lumbering and agriculture industries, and as an escape route for Colonials fleeing to Connecticut during the Revolutionary War.

In the spring of 1995, Barcelona Neck provided me with a passageway of an entirely different epic order: it was the place where I took the first fateful backswings to the future that signaled my return to competitive golf after a layoff of over a quarter of a century.

Back in 1970, at the shortsighted age of eighteen, I had resigned my number-one spot on the Harvard golf team to become a muckraking journalist instead of a trap-raking PGA Tour rabbit, vowing never to set spikes on a country club again. I had made this dubious decision on the otherwise fine spring day when the golf coach informed me that The Country Club in Brookline, Massachusetts, would revoke our team's playing privileges unless I got a haircut. The very next day all the colleges at Harvard went on strike to protest the war in Vietnam, and all final exams, athletic schedules, and haircuts were cancelled.

At the shorthaired and farsighted age of forty-three, having played an average of less than eighteen holes per annum in the intervening twenty-five years, I resolved to commence an intensive training program and tournament schedule under the tutelage of some of the country's top teaching pros with the goal of making it all the way to the PGA Tour at long last. I was acting out a sports fantasy shared by every amateur from Peoria to Perth who has ever birdied two holes in a row. In the parlance of the PGA Tour wannabes who toil on mini-tours and minor league circuits across the country and around the globe, I was "chasing the dream."

For me, the dream in question involved much more than resuming a postponed athletic challenge. It meant embarking on a challenging new adventure of the spirit amid the doldrums of middle age. Along with recovering my scratch handicap and a portion of my lost youth, I hoped to advance the ball—literally and figuratively—far beyond where I had ever hit it before. I aimed to exploit the new technology and the old-fashioned wisdom that were not available to me as a kid to shoot lower scores on the golf course and to achieve higher goals off the course. I was launching a quest to become not only a better player but also a better person.

I realized that the odds were against having it both ways. There was no guarantee that becoming a better player would make me become a better person or vice versa. In fact, there was a considerable risk of overloading my bag with too many pyschic clubs. But I was ready to take my shots and let them fall where they may. I did not expect to hook and slice myself into a mystic bliss. Nor did I view golf as a metaphor for life, or life as a metaphor for golf. I could only be certain that by making golf a part of my life again, life would inevitably become a part of my golf. As Percy Boomer, the British-born teaching pro's teaching pro of the first half of the century, used to say, "If you wish to hide your character, do not play golf."

Fortunately, Lee Trevino had articulated the practical method in this midlife madness. While age takes its toll on every athlete, it seems to matter much less in golf than in other major sports. The prime of a world-class tennis player seldom lasts beyond his thirtieth year. Most professional football, baseball, and basketball players burn out or suffer career-ending injuries before reaching even that modest milestone. But unlike more physically demanding and potentially debilitating sports, golf puts a far greater premium on mental discipline and experience than on exceptional speed or strength: your head and your heart count more than your biceps and triceps.

In fact, as Sam Snead once noted, for many players *Golf Begins at Forty*. Although Bobby Jones retired from competitive golf after winning the Grand Slam at age twenty-eight, Snead, Trevino, Julius Boros, Ben Hogan, Walter Hagen, Gene Sarazen, and Harry Vardon all won important championships in their forties. Jack Nicklaus won his sixth Masters in 1986 at age forty-six. Hale Irwin won his third U.S. Open in 1990 at age forty-five. Tom Kite won his first major, the 1992 U.S. Open, at age forty-two. Earlier in 1995, my former Texas junior golfing buddy, Ben Crenshaw, had won his second Masters at age forty-three.

Thanks to the advent of the Senior PGA Tour for players fifty and over, golf has become the only major sport a professional athlete can play into his golden years with the prospect of enjoying greater public recognition—and collecting more prize money—than he could have hoped for in his younger days. The Senior circuit was originally formed back in 1980 as a kind of frolicking sideshow featuring the sport's aging legends. But steady increases in the pot have now made it an almost irresistibly attractive alternative to retirement for veteran PGA Tour pros and a fantasized happy hunting ground for top amateurs. In 1995, the total prize money offered on the Senior Tour was in excess of $43 million, and there were five men who won over $1 million for the year.

Even so, the regular PGA Tour is still the true font of golfing fame and fortune. In 1995, the Tour offered over $73 million in official prize money, and a record nine players won over $1 million for the year. Several of the famous names on the Tour scored almost as much—and in some cases, even more—unofficial prize money in celebrity invitational events during the so-called Silly Season, following the end of the Tour schedule. U.S. Open champion Corey Pavin, for example, won $1.4 million in official prize money in 1995 but took home that much again in the postseason, most of it from a single $1 million tournament victory at Sun City, South Africa. Endorsement contracts with equipment makers, clothing manufacturers, and other commercial sponsors boosted the total collective 1995 incomes of PGA Tour regulars by tens of millions of dollars more.

The strategy I devised to get myself in on all this high-profile, highly profitable PGA action occurred to me in a kind of brainstorm inspired by the exposure I'd had to competitive golf as a kid. There were many reasons why I had quit the game, and two of the most prominent were named Ben Crenshaw and Bruce Lietzke. But the reasons why I decided to make a comeback—and the way I decided to go about it—were inextricably related to the reasons why I had originally taken up golf as a slow-footed, nearsighted ten-year-old in Houston, Texas.

Many golfers claim to have been drawn to the royal and ancient game because of its noble history and traditions, or the code of honor inherent in the rules. In my case, golf happened to be the only sport for which I was physically suited, and the main attraction was sensual. I loved the meaty smell of leather grips, the tartness of pine needles, the sweetness of freshly cut grass. I loved feeling the sun and wind burn my face, and hearing my spikes crunch the earth. Most of all, I loved the incredible, ineffable feeling of catching a ball smack in the middle of the clubface and the wondrous thrill of putting the once-stationary white orb into gravity-defying flight. As I found out later, golf was certainly not the same as sex. But in its purest form, as a solitary orgy of ball striking, golf was and would always remain more fun than anything else I did with my clothes on.

It mattered little that most of my contemporaries considered golf to be decidedly uncool compared to surfing, sailing, softball, or tennis. I followed my own instincts, and I seldom lacked companionship. Although I had been born and reared on what was supposed to be the right side of the tracks in Houston, I did not play there exclusively. I took lessons at River Oaks Country Club, where my parents were members, but I risked my spending allowance in money matches at nonexclusive public and semiprivate courses all over town, often against older kids who could and would pound me into a sand trap if I tried to welch on a bet.

Starting at the age of eleven, I spent my summers competing on the Texas junior golf circuit, the same high-powered spawning ground that produced Crenshaw, Lietzke, and Tom Kite. Although I always seemed to collapse like a castrated calf when I teed it up in the annual state junior championships, I won over twenty local and regional titles, including a citywide tournament for thirteen-to-fifteen-year-olds that I snuck into as a twelve-year-old after the head pro at River Oaks allowed that this was one instance in which it would be okay to lie about my age.

Then my parents got caught up in a variation of the "great expectations" syndrome. It wasn't that they started pushing me to excel in the hateful, moneygrubbing manner of some tennis parents. Just the opposite. Although Mom and Dad were duly proud of my accomplishments, they actively discouraged me from pursuing a professional golf career. My old man was afraid I was going to become what he called a "country club bum." My mother believed that I was too smart to become a golf pro. In the hope of broadening my horizons beyond the eighteenth hole at the family country club, she sent me off to the Choate School in Wallingford, Connecticut, at age thirteen.

My golf game then commenced a four-year-long slide from which it never fully recovered. Choate had a fairly decent team, and I lettered all four years. I was also the captain and the number-

one player in both my junior and senior years. But it wasn't the
same as going to school down in Texas. I had to put away my clubs
every September and hit the books until mid-March, when golf season began again. As a result, I kept losing about half a stroke per
semester to the kids who could play all year long.

I would never forget coming back to play in a Gulf Coast PGA-
sponsored regional junior tournament during the summer when I
was fourteen. I shot a 73 in the first round and thought I was pretty
hot stuff. When I looked at the scoreboard, however, I found that
I was only tied for the lead. I then shot three more rounds under
80. That put me thirteen strokes ahead of the closest player behind
me. Problem was, there was this one player ahead of me whom I'd
never heard of before. He was a tall skinny kid from Beaumont
who hit drives that seemed to roll forever. His name was Bruce
Lietzke, and he beat me by eight strokes.

Ben Crenshaw was even more amazing back then, a better all-
around player in many ways than in his current incarnation as a
PGA Tour pro and two-time Masters champion. Crenshaw won the
Texas state junior at the age of fifteen, beating the pants off a bunch
of big bad seventeen-year-olds who were twice his size. When we
all turned sixteen, most of us were expecting Ben to defend his
title, but he decided to play in a National Junior Chamber of Com-
merce tournament being held the same week in another state.
Bruce Lietzke won the Texas state junior that year while Ben was
off winning the Jaycees tournament. But the following year, Ben
came back and won a second Texas state junior championship.

The first time I ever played head-to-head with Ben Crenshaw
was in a practice round for a tournament at Houston Country Club
when we were seventeen. It so happened that I held the junior
club record of 70, which was two under par on a tricked-up track
that measured over 7,000 yards long. Ben had never even seen the
Houston Country Club course before, and he shot a 68. Everybody
used to talk about what a great putter Ben Crenshaw was and how
he had been taught the fundamentals at an early age by the late
great Harvey Penick. But a lot of it was just Ben's natural talent. I
remember standing there and watching the way he would swing
every club in the bag, saying to myself over and over, "Oh, so that's
how you're supposed to do it."

Despite my discouraging encounters with Crenshaw and
Lietzke, I tried to rehabilitate my golf game after graduating from
prep school. In the summer of 1969, I took a cross-country road

trip to play in a series of national-class amateur tournaments. My travel mate was a friend from the junior golf circuit named Bobby Walzel. Bobby, who was two years older, had been attending the University of Houston, then the nation's leading golf college and the former or future alma mater of such PGA stars as Phil Rogers, John Mahaffey, Fred Couples, and Steve Elkington.

While half a million nongolfing members of our generation were attending the Woodstock rock festival in upstate New York, Bobby and I drove all the way from Houston to Niagara Falls to play in the Porter Cup, the nation's most prestigious nonprofessional tournament save for the U.S. Amateur. Bobby had an exemption into the tournament because of his University of Houston golf team credentials, but I had to go through the thirty-six-hole qualifying. I surprised everybody by shooting a pretty slick 74-72, and nabbed the next-to-last available qualifier spot.

The Porter Cup simultaneously marked the zenith and the nadir of my golfing career. Back then there was no such thing as the Hogan Tour or the Nike Tour. The amateur circuit was basically the only place where you could tune up before you tried to make the PGA Tour. After the Porter Cup qualifying rounds, Bobby and a couple of other guys took me under their wings and tried to tutor me in the finer arts of big-time competitive play. I got tips on everything from trying to work the ball off the tee to missing away from sand traps and water hazards and getting extra backspin on my sand wedge. By the time the regular tournament rounds started, I was so dizzy with swing thoughts I couldn't break 80 anymore.

All those lessons eventually did sink in, after the fact. When I teed it up on the freshman team at Harvard the following spring, I averaged 73 in matches under very wet and messy course conditions. I was undefeated as the number-one man, and our team was undefeated, too. In those days, the NCAA wouldn't let freshmen play varsity sports, but just to prove that we were the best players in the school, the number-two man and I challenged the number-one and number-two varsity players to a match at The Country Club in Brookline, and gave them a good thrashing.

My run-in with the golf coach later that semester over getting a haircut to please the members of The Country Club was just the symbolic crowning blow in a long-running love-hate relationship with the country club culture in general. I had actually been thinking about quitting golf ever since the politicized summer of 1969, when I played in the Porter Cup. Although I hardly qualified as a member of an oppressed minority group, I had grown up playing with and against Mexicans, blacks, and a young lady named Mary Lou Dill, who won the U.S. Women's Amateur at age nineteen. The virulent racism, sexism, and elitism that seemed endemic to country clubs had had direct personal repercussions for my friends and me on more than a few occasions.

The decision to hang up my spikes, however, was ultimately based more on emotional and athletic considerations than political or social imperatives. Golf may be the hardest of all sports, given the dual demands it makes on mind and body. Michael Jordan, an avid amateur with a single-digit handicap, is arguably the world's greatest athlete, and yet he has collapsed more than once under the pressure of televised celebrity golf tournaments. Jack Nicklaus is inarguably the greatest professional golfer in history, with eighteen major championships to his credit. But like the lowliest duffer, even Nicklaus has been humbled by his share of double and triple bogeys, as witnessed by his debacle on the fourteenth hole at St. Andrews in the 1995 British Open.

"Golf . . . is the Great Mystery," P. G. Wodehouse observed in *The Heart of a Goof*. "Like some capricious goddess, it bestows its favors with what would appear an almost fat-headed lack of method and discrimination. . . . Men capable of governing empires fail to control a small white ball, which presents no difficulties whatever to others with one ounce more brain than a cuckoo-clock."

While I was never in danger of governing an empire, I considered golf an all-or-nothing proposition from a competitive point of view. Attending an Ivy League college posed the same predicament as prep school. I still had to quit every fall and try to pick up my game every spring while my buddies at the University of Texas and the University of Houston played year-round. Unlike Crenshaw and Lietzke, I might not have had the potential to become a Bobby Jones or a Jack Nicklaus. But I did not want to be a second-rate college player destined to become a second-rate pro for lack of proper competitive grooming and tournament experience.

Moreover, I had no patience for being a weekend golfer. For me, it was just no fun. I knew how well I could play, and if I didn't play well, it would infuriate me. I also knew that in order to maintain my standard of excellence, I needed to practice and play at least six days per week. Everyone does, including Michael Jordan and the great Jack Nicklaus. I could either spend my life on the course or off the course. There was no middle ground. I had taken up golf because of a naive love for the game. I could not keep at it unless I was able to give golf the constant attention and affection the game deserved. So I quit cold turkey.

Over the next two and a half decades, thanks partly to the aging of my fellow baby boomers, golf became the fastest growing sport on earth. The amateur population in the United States alone mushroomed from 17 million in 1985 to more than 25 million by 1995. The golf boom also democratized the game more effectively than any civil rights bill. Playing golf came to be considered way cool by almost every class of people from the guy at the Sag Harbor gas pump to celebrities such as Jack Nicholson, Bill Murray, Kevin Costner, Alice Cooper, and Hootie and the Blowfish.

In the event, I chose to return to golf not because it was cool or because everybody else in my generation seemed to be playing the game, but because I wanted to see if I could do it right the second time around. When I quit playing, woods were still made of wood and graphite was a No.2 pencil. At my best, I could shoot par consistently in tournament play, but I never reached the point of being able to break 70 except in practice rounds. Now there was an abundance of fancy, space age equipment designed to help golfers hit the ball farther and straighter than was ever possible before. And with the passage of years spanning these innovations, I had become older—and, I hoped, wiser as well.

Rather than merely turning back the clock, I wanted to see if I could raise my game to a whole new level. There had always been something special about the way Ben Crenshaw and Bruce Lietzke could play even when we were just teenagers. I could never put my finger on exactly what it was they had going for them. All I knew was they had it and I didn't. But my instincts told me that there just might be a chance to get a good firm Vardon grip on whatever it was that I had been lacking as a kid. If I could find that magical missing element, I could use it not only to lift my game but to fill the existential holes of middle age.

When it came time to formulate the specifics of my assault on the PGA Tour, I determined to go through the same basic steps any aspiring Tour pro must take to reach the big time. The process was roughly equivalent to starting at the Pony League level in baseball and working up through the A, AA, and AAA minor league professional ranks to the major leagues. First, I would resume my aborted career at the amateur tournament level. Then I would enter minitour and minor league professional tournaments of ever-increasing competitiveness from the Hooters Tour to the Nike Tour in preparation for the 252-hole torture test known as PGA Tour Qualifying School. If I failed in my first attempt at Q School, I would try to make the Tour by competing in the Monday qualifying rounds for selected PGA tournaments.

There was no way I could have predicted the excruciating twists and turns my golfing quest was destined to take any more than I could have predicted the course of my life from cradle to grave. Suffice it to say that the golf gods must have been watching over me. After starting like a flash, I plunged into the depths of despair as my golf game regressed along with my deteriorating physical and mental health. But just when it seemed all was lost, I managed to regroup with more than a little inspirational help from friends and loved ones. In the end, I was blessed with a hard won triumph that stunned all concerned, most especially me.

Out of convenience and nonincidental financial circumstances, I decided early on to make Barcelona Neck my home course, the place where I played my daily rounds and put my lessons into practice between road trips to compete in tournaments. My choice was inspired both in spite and because of the fact that Barcelona Neck seems at first glance to have almost nothing in common with such hallowed golfing enclaves as Augusta National, Pebble Beach, or any other PGA Tour stop.

The semimarshy land mass that forms the neck has the shape of a thin-billed seabird, encompassing some 340 acres hyphenated with a narrow spit that juts across the mouth of a little estuary called Northwest Creek. Most of the area is thickly forested with cedar, white pine, black pine, and oak. Blue jays, buntings, cardinals, chip mouses, finches, and sparrows nest in the branches. Deer, rabbits, squirrels, and battered golf balls proliferate in the underbrush. Offshore, the waters are rife with bluefish, cod, flounder, sea bass, scallops, and clams.

The treacherously seedy, Lyme tick–infested golf links at Barcelona Neck occupy less than 60 acres and offer only nine holes, the longest of which measures just 380 yards. The par is 70, but the course rating, a weighted projection of the average score an expert player might shoot under normal course and weather conditions, is a mere 65.9. The slope, a measurement of the relative difficulty of a course for nonexpert players, is a modest 105, several notches below the national average of 113 and barely a shadow of the top slope of 150. And yet, the unlikely layout I selected as the training camp for my comeback attempt boasts both a picaresque and surprisingly antique golfing pedigree.

Barcelona Neck is located within a short driving distance of several of the oldest and most famous golf courses in the country. Shinnecock Hills, which was opened for play around 1892 and has hosted three U.S. Opens, and the National Golf Links of America, designed by Charles Blair Macdonald, lies some fifteen miles to the west. The Maidstone Club, founded a year before Shinnecock, is about seven miles to the east. Also nearby are Montauk Downs, a Robert Trent Jones–designed track that ranks among the finest public courses in the nation; Atlantic Golf Club, a 1992-vintage course that rivals Shinnecock in length; Southampton Golf Club, which borders the eastern edge of Shinnecock's back nine; and Noyac Golf and Country Club, the most underrated and subtly challenging of the group.

Barcelona Neck survives as one of the last enclaves of blue-collar golf amid the silk-stocking citadels of eastern Long Island. Its origins trace to the founding of the Sag Harbor Golf Club in 1914 by a group of year-round local residents who lacked the income and social credentials for admission to the elite clubs formed by summer residents from the big cities. Over the next eight decades, while the white-shoed sons and daughters of the WASP artistocracy plied the well-manicured fairways of The Maidstone and Shinnecock, successive generations of plumbers, carpenters, bricklayers, barbers, and greenskeepers for the private golf courses did their hacking on the rough-and-tumble terra infirma at Barcelona Neck.

There are places like Barcelona Neck throughout the golfing kingdom, and they have existed for as long as the game itself. The exact origins of golf are lost in the mists of history, with various countries, clans, and cohort groups making foundational claims. But if the roots of the game as we know it trace to Scotland, so do two very distinct images of its provenance. One image is of a lazy, indulgent sport that provided royalty with a way to pass the time between feasts. The other—and probably more accurate—image depicts golf as one of the few recreations available to the working classes.

Like the modest little nine-hole track at Barcelona Neck, St. Andrews and other famous ancient golf courses were not laid out within castle walls but on waste areas. These so-called linkslands by the sea were marshy, uninhabitable places where sheep grazed amid howling winds and intermittent rains. The kind of people who knew the linkslands best were the folk who tended them, shepherds, fishermen, blacksmiths, coopers, and the like. Thanks to the light of the midnight sun during the summer months in Scotland, they could wander out from their homes after work and a home-cooked supper, and play for a good three to four hours, approximately the time it should take to complete a round of golf.

In America, courses that belong to the Barcelona Neck category are often referred to as "Goat Hill," a fictional name made famous by the writer Dan Jenkins in his bestselling golf novel *Dead Solid Perfect*. There is even a public course on Shelter Island, a short ferry ride from Sag Harbor, that literally goes by the name "Goat Hill." But Barcelona Neck, which until recently was distinguished by having some of the nation's last sand-surfaced putting greens, is different from all the other Goat Hills in charm and charter.

Thanks to an activist corps who kept it from being bulldozed out of existence, Barcelona Neck is a unique public-private hybrid. Although the entire property is presently owned by the State of New York as parkland, the Sag Harbor Golf Club is entrusted with the running and maintainance of the golf course on a year-to-year basis. The club itself is allowed to remain private, with membership by invitation only, but the links are open to anyone who can ante up a $10 daily green fee. Access to the surrounding three hundred acres of forests and beaches is open to the public without charge throughout the year.

I learned about how all this came to pass and about the related battle over Barcelona Neck that saved the links when I was invited to play in the 1995 Sag Harbor Golf Club member-guest tournament with a uniquely gifted partner. His given name is Tom Sabloski, but he is known to all his golfing buddies as Toad. And it was in partnership with Toad that my quest for the PGA Tour commenced with a sudden death shootout and an impromptu crash course in certain unwritten rules of etiquette, that reminded both of us that, as the writer John Updike once observed, "On the golf course as nowhere else, the tyranny of causality is suspended and life is like a dream."

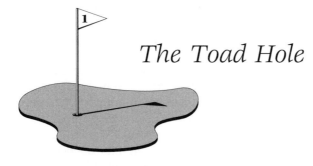

The Toad Hole

the saga of Hurt and Toad began early on the morning of June 3, 1995, less than three weeks prior to the centennial United States Open Championship at Shinnecock Hills, when I awoke to the sounds of a thundering, lightning downpour. Hailstones the size of Titleists were pounding on my roof. A gale-force wind was bowing the backyard trees like a long hitter bending low-torque graphite shafts. It was not easy, perhaps not even prudent, to get out of bed.

The annual Sag Harbor Golf Club member-guest tournament was scheduled to tee off with an 8:30 A.M. shotgun start. But I felt sure that the first competitive step in my golfing comeback would be canceled or at least postponed. The earsplitting electric bolts riffling across the sky posed a serious hazard to human life, as well as a worrisome distraction to anyone who might attempt to wield a metal-headed driver.

Just as I determined to seek refuge back underneath the covers, however, the storm suddenly broke, and the sun started to poke through the clouds. I realized that I'd better get my ass in rain gear and haul it over to Barcelona Neck or there would be hell to pay in the person of Toad, the member with whom I was partnered but had yet to meet.

I jumped into my Jeep and raced out of Sag Harbor on Highway 114, covering the 1.1 miles between my house and the entrance to Barcelona Neck in less than two minutes. Then I veered off on a deeply rutted asphalt trail lined with pine trees and dense underbrush. The sky clouded over again, and a steady drizzle descended on the windshield. I saw steam rising from the thickets on either side of the trail. A startled pheasant scurried for cover as I bounced past a yellow-lettered sign that read CAUTION GOLFERS AHEAD.

When I reached the clearing where the pavement crossed the fifth and fourth fairways, the clubhouse came into view behind an S-curve. It was a one-story, gray clapboard cottage topped with shingle roof, a tin chimney, and a five-pronged TV antenna. There were two sliding glass doors on the near side that opened onto a wraparound porch sheltered by a green-and-white awning. A fleet of battered old golf carts was parked next to the practice putting green, and upwards of fifty men with considerably fewer than fifty golf umbrellas were milling about in the drizzle.

I slid around the S-curve, bypassing a tree-shaded graveyard guarded by a double-railed white wooden fence. The graveyard held the remains of the Russell family, the property's original owners. There were sixteen tombstones ranging from a foursome of four-foot-high engraved stone tablets to an assemblage of crumbling rock markers. The oldest tablet, dated 1797, identified the tomb of the patriarch, David Russell. One could only wonder if old man Russell's role in helping his fellow settlers flee invading British Redcoats some two centuries before was what earned him this final resting place overlooking a golf course.

As I steered the Jeep into the parking lot on the far side of the clubhouse, I was almost blinded by the sight of Judge Paul Bailey, the Sag Harbor Golf Club's tournament director. Bailey was a tall, narrow-framed former state trooper turned attorney and arbitration panelist, but he was dressed up like a Tyrolean yodeler in a plumed alpine hat and a pair of chartreuse shorts suspended with rainbow-striped braces. His deep-set brown eyes were flashing like landing lights behind a pair of wire-rimmed aviator glasses as he hoisted a beer mug above his head to toast my arrival. He was the man who had been responsible for entering me in the tournament and pairing me with my member-partner Toad.

"About time you got here, bub," Bailey declared. "Toad was fixin' to bet me you weren't gonna show."

"No such luck," I muttered.

"I been tellin' everybody that you guys got a good chance of winnin' this thing," Bailey said, smiling conspiratorially. He raised his beer mug again and took a sip. "Good luck."

I stared back at him, wondering how he could handle a brew so early in the morning and whether I could handle the pressure of being the favorite.

"Thanks a lot, Judge," I said at last. "We're gonna need all the luck we can get."

I sat down on the tailgate of the Jeep and put on my spikes, scanning the porch to check out the competition. I recognized only a handful of players, most of them guys who played in the regular Saturday morning scrambles. There was Frankie the barber, a chain-smoking high-handicapper in his late forties, and Val, the volunteer fireman. They were huddled under an umbrella next to Whitey King, a snow-haired construction foreman dressed in denim overalls and work boots. Next to them was young Marshall Garypie III, the son of a former club champion and himself a low-handicapper, nattily attired in cream-colored shorts and blue Ashworth shirt.

Most of the other guys I knew were crowding under the awning. There was Jimmy Schiavoni, a plumber with forearms the size of sewer pipes and a heart bigger than Peconic Bay. There was Little John, also known as Cheech, a short and portly retiree afflicted with throat cancer who spoke with the aid of a voice box. There was Ace, a jug-eared jokester in his seventies who kept warning that he would one day shoot his age. And there was Jack Somers, a weather-beaten sixty-nine-year-old former baseball player who mowed the fairways and raked the traps at The Maidstone Club. In days gone by, he had earned the nickname Jack the Rat for his mastery of Barcelona Neck's long-since-grassed-over sand-surfaced greens.

Bailey hovered close by the Jeep until I had finished sorting through the fourteen clubs I was going to use, all of which were so old and obsolete they looked like they belonged on a plaque in an antique golf equipment museum. Then he led me around the front of the clubhouse to look for my partner.

I didn't dare ask how Toad got his nickname, and I didn't have to. We found him hunkering beneath the overhang beside the front door of the clubhouse in a characteristic frog crouch, chatting with a couple of buddies in a loud croaky voice. Balding, broad-shouldered, and olive-skinned, he was wearing cutoff jeans that revealed a pair of widely splayed legs, and a nylon knit shirt that barely concealed his pouchy belly. I'd been told that he was a few years on the far side of fifty, but in the greenish yellow glow of the porch light he alternately appeared to be older and younger than his actual age, as well as both more and less amphibian.

"Nice to meet ya, Mr. Hurt," he said, springing up to pump my hand. "But I gotta admit I was kinda worried when Bailey told me your last name."

"Why's that?" I asked.

Toad grinned. "I thought your first name might be Dick."

One of Toad's buddies rolled his eyes. Then he grabbed me by the arm and ushered me toward a beer keg stationed by the practice putting green.

"Name's Buck," he said. "We're playin' in the same foursome."

I watched Buck lean over the keg and draw a beer. He was a pink-cheeked fellow with the rough-hewn hands of a ditchdigger.

"We got three of these puppies this year," Buck informed me as he tapped the keg. "Better try all of 'em. You're gonna have a long day."

I allowed that coffee was more my style at this hour, though the beer was probably better for my swing tempo.

"Sorry, Harry," Toad called after us. "Gotta keep up my reputation. I'm the number-one ball buster in this club."

"Yup," Buck burped through his cup. "And he don't mean golf balls, neither."

Moments later, Bailey announced that it was time for all contestants to report to their starting holes. I fell in step behind Buck and Toad, who were towing their golf bags on pull carts. As we ambled toward our designated tee, I learned that my partner was a housepainter of Polish descent with a convoluted family history and a protracted bitter divorce on his hands. He claimed that he had briefly studied "real painting" under locally resident modern art master Willem de Kooning, only to be advised not to quit his day job. Along with hitting big drives, Toad prided in catching big fish. In fact, he was the newly crowned "Flounder King" of eastern Long Island, the winner of both first and second places in the previous month's Sag Harbor Flounder Derby. I also learned that he was still feeling the after effects of the night before.

"Some of the guys took your partner power-drinking at The Corner Bar," Buck confided, chuckling. "They wanted him to be nice and loose for this mornin'."

"Sheet," Toad retorted, spitting over his shoulder. "I play better with a hangover. Just wait."

İt did not take long for Toad to prove himself. Our foursome had drawn the double-edged lot of starting on number six, a 315-yard par four. The sixth was the only true dogleg at Barcelona Neck, which made it, in my view, the most challenging hole on the course. The design resembled the track of a narrow-gauge amusement park ride that climbed, dipped, and curved through a maze of dense forests. Approximately 200 yards up the slight incline that ascended from the tee, there was a lonely cedar tree planted smack in the middle of the fairway. The cedar marked the apex of the dogleg, which at that point dove to the right down a steep hill protecting a postage-stamp green.

The condition of the tee ground on number six added to the natural and architectural hazards. All the other holes except for the par-three third hole had tee boxes covered with a green synthetic outdoor carpeting that was, as Jack the Rat vividly if rather indelicately described it, "harder than a wedding cock." The carpeting could crack or break the wrists of golfers who dared to penetrate it without first whittling their tee points to the sharpness of industrial-grade ice picks, but it at least afforded stable footing to those who wore steel-cleated golf shoes. The sixth tee was basically a sand dune slung down in a chute of pines, and it was, to use Somers's phrase, "softer than newborn baby shit" and similarly slippery.

In keeping with the spirit of the Royal and Ancient Golf Club of St. Andrews, Scotland, I had privately christened each of the holes at Barcelona Neck with a distinctive name. I had dubbed number six Lyme Tick. Anything other than a perfectly faded tee shot—for example, a drive hooked, sliced, or hit dead straight—would land you in one of the surrounding forests, all of which were overrun with tick-carrying deer that could not legally be shot at or shooed away despite their well-documented infectiousness.

As the member partner of our team, Toad assumed the honor of hitting first. I watched with chagrin as he spread his widely splayed legs as far apart as possible, hooded the face of his driver, and yanked the club back and through as if he were flailing a whaler's harpoon. His ball started out on a low beeline toward the cedar tree in the middle of the fairway, then ducked sharply to the left and bounded into a patch of rough littered with pine needles and scrub.

"That's showin' him the way," Buck chortled as I stepped up to the tee.

"Yeah, yeah," chimed his partner, a ham-handed local pharmacist named Artie. "Nice drive, Toad."

Toad gestured at them with his middle finger, then turned to me.

"Give 'em hell, Harry."

The instant I took my stance, I felt the familiar feeling that had haunted me every time I'd begun a competitive round in years gone by—a combination of nausea and sheer terror. I kept reminding myself that this was only a blue-collar member-guest tournament, not the U.S. Goddamn Open. It didn't matter. My hands kept trembling and my heart leaped into the back of my throat. But thanks to muscle memory, pure luck, or some unconscious combination of the two, I managed to launch a Lyme Tick–appropriate high fade that cut the corner of the dogleg and skidded past the cedar tree with room to spare.

"Good thing you got yourself a partner, Toad," jeered one of the guys in the foursome behind us.

"Eat your heart out, bub," Toad returned. Then we took off to find his ball.

It was not a pretty sight. Toad's tee shot had lodged quite firmly between the roots of a scrub in the left rough. He had no choice but to take an unplayable lie, which, in turn, meant incurring a one-stroke penalty. Muttering under his breath, he dropped two club lengths back of the scrub, pulled out a nine iron, and punched his ball blindly over the hill toward the green.

"Don't worry, partner," I assured him. "We'll still make four or better."

Then I stepped up to my perfectly positioned drive, took pitching wedge in hand, and went prospecting for a patch of smooth grass. There wasn't one. The fairways at Barcelona Neck had less vegetation than some portions of the asphalt road connecting the clubhouse to the highway. Although winter rules applied year-round, the best you could hope for was a marginally improved lie. I finally settled on a mound of dusty sprigs, whipped back my pitching wedge, and topped my second shot about fifty yards.

I sprinted after the ball as if I were chasing a pickpocket. For all intents and purposes, I felt like someone had just stolen my first birdie opportunity, and that someone happened to be me.

When I reached the crest of the hill, my stomach turned a somersault. There was a ball lying twenty yards short of the green on a patch of hardpan; that one had to be mine. But there was another ball about six feet from the pin. I prayed that it was my partner's.

"Guess we're looking at a routine four," Toad said, grinning as he identified and marked the ball on the green.

I nodded, and promptly sculled my third shot fifteen feet past the hole.

The foozled chip left me with virtually no chance of making four. Although the Sag Harbor Golf Club's new greens were supposedly superior to the old sand-surfaced ones, they often had less grass on them than the fairways. In fact, most of what lay between my ball and the cup was either weeds or wormholes. My par putt got airborne in the first three inches and hip-hopped hopelessly off-line about two feet short of the lip.

"Rest of that's good," Buck declared with a smug smile. "Kick him away."

I retreated to the edge of the green, silently cursing myself. Though I tried to look away in shame, I couldn't help watching Toad strike his par putt out of the corner of my eye. Like an instant replay of my feeble effort, his ball got airborne and skipped off-line in the first couple of inches. But just as it appeared to be slipping past the cup, it clipped a patch of crabgrass, caromed forty-five degrees to the left, and plopped into the hole.

"Lucky fuckin' break," Buck growled. "Better stick the pin back in before it jumps back out on ya."

Toad simply sighed. "Like I said, just a routine four."

Not surprisingly, I approached our second hole of the day with mixed emotions predominated by anguish and anxiety. Number seven measured just 380 yards via the inside edge of its ever-so-slight dogleg right, but it was the longest hole at Barcelona Neck, and it was listed on the scorecard as a par five. In my St. Andrewsian nomenclature, number seven was variously known as Eagle's Nest and/or Bird Brain. It presented a perfect opportunity for me to redeem the team of Hurt and Toad from the near disaster at Lyme Tick—at the risk of making an even greater fool of myself.

The major hazards on number seven were another thick forest that extended down the entire right side of the fairway, and a cluster of sand traps backstopped by a line of oaks about 220 yards off the tee on the left. If you sliced your tee shot into the woods on the right in an overly aggressive attempt to hug the inside edge of the dogleg, you were a bird brain who deserved to make bogey or worse. On the other hand, if you drove it down the middle or simply bailed out long and left beyond the traps and the oak trees, you were looking at a very easy birdie and a fair go at nesting an eagle.

After Toad pushed his tee shot into the right rough precariously close to the tree line, I set up to hit my ball way left, and endeavored to swing with plenty of hand speed to promote a draw. It appeared for a split second that my drive was going to duck hook all the way over the sand traps and into an adjacent set of bunkers beside the eighth green. Instead, it kicked off an oak root and skipped out into a clearing beyond the trees.

While Buck continued to grumble about our undeserved good fortune, I pulled out an eight iron and knocked it stiff. The next thing I knew, I was tapping in for an eagle three. That put the team of Hurt and Toad at two under after two holes. If we maintained this torrid pace for the rest of the day, we could, at least theoretically, shoot an eighteen-hole total of 52, or eighteen under par, a fact that was not lost on my ebullient partner.

"Way to go, Dick," Toad chortled, jabbing his putter in the direction of my groin. "All we gotta do is get by the par threes and we're gonna lap the field."

We quickly discovered, however, that the two foursomes ahead of us were still gridlocked on number eight, the first of the par threes. The group waiting on the eighth tee was led by Jim Schiavoni, the plumber with the sewer pipe forearms and Peconic Bay heart. When they finally hit off and started toward the green, Toad sauntered over to Schiavoni and tapped him on the shoulder.

"Excuse me, sir. Do you think you could pick up the pace a little bit? There's a two-stroke penalty for slow play."

Schiavoni didn't even flinch. "Eat shit, you Polack bastard."

Toad gasped in mock horror. "Oh, my. I thought this was supposed to be a gentleman's game."

Buck's guest partner, Artie, who evidently rankled from a prior encounter with Schiavoni down at the local drugstore, started waving his arms and returning epithets in kind.

"Yeah, come on, ya goddamn dago. Move that meatball ass of yours."

I thought for a fleeting moment that Schiavoni was going to turn around and punch Artie in the mouth, and I wouldn't have blamed him if he had. But it wasn't necessary. Toad pulled a five iron out of his bag and began making practice swings that came frighteningly close to Artie's head.

"Watch your fuckin' language, bub," Toad ordered. "Like I said, this is supposed to be a gentleman's game."

Artie grimaced in fear. "Okay, okay, for christsake. I was just fuckin' kiddin' the guy. Quit swingin' that thing at me, damn it."

Toad finally agreed to stop only after Artie promised to apologize to Schiavoni when they got back to the clubhouse.

"If it weren't for Jimmy, ain't none of you fuckers would be playin' golf out here today," Toad declared, "includin' me."

"What the hell are you talking about?" Artie asked.

"Jimmy's the guy who helped save this club from bein' bulldozed out of existence," Toad replied, dropping his five iron and plopping down on a bench next to a conveniently positioned beer keg. "One of the guys, anyway."

Toad reminded us that the Sag Harbor Golf Club had been founded by and for working stiffs like Schiavoni and himself. But throughout its long history, the club had always been threatened with extinction at one time or another.

"The first time was way back in 1935 when the original clubhouse, which was a three-story farmhouse, burned down in a mysterious fire," Toad recalled. "The members didn't have enough money to build a new clubhouse from scratch, so they temporarily replaced it with a damn chicken coop. Then they bought this beatup old barn out in Montauk for a hundred bucks, moved it onto the property, and got a brick mason from town to help 'em restore it.

"Twenty years later, almost to the day, that damn clubhouse burned down, too," Toad continued. "Everybody suspected it was arson, but it could never be proved. Anyway, the club members got together and scraped up just enough money to build a new one. It didn't amount to much, but it's the clubhouse we got today. And it's still hangin' in there just fine, mostly because guys like Jimmy and me and some of the carpenters who belong to the club here keep fixin' it up. But that's a whole other story."

Toad stopped to see if the eighth green had cleared yet—it hadn't—then he resumed his monologue.

"Anyway, like I was sayin', the reason we're playin' golf here today is because of somethin' else that happened involvin' Schiavoni. Ya see, over the years, the ownership of the Barcelona Neck property kept changin' hands. You had the Russell family, who owned it way back at the very beginning and are buried over there in the graveyard by number four tee. Then they sold it to someone, who sold it to someone else, and so on. Sooner or later, there was big real estate companies involved, and then they went under, and so you had banks involved. All of 'em had plans to make something here besides a golf course. At one point, Grumman Aircraft was even thinking about using the place to build hospital ships, but nothing ever came of it.

"Finally, along about 1982, this big real estate developer by the name of Ben Heller buys the property from a bank or somebody for about six million. Heller was livin' over in Easthampton at the time, and he owned a bunch of other big tracts on the East End like the old Grace Estate. Anyhow, Heller supposedly had plans to build some kind of subdivision on this property, maybe around the golf course and maybe right on top of it. But for whatever reason, the subdivision scheme never got off the ground. Then in the fall of 1989, more or less out of the blue, Heller sold the property to the State of New York for somethin' like fifteen million. And that's when all hell broke loose."

Toad paused long enough to grab his five iron again. He strode back to the eighth tee, making practice swings, picking up where he had left off.

"What happened, ya see, is that the State purchased Barcelona Neck with funds provided from the Department of Environmental Conservation. Then the damn DEC announces that they're plannin' to close the golf course by the end of the year. According to the DEC, a golf course ain't compatible with the Open Spaces Act, and besides, they ain't got the personnel to run a golf course even if they wanted to. They say they want to tear up all the holes and turn the place into a nature preserve, maybe even lease it for huntin'. At one of the public meetings, somebody gets up and asks 'em, 'You mean that it'll be all right to shoot a deer out here, but we can't hit golf balls?' And they say, 'Yes, that's exactly right.'

"Well, that didn't go down so good with the members of the club," Toad noted. "But it wasn't just us. A lot of people around

here who don't even play golf were mad about what the DEC was
goin' to do. So we organized this big rally at the VFW hall in Sag
Harbor on Thanksgiving Day. The club's only got about four hundred members, but somethin' like eight hundred people showed up
at the rally, includin' a bunch of local politicians who were with us
on this thing. The politicians told us that we needed to make ourselves heard by signin' petitions and writin' letters and stuff.

"This is where Jimmy got on the case big time. Schiavoni helps
organize this petition drive, which collects three thousand signa-
tures sayin' the State should save the golf course. Then he hooks
up with this business service in town, and they start crankin' out
letters on a word processor. We're talkin' bags full of letters. As I
remember, he was sendin' out somethin' like two hundred letters
every other day to the DEC and to Governor Mario Cuomo up in
Albany. They were up to their asses in letters about Barcelona
Neck."

Toad quit practice swinging and started laughing and shaking
his head.

"They say I'm the club's number-one ball buster, but Schiavoni
is a fuckin' piece of work himself. Anyway, it gets to the point
where Cuomo sends down the word that the State don't need to
get no more letters. Right before Christmas, the DEC announces
that it's gonna hold off on its plans to close down the golf course.
Then they start negotiatin' with the club and the politicians who
are supportin' us. This goes on for almost a year until the DEC
agrees to a compromise."

By now the eighth green had finally cleared, and Toad got
ready to hit his tee shot. I made him hold up.

"So how does it stand now? You didn't say what the compromise was."

"The DEC agreed that the Sag Harbor Golf Club can keep run-
nin' the golf course because it's always been here for the working
people and the senior citizens," Toad informed me. "But they said
they'd only lease it to us one year at a time. That makes it kind of
tough for us to plan anything or put money into long-term improvements of the golf course."

"You mean, the DEC could just decide not to renew the lease?"
Artie asked.

Toad stepped back up to the tee, nodding. "Yep. Everything's
still touch-and-go."

*   *   *

The same applied to the team of Hurt and Toad. The long wait on the eighth tee might have strengthened the bond between us, but it definitely weakened our golf games. We both bogeyed the first of Barcelona Neck's par threes, a tricky little 175-yarder up a slight incline and against the prevailing wind that I had variously dubbed Crepe or Crap, depending on my mood. The cause of our first team foul-up was putting: each of us missed five-footers for par.

Number eight set the tone for the rest of the day. We rallied with a triplicate of birdies on number nine, number one, and number two, all of which were par fours. But we gave strokes back both times we played the third hole, a 150-yard par three, and the second time we played number eight. In each instance, the source of our bogeys was poor putting. Along the way, Toad also lipped out makable birdies on the fourth and the fifth, while I flubbed a six-footer for eagle the second time we played the seventh and a five-footer for birdie on our second pass at Lyme Tick. By the end of our eighteen-hole day, the team of Hurt and Toad was at exactly the same place it had been after the second hole—two under par.

"Afraid we putted ourselves out of it, Dick," my partner said, sighing, as we marched off the final green. "It's gonna take at least four under to win."

But the inclement weather and unyielding greens had apparently hobbled the rest of the field, as well. Upon returning to the clubhouse, we discovered that our team was tied for first place with the twosome of Rodriguez and Bistrian. I half expected that the deadlock would be broken by comparing scorecards hole by hole in match play fashion or by counting total birdies. However, Judge Bailey, the tournament director, insisted that there had to be a sudden death playoff. His decision was controversial, to say the least.

Although the drizzle had slackened, the sky was darkening again, and most of the other contestants were growing surly and boisterous, which was certainly understandable given the recreational and gastronomical opportunities at hand. Unlike its counterparts at Shinnecock Hills and The Maidstone, the nineteenth hole at Barcelona Neck was typically furnished with a fine-blue-felt-covered poker table complete with slots for chips and cards. But the poker table had been made inaccessible by a member-guest tournament buffet spread consisting of fried chicken, buttered rolls, and some kind of goulash whose colors and consistency resembled those of the turtle pond in the woods next to the parking lot.

To make matters worse, the beer kegs were running dry, the hard stuff was still locked up in the cabinet behind the kitchenette, and Bailey had officiously decreed that no one could have a bite of food or a drop of booze until the playoff was completed. Bailey further stipulated that the format for deciding the winner would be a sudden death shootout beginning on number one, which promised only to further delay the posttournament feast.

I had irreverently dubbed number one the Road Hole. The seventeenth at St. Andrews, for which it had been named, was a long and dangerous dogleg right par four flanked by a hotel and a rock-walled thoroughfare. By contrast, the first at Barcelona Neck was a very short straightaway par four with an extraordinarily wide fairway bisected by a narrow dirt trail leading from the clubhouse to the beach. The relative lack of difficulty presented by this Road Hole meant that at least one or two extra holes would probably be required to decide the playoff. But for reasons that soon became painfully obvious, I would hereafter refer to number one as the Toad Hole.

Amid a chorus of jeers and single-fingered gestures, Bailey led the way back to the first tee, where he put down his beer mug just long enough to flip a coin into the air. Toad called heads, and won the toss for our team. He elected to hit first, hoping to apply added pressure to our opponents. Instead, he promptly duck hooked his tee shot deep into the woods on the left. I followed with a towering draw of well over 280 yards, but my ball landed on a patch of hardpan, hopped leftward, and dribbled into a clump of weeds about 30 yards short of the green.

Lenny Rodriguez, a southpawed Sag Harbor carpenter with a chestnut-brown complexion and a sad-sack facial expression, led off for the competition just as the wind began to whip up. He drew his club back slowly, but came down with a much-too-open left hand, hammering his ball into the left woods near Toad's. The shot apparently rattled his guest partner, Pat Bistrian, an excavation contractor from Amagansett, who proceeded to blast his ball even farther left into the adjacent fairway.

After a series of beery and embarrassing miss-hits, all four of us wound up on or near the green in three strokes. Rodriguez then chunked two chip shots from the apron and picked up his ball, signaling his partner to go it alone. Bistrian had a six-foot sidehiller for par. Toad and I were looking at seven-footers from below and above the hole.

What happened next does not bear blow-by-blow recounting in any respectable golfing forum from Sag Harbor to St. Andrews. The bottom line was that the opposing team got their par and the team of Hurt and Toad did not. The same thing that had kept us from winning a clear victory after eighteen holes also caused us to lose the playoff on the Toad Hole—abysmally poor putting.

Back at the clubhouse, the awards ceremony was brief and appropriately ironic. Rodriguez and Bistrian were duly presented with the first-place prizes: two Footjoy shoe boxes containing $75 in cash. Toad and I were awarded second-place prizes, which turned out to be—what else?—a pair of MacGregor "Smoothie" putters with offset heads and the price stickers still attached. The sticker on Toad's putter read "$75." The sticker on the identical model I received had been marked down to "$40."

$\mathbf{a}$lthough I had wound up with a justly deserved booby prize in my competitive debut in the Sag Harbor member-guest, the experience had provided me with an invaluable refresher course in playing under tournament pressure for the first time in twenty-five years. Following the awards ceremony, I conferred with Judge Bailey and Jack Somers about a potential obstacle confronting my quest to make it all the way to the PGA Tour. The problem, I explained, was qualifying myself for future outside competitions in accordance with United States Golf Association statutes.

In order to become eligible to enter professional tournaments and most of the top amateur events, I had to establish a bona fide USGA handicap of two or less. Once upon a time, you could simply fudge your handicap or get a friendly club pro to sign off on it. With the advent of nationwide computerization systems, that was no longer possible. The USGA now mandated that every golfer obtain an identification number registered with the Golf Handicap Information Network (GHIN). And unless you belonged to a USGA-registered golf club, you couldn't get a GHIN or establish a bona fide handicap.

Bailey and Somers offered to help me circumvent this catch-22 with characteristic Barcelona Neck aplomb. They noted that I could not even be proposed for official membership in the Sag Harbor Golf Club until the following December. In the meantime, though, I could purchase a year-round ticket for $285. For an additional $10 handling fee, they would simply add my name to the monthly handicapping list the club sent in to the USGA.

"Whaddya shoot on your own ball today, bub?" Somers asked me.

"Something like a 72."

"I seen ya out here on the course practicin' up for the tournament. Do ya remember five other scores from before today?"

I bit my lip, nodding. "Sure, I can think of a few. How about 69, 68, 70, 69, 70?"

"Perfect," Bailey said, jotting down the numbers on the back of a bar napkin. "We can probably get you a two on the board in a couple of weeks."

By this time, the hard stuff had been brought out, and the post-tournament celebration began to degenerate into a round of inebriated, semibegrudging apologies. Under Toad's watchful glare, Artie tracked down Jimmy Schiavoni and apologized for calling him a fuckin' dago. I apologized to Judge Bailey for not winning the tournament and thanked him and Jack the Rat for their help with my handicap problem. Toad apologized to me for putting so poorly. I apologized to Toad for the same thing.

Then Jimmy Schiavoni came over to me and apologized for Toad. I told Schiavoni that no apologies were necessary, adding that Toad had given him major credit for saving the Sag Harbor Golf Club.

"Hey, Toad," Schiavoni shouted. "You really say that about me?"

Toad nodded. "Yep, just ask Dick over there."

Schiavoni guzzled down a strong-smelling cup of clear liquid, then looked back at me, winking and shaking his head.

"No wonder you guys lost," he said. "That fuckhead partner of yours don't even know who the hell he's been playin' with."

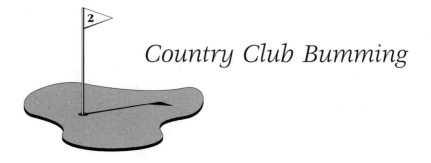

Country Club Bumming

i stared at the televison screen as a blond guy with a beer gut attempted to hit a three iron shot, muttering under my breath in gape-mouthed horror.

"What the hell is wrong with this picture?"

The answer was just about everything—and then some.

The guy hunkered over the ball like the Hunchback of Notre Dame, his shoulders sagging and his head drooping. His stance was too wide and his grip was too weak. He yanked the club back in a kind of drag sweep, then snatched it inside and up to the top, where the flange nearly flopped over onto his left ear.

He started his downswing with a spasmodic sideways lunge. Then he flung his right shoulder out and around, rolled his wrists, and jerked through the ball with both knees bent and thrusting forward as if he were trying to push a wheelbarrow.

The best thing about the guy's swing appeared to be the pose he struck at the finish, as he belatedly straightened his left side and spun his chest toward the target, smiling for the camera.

The worst thing about his swing was that it happened to be my own.

"God, that's ugly," I blurted. "Get this guy outta here."

"We'll try," said a laughing voice behind me.

I was sitting in the pro shop at The Maidstone Club in East-hampton, New York, on the second Tuesday following the Sag Harbor Golf Club member-guest tournament reviewing a videotape the head pro, Eden Foster, had just shot out on the practice range. The geographic locale was barely half a dozen miles southeast of Barcelona Neck as the seagulls fly, but it might as well have been on another planet. For if the Sag Harbor Golf Club embodied the archetypal characteristics of a Goat Hill, The Maidstone Club ranked in relative terms as a sacred shrine in the Himalayas.

Nestled on a steeply rising incline overlooking the Atlantic Ocean, The Maidstone had been established in 1891, four years before the formation of the United States Golf Association. It was a classic seaside links that included a 6,390-yard, par 72 championship track and a separate nine-hole practice track, the latter a vestige of the original thirty-six-hole layout designed by the renowned John Park and Willie Park Jr. The editors of *Golf Digest* had listed The Maidstone at number thirty-eight in their most recent roster of "America's Top 100 Golf Courses," but the club claimed a far loftier position in historic provenance, WASPish social prestige, and pristine beauty.

If the Parks were the Monets of golf architecture, The Maidstone was their version of *The Water Lilies*. Everything about the place bespoke the eternal values of tradition and understated taste. The rambling double-chimneyed clubhouse with its vine-covered stucco walls and multiple eaves loomed like an ancient galleon grounded on the rocky shelf above the first tee. In its shadow stood a single-chimneyed stucco pro shop that was roughly twice the size of the clapboard cottage at Barcelona Neck, and yet, through lack of identifying signage or outdoor product displays, more closely resembled a cozy summer love nest than one of the garish commercial emporiums at so many other golfing meccas.

Throughout the linksland below, the forces of man and nature had conspired in the creation of delicately balanced, blithely untamed harmony. The meticulously manicured fairways were perfect, and so were the greens; both were composed of bent grass that smelled fresh and sweet enough to eat. At the same time, you could see and feel and hear the raw power of the primeval elements in the towering beachfront dunes that bordered the outlying holes, in the kettle ponds deposited by retreating glaciers amid the incoming holes, and in the swirling maritime winds that prevailed in the high season.

I had come to The Maidstone Club by virtue of a chain of circumstantial events that sounded like something out of a Charles Dickens novel. Having found a way to establish a two handicap, I needed to find some first-class coaching that would enable me to play like a true two. Once again, the boys at Barcelona Neck delivered for me. The day after the Sag Harbor member-guest, Jack Somers, the former baseball player turned groundskeeper, told me that The Maidstone had hired a new head pro. He was a young guy from somewhere down south who seemed to have a real gift for teaching beginners and advanced players alike.

I knew that even with the best of connections getting into The Maidstone Club as a full-fledged member would take years and cost tens of thousands of dollars in initiation fees. But in following up on the tip I had gotten from Jack the Rat, I happened to renew an acquaintance with a friend who already belonged to the club. He agreed to act as a kind of anonymous benefactor. He took me on a golfing outing to The Maidstone and introduced me to the club's new head pro, who, in turn, accepted me as a guest pupil.

Eden Foster looked like a young adult version of dozens of guys I'd played against on the junior golf circuit. He was trim and tanned, broad-shouldered but not too tall, with sun-bleached hair and darting brown eyes. He dressed in neatly pressed tan slacks and golf shirts with The Maidstone Club's logo. And as he sat in the pro shop listening to me outline the upcoming competitive steps in my quest, his grin stretched nearly from ear to ear.

I told Eden that the first major target date on my tournament calendar was the thirty-six-hole New York regional qualifier for the 1995 U.S. Amateur Championship on August 7. If I won one of the five available qualifying spots, I would have the dubious privilege of playing against defending champion Tiger Woods at Newport Country Club. Either way, I planned to enter my first professional tournaments in early September. The penultimate event on my calendar, Stage One of the PGA Tour Qualifying School tournament, was scheduled for mid-October.

"Don't expect miracles," Eden warned. "It's gonna take some time."

"Hallelujah, praise the Lord," I rejoined. "You're preachin' to the choir, Reverend Foster. I have been here before, and I know the darkness that comes before the light. I also know that if and when the light ever comes, it's more than likely gonna go out on you before you know it."

Eden frowned at me. "Come again?"

"What I'm trying to say is, my hopes are high but my expectations remain in check. I know there's no way to become the new Jack Nicklaus in less than three months. What this project is all about is trying. It's about trying like hell to get my game in shape and trying like hell to play big-league pro golf just to see what it's really like. I realize the odds are long, and so is the road to making a comeback. God knows, it took a lifetime for me to groove that ugly swing we just saw on the videotape."

"Well, if it's any consolation to you," Eden said, "that swing is not all your fault."

Eden explained that over the past decade or so the theories of the golf swing had undergone a technology-driven transformation analogous to what had happened in tennis following the switch from wooden rackets to high-tech frames. He said he could tell just from looking at the videotape that I was the well-trained product of the postwar steel shaft era. Back when I was growing up, most respected teaching pros instructed you to bend steel shafts in much the same manner as their predecessors had endeavored to manhandle the old hickory shafts. The so-called small muscles dominated the swing. You were supposed to control the club by "pronating" your wrists like Ben Hogan, and power the shot by "hitting with your hands" like Tommy Armour and "driving your legs" like Nicklaus.

In the modern age of graphite and titanium, the leading gurus of the golf swing now advocated the so-called big muscle motion pioneered by the likes of David Leadbetter and his star pupils Nick Price and Nick Faldo. The keys were synchronization and keeping the club "on plane" while effecting a "lateral rotation" around a set of imaginary double axises aligned with each armpit. Your hands and arms served merely as "connectors" to the club. You were supposed to keep your wrists and knees "quiet." Both power and control were produced by the coordinated turning of the hips and shoulders around the right axis on the way back and the left axis on the way through.

"There are plenty of guys around like Nicklaus and Johnny Miller who still swing the old-fashioned way," Eden noted. "The problem is, it's a high-maintainence swing that requires perfect timing because there are so many moving parts. Unless you have the time to practice it every single day, you're gonna lose it at some time or other when you're out on the course, especially if you're playing under pressure. Once you learn it, the new method is much simpler, much lower maintainence. I know because I've tried 'em both."

"How's that?" I asked. "Jack Somers told me you were only thirty years old. I assumed you learned to swing the new way when you were starting out as a kid."

Eden smiled, shrugging his shoulders. "I grew up in a small town in New Mexico. Guess the news just got there late."

As he led the way back to the practice range, I discovered that we had more in common than similar swing change problems. In fact, the two of us shared roughly parallel backgrounds and golfing histories, as well as youthful aspirations of making the PGA Tour. Listening to Eden recount his story, I couldn't help but wonder if his experiences somehow foreshadowed what might be in store for me in the months ahead.

Eden hailed from a central New Mexico desert county seat called Socorro. Where my father had been a wildcatter, his dad was an oil-finding geologist. His mother, who had raised Eden and two daughters, shared my own mom's love for cooking picante. Like me, Eden had taken up golf at about age ten and cut his teeth playing against older kids in one of the most competitive environments in the Southwest. "The population of Socorro is only about seven thousand people, but it's turned out something like twenty-three golf pros," he told me. "Our high school golf team won eighteen state championships between 1965 and 1986."

Eden had also suffered through a roller-coastering amateur and college golf career much like mine. After starring on his high school team, he had enrolled at New Mexico Junior College under the tutelage of coach Jesse Blackwelder, whose students included PGA journeyman Ronnie Black. Eden was expected to become the number-one or -two man his sophomore year, but after Blackwelder insisted that he replace his natural hook with a fade, his swing fell apart and his scores skyrocketed. In the hope of starting afresh, he transferred to Eastern New Mexico University, the seventh-ranked small college in the nation, and promptly tore a ligament playing in a pickup basketball game.

"I kept trying to get back on track after the injury, but it never happened," he recalled. "The competition was too stiff unless you could play at the top of your game. I shot two under par in the team qualifying tournament and didn't make it. But I still kept thinking that if I could somehow pull it all together, I might be good enough to play on the Tour."

After graduating from college with a finance degree, Eden surveyed the country for a place where he could earn a living in the golf business and work on his game at the same time. In the summer of 1988, he found employment as a second-level assistant pro at Silver Spring Country Club in Ridgefield, Connecticut. That winter, he trekked down to Naples, Florida, where he got a part-time job working in the bag room of a local golf club for $5.50 an hour and tried to rebuild his swing. "The five-fifty an hour didn't mean a thing to me," he confided. "All I wanted to do was tee it."

Back at Silver Springs C.C. the following summer, Eden discovered that he had a hidden talent for teaching. The head pro had originally assigned him to work behind the counter in the shop, but after volunteering to help a few of the members out on the range, he was under ever-increasing demand to give lessons. Unable to find sufficient time to practice, he saw his own game begin to slip even further. He finally decided that he owed himself one more shot at the big time. In appreciation for his services, the members at Silver Springs raised $14,000 to finance his bid to become a touring pro.

"That really touched me," he said, almost watery-eyed at the memory. "I wrote out a hundred and seventy thank-you cards by hand with a special note to each member."

Eden then drove down to Florida and spent the next six months playing on the Tommy Armour Tour with painfully sobering results. "I knew after the very first round that being a touring pro wasn't for me," he admitted. "I was playing in a tournament at Grenelefe, which is a Robert Trent Jones course about seventy-four hundred yards long, and there was a forty-mile-an-hour wind blowing. I hit the ball as well as I could and shot a 75, but a guy named Clark Burroughs shot 65. I knew right then that I didn't have a 65 in my bag.

"I went on to play in about five or six more Tommy Armour tournaments anyway. At the time, I was driving a '91 Ford Thunderbird and dressing in Polo pants and Ashford shirts. The guys I was playing against were driving 1975 Honda Civics, sleeping in their cars, and wearing the same clothes four days in a row—and they were beating me. Finally, I said to myself, 'There's got to be a better way. I just can't see myself living this life.'"

In the spring of 1993, Eden sent his résumé to Jim Gerber, who had recently been hired as the head pro at The Maidstone Club. They hit it off immediately, and Eden joined Gerber's staff as the top teaching assistant. Then, in the fall of 1994, Gerber was offered the widely envied task of restoring Eastlake Country Club in Atlanta, the fabled former home course of Bobby Jones. Although he had just turned thirty, Eden applied for the vacated head pro slot at The Maidstone Club and managed to convince the search committee he was the best man for the job.

"I told the search committee that The Maidstone was a great club that needed to have some continuity," he recalled. "I said that I intended to stay here for the long haul."

"That's certainly reassuring from my point of view," I said, gripping a three iron again as we arrived at The Maidstone Club practice range. "And I know it'll come as good news to that guy we just saw on the videotape back in the pro shop."

Eden emptied a basket of range balls beside my feet. "Okay, then, let's see what we can do to make that guy go away—or at least look a little better while he's here."

Eden began by telling me to do virtually the exact opposite of everything I'd been taught as a junior golfer. He advised me to narrow my stance and simply let my arms hang without hunching my shoulders so much. Then he instructed me to relax my left-hand grip and pick up the club with my right hand while he helped me guide it back on an angle that seemed to point forty-five degrees away from my right knee.

"You're gonna feel like you're taking it back way outside, like you'd do if you were trying to cut the ball," he said. "But trust me, you're really just on plane rather than too far inside like you used to be."

When I got the club to the top of the backswing, Eden stopped me again. He grasped my right arm, stretched it out from its folded tuck, and raised my right elbow. Then he instructed me to start my downswing with only two thoughts in mind: clearing my hips and straightening my left leg through impact.

"Don't focus on shifting your weight off the right side for the time being," he said. "You're doing a good job of that already. In fact, you're overdoing it. The thing we've really gotta work on is getting rid of your sliding motion when you come through the ball. You'll hear some of the younger teaching pros talk about 'squeezing the ball' or 'trapping it left.' The older guys used to talk about 'hitting the ball down the line.' That's what I want you to feel. But the line isn't the first base line or the third base line. I want you to hit it on a line straight to the shortstop."

I backed off for a second, then renarrowed my stance and attempted to swing the club as instructed. I felt like I was going to hit the ball dead right. Instead, I topped it dead straight.

"That was better," Eden allowed, "at least on your backswing."

"Then what went wrong? Why did I top it?"

He feigned puzzlement. "Couldn't tell you without replaying the video in slow-mo. The downswing was too fast to see with the naked eye."

For the next forty-five minutes that day, Eden and I worked on reducing my notoriously quick tempo, increasing the extension of my backswing, and eliminating my leg slide in the impact zone. But my bad habits were so deeply ingrained and so obstinate in their refusal to change that he agreed to make himself available to tutor me at least twice a week for the next forty-five days.

The formation of my student-teacher alliance with Eden Foster marked a major turning point in my quest to qualify for the PGA Tour. It was so happy and fateful a coincidence it reminded me of Pip's first meeting with Miss Havisham in the opening pages of *Great Expectations.* When I returned home to Sag Harbor later that evening, I reread the famous passage in which Pip divined the import of that encounter in terms that applied to my initial coaching session with Eden Foster.

> That was a memorable day to me, for it made great changes in me. But it is the same with any life. Imagine one selected day struck out of it, and think how different its course would have been. Pause you who read this, and think for a moment of the long chain of iron or gold, or thorns or flowers, that would never have bound you, but for the formation of the first link on one memorable day.

as my lessons with Eden progressed, I tried to put them to proper use by finding places to practice and play at least six times a week. That turned out to be much harder than I had anticipated. My home course at Barcelona Neck offered plenty of room to hit drivers, but there was no practice range per se. Most of the holes were too short, and all of the fairways too bare, to work on medium or long iron shots. Likewise, the greens at Barcelona Neck were so beat up and uneven that you'd go half crazy trying to find a truly straight putt for the purposes of grooving your stroke.

I turned by default to Poxabogue Golf Course out on Highway 27 near Bridgehampton, a place whose name suited its problematic clientele. Poxabogue boasted a surprisingly well-watered nine-hole course, most of which consisted of short par threes, and the only public practice range in the Hamptons where you could hit off grass as well as off plastic mats. It also had a funky little restaurant in a red-shingled shack adjoining the pro shop that served hearty breakfasts starting at 7:30 A.M. and home-cooked light lunches until just prior to closing time, 6:30 P.M.

Unfortunately, the entire facility suffered from a pox of over-popularity among hip-chic summer residents from New York City and itinerant hackers from trailer parks across the nation. Lacking even the most basic ball-striking skills and blithely ignorant of the rules of etiquette, they endangered all human life within shanking distance on the nine-hole course, and so severely bogged down play that it could take over two hours to complete what should have been a forty-five-minute round. The grassy expanses on the prac-tice range likewise wilted amid the seasonal drought and the tourist onslaught. All the flat spots got chewed up by divots before the middle of June, exposing a subsurface harder than the concrete beneath the plastic mats.

I guessed that my role model, Lee Trevino, who had reportedly learned the game by hitting balls off cacti and cow chips, would only mock my complaints about Poxabogue as the crybaby whining of a former country club brat. Then again, Trevino had never taken a shank on the shins out there as I did two days in a row. As the summer wore on, I found that the best way to survive my perilous practice sessions at Poxabogue was by pretending that I was suiting up for a televised bout against the American Gladiators. I would tape my wrists and ankles, cover my eyes with wraparound Bolle sunglasses, position my golf bag to guard my shins, then grit my teeth and flinch my back muscles every time I heard the whistling sounds of someone else's shots.

After a couple of weeks of hitting a couple of hundred range balls a day, my callused palms began to resemble a topographic map of the Rocky Mountains, and my entire torso ached from excessive twisting and vibratory aftershocks. I sorely needed some R&R to repair my body and replenish my morale. So, with the help of Eden and a couple of other well-connected friends, I secured clubhouse passes to the 1995 United States Open Championship slated for June 15 to 18 at Shinnecock Hills in Southampton.

From the moment I passed through the Open ticket gates, I felt like a little kid attending the world's greatest sports carnival in the company of 25,000 fellow spectators. Although the tournament happened to be run by the avowedly amateur-minded United States Golf Association rather than by the PGA Tour, the unabashed commercialism overwhelmed the official emphasis on "open" competition and volunteer marshals. And yet, only a politically correct curmudgeon with his posterior impaled on an L-wedge could fail to have a good time amid the folly that had befallen such a stately setting.

Shinnecock's gray-shingled clubhouse with the white-columned porticoes designed by Stanford White peered down from its foundation atop a humpbacked former Indian burial mound eroded by crosswinds from the ocean to the south and the bay to the north. In the hollows below its aristocratic profile there was now a boisterous city of canvas tents, including over forty lavishly appointed corporate tepees. Not coincidentally, the largest of these portable palaces was the merchandise tent, which ran close to half the length of the practice range and reportedly grossed sales on the order of $1 million a day.

I purchased more than my share of commemorative shirts and hats prior to the opening round on Thursday, then spent the next three and a half days traipsing across the 6,912-yard, par 70 combat zone trying to learn something that would help my own game. I failed to get my first glimpse of teenage phenomenon Tiger Woods before an injury forced him to withdraw. But I did get the chance to follow Greg Norman, Nick Faldo, and Nick Price close on the heels of the ubiquitous David Leadbetter, elbowing my way through the crowds at each tee so I could get a close-up view of their "big muscle" swing methods.

During the final round, I plopped down behind the green of the 408-yard par-four fifteenth hole, a downhill tricky dogleg right, whispering to another spectator that whoever passed through in the lead was going to win. I cheered Corey Pavin when he sank the birdie putt that got him back to even par. I waited patiently for Norman to mount a charge, only to groan in sympathy as he lipped out a birdie putt on the fifteenth to remain at two over. Then I rushed over to the eighteenth hole just in time to watch from the upslope near the green as Pavin hit the fantastic four wood shot to five feet that clinched his first major tournament victory.

The highlight of the Open for me, however, was a brief reunion with my former Texas junior golfing buddy Ben Crenshaw. Back in April, I had watched on television as Crenshaw won his second Masters, a uniquely inspirational triumph that came on the week-end following the death of his mentor, Harvey Penick. He had al-most fallen to his knees crying tears of joy and grief after putting out on the final hole. "I felt like I was carrying a fifteenth club in my bag all week," he had said afterward, referring to the unseen influence of the late Penick.

When I met up with Crenshaw in the clubhouse on the second day of the Open, I was immediately reminded of why he had earned the nickname Gentle Ben. Although he had just made the cut, he had pretty much knocked himself out of contention to win due to uncharacteristically poor chipping and putting. But rather than bemoan his scores, he told me he was having the best year of his life, thanked me for the note I'd sent congratulating him on his Masters victory, and asked how I was doing.

With considerable temerity, I gave Crenshaw an outline of my comeback attempt to qualify for the PGA Tour and asked if he could offer any advice. I wouldn't have blamed him if he had just laughed me off. Instead, he reacted to my quest even more seri-ously and specifically than I had any right to expect.

"First of all, I think what you're doing is wonderful," he said, adding with startling recall that dated back almost thirty years, "When I watched you play at Houston Country Club, I could tell you had been taught properly. You had a good grip and a smooth swing. You've got to keep training and practicing, and remember to keep making a good shoulder turn. When it's time to get ready for PGA Qualifying School, break down the courses you have to play hole by hole, so you know where you have a good chance of making birdies and where you're best off just trying to get away with a par."

I mentioned that everything about golf from the clubs to the swing had changed so radically since we were kids that it made me feel like Rip Van Winkle.

"I know," Crenshaw replied, smiling. "Everybody's got this space age technology nowadays. I've started playing with King Cobra metal woods, and they're incredible. But what it all comes down to is, you've just got to trust your ability. Try to remember the things that got you started in golf. And any amount of time you can put in on your short game will help. Chipping and putting don't change."

I returned to my long-shot labors on the Monday following the U.S. Open with an upbeat attitude inspired by Crenshaw's encouraging words and a renewed determination to get with the program he had outlined. The first step was cleaning out a set of skeletons that had been in my closet for far too long—namely, the outmoded equipment I had been using. I knew better than to blame my minor injuries or my continuing swing problems on my golf clubs alone. That was the classic cop-out of every inveterate duffer. But I also knew that the particular sticks in my mismatched bag didn't help matters much.

Upon quitting the Harvard golf team, I had traded my custom-made persimmon woods and pro model Spalding irons to a classmate in exchange for a large quantity of imported contraband. The day before my first lesson with Eden Foster, my younger brother, Bill, had sent me a metal-headed Big Bertha driver and a metal-headed Big Bertha three wood as his contribution to my comeback efforts. I was still stuck, however, with a hodgepodge of hand-me-down irons that I had inherited from my late father and that ranged in age and obsolescence from a Ben Hogan Equalizer to an assortment of Lynx Master Models missing the six and the nine. The only old clubs worth keeping were a 58 degree Spalding Dynamiter sand wedge and my poppa's putter, a copper-headed heel-shafted Ping whose design dated it to 1966.

One visit to a local sporting goods emporium convinced me that there was no way I could try out the entire panoply of new high-tech irons produced in response to the worldwide golf boom. Golf equipment had become a $2.2 billion a year business with hundreds of major and minor brands on the market, each of which claimed to have discovered a state-of-the-art gizmo or gimmick guaranteed to produce lower scores. Some of the clubs literally looked like they had landed from outer space; one in particular, the "Alien" wedge, even had a double oval face that resembled E.T., the Hollywood movie extraterrestrial.

At the end of the day, I realized that when all the daffy club designs were discarded, I basically had two major types of irons to choose from: the old kind and the new kind. The technical term for the old kind I'd grown up playing with was "forged" irons, most of which were also shaped like and referred to as "blades." As this name implied, blades had relatively small, thin club faces. Many veteran pros and top amateurs still preferred blades because they supposedly allowed you to work the ball left or right more easily and had a deliciously sweet feel when struck dead center.

The new "cast" irons, on the other hand, were touted as being easier to hit straight. Most of these were "cavity backed" and/or "perimeter weighted," meaning that they had thicker faces than blades buttressed by metal-lined cavities on the back sides of the club heads that distributed the weight along the outer edges. The top-selling cast irons typically came in two club head models, mid-size and oversize, both of which were much bigger than blades. They could be fitted with either steel shafts or graphite, which cost about 50 percent more. Their generous dimensions coupled with their scientific weight balancing supposedly made them far more forgiving on mishits.

Despite my limited budget, performance mattered to me more than price, and the ineffable element of feel counted most of all. A friend had let me hit a couple of his graphite-shafted Big Bertha irons, which retailed for over $1,000 a set. But the Berthas were so damn big that it seemed to require an amazing feat of muscular manipulation to close the club face enough to hit an intentional draw. I'd had better luck drawing the ball with another friend's set of King Cobra oversize irons, which sold for about $580 a set with steel shafts. But those clubs featured reverse L-shaped offset hosels designed to eliminate slices that also made it more difficult to hit an intentional fade.

"Try one of mine," Eden suggested one afternoon out on The Maidstone Club practice range. "Could be the best of both worlds."

He handed me a King Cobra five iron that appeared identical to the kind I'd already tested except for the hosel, which was straight, like the hosel of a blade, rather than offset.

I proceeded to hit one of the most solid feeling shots of my life right at the 175 yard marker. Then I attempted to shape an intentional draw followed by an intentional fade. Both shots flew precisely as targeted.

"These are terrific," I shouted out. "Where can you buy a set?"

"You can't," Eden replied. "They're Tour Model irons designed for the pros. Cobra doesn't encourage the big golf stores to carry them in stock because most amateurs like the offset models. If you want a set, you've got to order them direct, and that can take up to six weeks."

I groaned. "Then we're shit out of luck. The U.S. Amateur qualifier is coming up in less than six weeks."

"Lemme make a few calls," Eden offered, politely reclaiming his five iron before I could make off with it. "The Cobra people have been talking to me about joining their club pro staff. Maybe we can find a way to rush-order a set."

While I waited with bated breath to see if Eden could secure me a set of the coveted Cobra irons, I began to devote more and more time to the old-fashioned art of country club bumming, an incessant networking effort to gain access to the finer courses of eastern Long Island by calling favors from friends, friends of friends, and even total strangers. The best public course in the area was Montauk Downs, a formerly private track designed by Robert Trent Jones. At only $20 per round, the greens fees were the best bargain since the sale of Manhattan for a string of beads. But Montauk was nearly forty-five minutes from Sag Harbor, and it was so oversubscribed during the summer that you had to get up at 4:30 A.M. to schedule tee times a week in advance.

I had better luck conning my way onto the more prestigious private courses, though not without paying some pretty exorbitant prices. A single round on the U.S. Open layout at Shinnecock Hills, authorized by a member friendly with my wife's family, cost a cool $150. A fellow writer who belonged to the National Golf Links of America arranged for me to play half a dozen rounds there—but at a total cost of over $450 in greens fees alone, guesting at the National did not come cheap. Neither did playing Noyac Golf and Country Club. The starter at Noyac charged $85 per eighteen holes, and allowed me to tee off only after receiving a phone call from

the Sag Harbor police chief, another friend from a previous jour-
nalism project who was chairman of the greens committee.

After a series of frustrating runarounds, I found that the best
country club bumming was to be had at the Southampton Golf
Club. Though neither as famous as the National nor as exclusive
as The Maidstone, the Southampton Golf Club was located right
next door to Shinnecock Hills, and its 6,287-yard, par 70 course had
been designed by the preeminent local architect, Seth Raynor. Unlike Shinnecock, where I spent most of my round in waist-high
fescue weeds, Southampton had fairways wide enough for me to
hit and just enough rough to keep me sharp.

Perhaps even more important, the guest fees at Southampton
Golf Club were only $45 a pop, and the membership, which con-
sisted mostly of year-round resident "townies," included several of
my local drinking buddies. One of them was Paul Babcock, a fifty-
two-year-old former Eastern Airlines pilot turned real estate agent
with a single-digit handicap who had studied Harvey Penick's *Little
Red Book* as closely as he once studied flight manuals. Babcock took
an avid interest in my comeback quest and inspired me to play
some of my best golf. That moved me to ask if he would consider
caddying for me in the U.S. Amateur qualifier. He consented with
two conditions attached.

"First, you've got to promise me you'll take 'dead aim' on every
shot," he said, alluding to Penick's guiding principle. "And second,
you've got to practice your putting for at least thirty minutes every
day from now on."

I soon discovered that abiding by the terms of Babcock's caddying contract would cost me dearly in financial terms as well as
in time. I had been hoping to keep my day job as a freelance journalist until late summer. But it proved impossible to serve two masters with one mind and body. In order to take lessons, practice,
arrange access to good courses, and actually play the game, I had
to spend at least seven hours of every day on golf. In the evenings,
I had to write appropriately pithy accounts of my activities in the
journal I was keeping as background material for this book. At the
same time, I also had to attend to the kind of niggling paperwork
and perpetually changing itineraries that compel every successful
touring pro to hire an office manager.

In early July, the first important entry form to cross my desk—
the application for the U.S. Amateur qualifier on August 7—put the
fear of the golf gods in me. By this time, I had received a USGA
card via the Barcelona Neck clubhouse certifying my handicap at

a nice round 2.0, well below the minimum 3.4 handicap required to compete in the Amateur. The $80 entry fee seemed like a pittance compared to what I had already spent on greens fees in my country club bumming. Travel expenses promised to be nominal, since the qualifying site for my region was Southward Ho Country Club in Bay Shore, about an hour's drive from Sag Harbor.

But a boilerplate clause on the U.S. Amateur application under the heading "PERFORMANCE IN LOCAL QUALIFYING" warned in bold-faced type:

> If a player fails to return a score within 12 strokes of the USGA course rating of the course, an entry filed by him for a future Amateur, Mid-Amateur, or Senior Open Championship will be declined unless the player can document that he is capable of competing at the national championship level.

All of a sudden, the white lies I had told to expedite establishing my handicap at Barcelona Neck came back to haunt me. I had actually gone on to shoot the rounds of 69, 68, 70, 69, and 70 that I had rattled off to Judge Bailey and Jack Somers following the Sag Harbor Golf Club member-guest. I had even turned in a bona fide 64 tabulated in strict accordance with USGA rules by totaling up my scores in two separate nine-hole rounds played on successive days. What scared me was that I had yet to break 75 on any of the "real" courses where I had been country club bumming.

In fact, I figured that my scores at Southampton Golf Club, excluding mulligans and gimme putts, probably averaged in the low 80s. That scoring average was dangerously close to being twelve strokes over the course rating at Southward Ho. Although I had shown flashes of my youthful brilliance from round to round, I needed to regain the all-too-elusive consistency I'd had as a kid before it was too late. If I failed to break the lows 80s in two rounds at Southward Ho, I faced the prospect of being banned from all future USGA events as an imposter before my quest for the PGA Tour got off the ground.

In mid-July, I nevertheless received conditional confirmation of my application for the Amateur qualifier. The good news was that no one had questioned my handicap or disputed my ad hoc affiliation with the Sag Harbor Golf Club. The bad news was that I had been assigned to the first group off number-one tee in the morning round. Our starting time was scheduled for 7:30 A.M., well before I customarily opened my eyes and far too early to allow me to spend the night before the tournament in my own bed in Sag Harbor.

I rushed over to The Maidstone Club for another lesson with Eden Foster, hoping he could help me regain my confidence and raise my level of play. He greeted me with exactly what he had rush-ordered a few short weeks before: a set of King Cobra Tour Model irons. Anxious to try out my new sticks and show off the progress I had made under his tutelage, I marched him directly to the practice range and started swinging away with gleeful abandon.

For the first couple of shots, I performed like a champ, keeping the club on the proper plane and hitting the ball down the line. My new King Cobra Tour Model irons felt like wonder sticks. I simply couldn't miss. Then, all of a sudden, my dreaded drag sweep reappeared out of nowhere, tripping the club head on tufts of grass in mid-backswing six times in a row. Eden told me to take a break.

"Remember that ugly old guy on the videotape?" he asked.

I sighed mournfully. "Sure do."

"Well, he's just like Jason in *Friday the Thirteenth*. He's baaack—and it looks like he's gonna be with you for a long time."

Despite that dispiriting forecast, we kept plugging away on the practice range until my evil twin from the videotape temporarily went back into hiding. Then I broached the subject of my starting time in the Amateur qualifier, complaining long and loudly about the fact that I'd have to get up before sunrise.

"You must have forgotten what a blessing it is to tee off in the first group in a tournament," Eden chided. "You'll have the whole course open in front of you, no one to hold you up. Plus, you'll be the first one on the greens. They'll be freshly mowed, and there won't be any spike marks on 'em yet."

"Fabulous," I said. "Maybe I'll play better if I practice sleep-walking."

Eden ignored my sarcasm. "We're gonna have to get you on a revised schedule right away. I want you to get up at six-thirty every morning between now and the day of the qualifier so you get used to hitting balls at that hour. Trust me, it's worth it."

As usual, Eden knew what he was talking about. Taking his advice to heart, I joined the ranks of the local postdawn dewsweepers, and once I got used to it, the new routine did wonders for my golf. Every morning the holes in front of me were clear, and so was my mind. I gradually regained some consistency, which, in turn, lowered my scores to the middle 70s and boosted my hopes of playing well enough in the Amateur qualifier not to be banned from future USGA competitions.

Then, about a week before the tournament, my loose-knit support crew began to unravel. Eden had to cancel our last two pre-tournament lessons to supervise teaching clinics for members at The Maidstone. Paul Babcock had to cancel our dress rehearsal caddying round because of a pending real estate deal. Two afternoons later, Babcock called again. His real estate deal was set to close on Monday, the day of the Amateur qualifier; he informed me with regret that I'd have to find another caddy. In desperation, I turned to Toad.

"You gotta be fuckin' kiddin'," Toad scoffed when we met for a beer at Barcelona Neck. "I wouldn't tote a goddamn golf bag for a million dollars. Besides, I just ran into this lady I used to go to high school with. She just got divorced a couple of months ago. I told her we'd go out on my boat Monday afternoon. I can't be blowin' her off to caddy for you at some mucky-muck country club upisland."

I thought about recruiting my wife, Alison, and quickly concluded that caddying for me was far beyond the call of her matrimonial duty. Alison was a hardworking restauranteuse with her own business to run. She had already suffered enough secondhand trauma from hearing me bitch about my golfing setbacks, and for better or worse, she didn't know a sand wedge from a sandwich. It was clear that I would have to face the U.S. Amateur qualifier in the same way every golfer must ultimately face his inner and outer demons—alone.

Like Crenshaw on the eighteenth green at Augusta National, I suddenly broke down in tears when I got into the Jeep to drive to Bay Shore to play my first practice round. Alison was standing on the front steps of our house wearing a white bathing suit with a blue-and-white-striped sailor's shirt tied around her waist. Her blond hair shone like a halo in the morning sun.

"Whack 'em good, honey," she said, waving good-bye. "And remember, I love you and my heart will be right there with you no matter what."

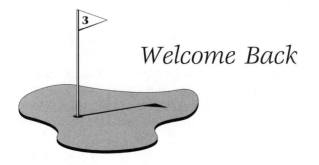

Welcome Back

On or about eleven A.M. on Monday, August 7, I stood on the sixteenth tee at Southward Ho Country Club making the Sign of the Cross. My entire body trembled at the sight of the hundred-foot-tall pine trees lining both sides of the fairway in front of me. I gulped for breath as rushes of adrenaline surged through my veins. Then I Crossed myself once more.

There were just three holes left to play in the opening round of the New York regional qualifier for the 1995 United States Amateur Championship. To the awestruck disbelief of both my playing partners and myself, I was even par on the day. And the only way I could account for my performance or hope to keep it up was through continuing Acts of Divine Intervention.

Overnight, a preautumn cold front had dropped the temperature from the low nineties to the middle seventies. It had also reversed the direction of the prevailing winds and turned the strategic challenges of the 6,582-yard, par 71 Albert W. Tillinghast course upside down. The par fives had become unreachable in two shots for even the biggest hitters, while the long par fours were well within mid-iron approach shot range for relatively short knockers like me.

Number sixteen, the hole at hand, happened to be exceptionally demanding under any weather conditions. It was an elegantly uncluttered 419-yard par four with a kidney-shaped lake at the end of the tree line on the left and out of bounds on the right. Like most of the greens at Winged Foot and other Tillinghast-designed courses, the sixteenth green was guarded by bunkers on both sides and sloped sharply downward from back to front, ready to penalize a second shot hit left, right, or long.

I made a third Sign of the Cross, a gesture I had not performed once, much less thrice, in a single day for an even longer time than I'd laid off from competitive golf. Then I took my stance and proceeded to hit one of my most sinful drives so far. The little devil started down the left side and faded gracelessly across the entire width of the fairway toward a patch of Bermuda rough. I grunted with vexation as my ball came to rest a few inches short of the tall grass but also a good 180 yards short of the green.

Swinging a four iron on the strength of another adrenaline rush, I struck my approach shot so thinly that it failed to rise high enough to catch the following wind. I watched my ball peter out on a narrow incline about three yards below the putting surface and maybe 25 feet from the pin. My chances of finishing round one at even par now depended on getting up and down, since both the seventeenth and eighteenth holes were even more difficult than the sixteenth, and I had little hope of birdieing either one of them.

Given my state of hypertension, I knew there was no way to summon the soft touch required for a conventional pitch and run, so I clutched my poppa's antique Ping putter and prepared to hit a "Texas wedge" from off the green.

"O, Lord, please just let me get this close," I whispered. "If you'll just let me make par, I swear I'll go to church on Sunday."

I jabbed at my ball with what could only be described as teleological trepidation, and looked up just in time to see it hit the pin and drop in for a miraculous birdie three. That put me at one under with only two holes to go.

"Jesus Christ!" exclaimed one of my playing partners, a short, stocky, stubble-faced twenty-seven-year-old Italian food scion named Matthew Esposito who was about to go five over on the day. "How did you do that? My putts keep lipping out and yours roll straight in."

I made another quick Sign of the Cross and looked him in the eye. The last time I had played in a tournament of this caliber Esposito had been only two years old, and the third member of our group, a wiry twenty-five-year-old health claims executive named Daniel Goldstein, who could outdrive both of us by forty yards, had not yet been born.

"You're a good Catholic, aren't you, Espo?" I said at last.

"Yep."

"Well, then, do like your Uncle Harry and pray."

"I have been praying," Esposito admitted. "But my putts still won't drop."

"Then pray harder."

In retrospect, I probably should have promised to enter the priesthood in exchange for another God-given stroke of luck like the birdie on sixteen. We had to hit directly into the wind on the 214-yard, par three seventeenth, which made the hole effectively play like 230 yards. After pulling my seven wood tee shot into the greenside trap on the left, I bladed a sand wedge twenty-five feet past the pin and three putted for a double-bogey five.

Somehow, I managed to shake off the costly errors at seventeen, and limped home on eighteen with one of those pars that could've been a birdie if I'd just hit a bolder putt. My first round score added up to a one over par 72, a much lower number than I had any right to expect under the circumstances. And although I couldn't help rankling over my blunders on the next-to-last hole, my remorse was far outweighed by my relief at coming in well below the twelve over par score that would have prompted the USGA to ban me from future national-class competitions.

My relief soon turned to outright elation as I realized that I had become the leader in the clubhouse and was destined to remain so for a good half hour. That was only partly because I had been in the first group off the number-one tee that morning. Esposito and Goldstein had shot 77 and 76, respectively. A loudmouthed guy in the group behind us matched my 72. He and I remained tied for the lead until a 69 came in, followed by a 70 and a few 71s. But it looked like nobody else was going to do better.

"Well, hot shit," I muttered under my breath. "Hot, hot fuckin' shit."

I watched an elderly lady wearing a USGA cap print my name on the leader board next to the other low scorers, overhearing her grumble that the afternoon tee times were going to be a good twenty minutes behind schedule because of slow play in the morning round. Then I wolfed down a $13 buffet sandwich in the clubhouse bar and decided to go over to the driving range until my threesome was called to the tee.

I hoped that by hitting a few balls I might be able to keep my muscles loose and my attention focused on the present. But my mind kept replaying the remarkable round I had just shot and the equally unlikely chain of events that had transpired over the preceding seventy-two hours. As I finished one small bucket and started in on another, I remained blissfully unaware that I was setting myself up for a disaster far worse than my double on seventeen.

" **G**olf is the reason for being."

E. Parker "Skip" Yutzler Jr. grinned into the dimming twilight as we hurried along the back nine at Southward Ho on the Sunday evening before the Amateur qualifier, muttering the aphorisms of a dearly departed fellow club member.

"We work so that we may live," he declared, "and we live so that we may play the game."

Skip appeared to be in his late forties or early fifties. He had mischievous blue eyes and a roundish, clean-shaven face shaded by a University of Virginia baseball cap. Like me, he was wearing a thin cotton golf shirt and Bermuda shorts in response to the unrelenting heat wave that had hung over Long Island for the past month and a half.

Skip handed over a business card that identified the firm of E. Parker Yutzler, Inc. as "Recreation Specialists." I gleaned from our conversation that he supplied and marketed various types of playground equipment. I also learned that he was a six-handicapper who had won several intramural tournaments at Southward Ho, though never the club championship itself, and that he had amassed a wealth of insider information about the deceptive subtleties of his home course.

"The greens here roll pretty smooth, but they're tricky to read," he informed me as we teed off on number twelve. "They never break as much as it looks like. So when in doubt, don't give away the hole."

I nodded, jotting down his remarks in a pocket-size spiral notebook as faithfully as a Bible scholar. Although I was genuinely grateful for the advice, my note taking happened to be a little disingenuous. In a previous visit to Southward Ho, I had already formulated a putting strategy that coincided with Skip's. I had to give him the impression, however, that I had never seen the course before. According to the procedural sheet sent out by Metropolitan Golf Association officials co-organizing the Amateur qualifier on behalf of the USGA, competitors were permitted only one practice round, in which they could play only one ball.

The MGA's arbitrary limitation on practice rounds, which I was surreptitiously violating that Sunday evening, didn't seem fair to me for several reasons. Three of the names listed on the tee time sheets were members of Southward Ho who could play the course every day. At least twenty other entrants lived in nearby towns; as I later learned in confirmation of my suspicions, they had also gained access to the course on more than one previous occasion. I felt that I likewise deserved another go since my previous practice round had been an extemely unnerving experience.

I had actually gotten my first look at the site of the Amateur qualifier the previous Tuesday shortly after my golfing/drinking buddy Paul Babcock had called to renege on his promise to caddy for me. I remembered rumbling up Southward Ho's gray stone driveway feeling lonelier than a clump of crabgrass on the putting green at Shinnecock Hills. I passed by a swimming pool, tennis courts, and a band of preteen summer campers frolicking beneath some shady oaks, twinging at the thought of my own country club–oriented youth. Then I came to the end of the driveway to find a two-story brown-shingled building with white-columned porticoes that looked like a quarter-scale imitation of the Shinnecock clubhouse.

The starter on duty that afternoon assigned me to play my practice round in the company of a female golf pro whose name I never caught and a middle-aged fellow who introduced himself as Bill Bartels with a firm and overly energetic handshake. I could tell at first sight that Bartels was a player, quite possibly a touring pro. Somewhere around six feet tall with dark brown hair and a trim mustache, he had the sloping shoulders, deeply tanned forearms, and lumbering gait of a guy who spent most of his daylight hours on a golf course. He was wearing a pair of khaki-colored Dockers, a blue golf shirt mottled with perspiration, and a cap emblazoned with the Ping logo.

Bartels proved that I'd guessed right about his golfing abilities on the very first hole we played together, the 546-yard, par five tenth. I absolutely crushed my tee shot down the left side of the fairway, expecting to outdrive him by a good fifteen paces. Instead, I discovered that our balls were dead even in the fairway for what turned out to be the first and last time of the day. A solidly struck three wood left me a good 30 yards short of the green. Bartels knocked his ball all the way to the fringe with a four wood. I muffed an easy wedge shot, then three putted for bogey. He almost chipped in for eagle.

As our practice round wore on, my game grew wilder and wilder, while Bartels settled into a smooth swinging groove. He not only outdrove me on every hole, he outclassed me with his long and medium irons, his short approach shots, and his trap play. The only aspect of his game that seemed a wee bit off was his putting. By my count, he missed half a dozen birdie attempts from the twenty-foot range by a total combined margin of under six inches, including three that hung on the lip. And that was just on our first eight holes of the day. I, meanwhile, found myself hard-pressed to get up and down for a handful of pars.

"How long have you been on the Tour?" I finally asked as we walked up the eighteenth fairway, completing our first nine holes.

Bartels chuckled, shaking his head from side to side. "I may be crazy, but not crazy enough to turn pro. I'm just trying to tune up for the U.S. Amateur qualifier they're having here on Monday."

As I blanched with dismay, Bartels went on to tell me that he had never played junior or even college golf. Though he had taken up the sport at age seven or eight, he had not played competitively until age twenty-five, when he had joined a club out in Denver following graduation from the University of Colorado. Now a wizened forty-two-year-old, he worked as a salesman for a heavy-duty equipment company in nearby Seaford, Long Island. His only significant golfing victory had been winning the 1978 Denver city championship. Monday would mark his third attempt to qualify for the U.S. Amateur after two previous near misses.

Bartels's admittedly modest competitive biography belied his obvious talent, which, in turn, put my meager efforts to shame and filled me with a lockjawed dread of what lay ahead. I figured that he shot no worse than even par that afternoon, and maybe as low as one or two under, while strictly observing the MGA mandate to play only one ball. I played mulligans and practice shots whenever possible, and still barely managed to break 80. If Bartels was representative of the kind of accomplished ball strikers I would face in the Amateur qualifier, I was likely to be in for a very humbling day.

On the Wednesday afternoon following my practice round with Bartels, I decided to go looking for an insider's edge, a dubious pursuit that led me to an even more dubious place called the Oakdale Golf Center. Located on Highway 27 several miles east of Southward Ho, Oakdale was one of those gaudy goofball parks spawned by the late-twentieth-century golf boom that must have made the ghost of Bobby Jones turn in his grave. It featured a fanciful putt-putt course and a Japanese-style double-decker driving range covered with plastic mats. A block-lettered sign informed prospective patrons that they were not allowed to wear golf shoes on the premises and that anyone who deliberately hit a ball over the safety net surrounding the range would be ejected.

I came to Oakdale in search of one Joe Malloy, a proud and square-shouldered ex-Marine with a shock of white hair and a pair of prescription sunglasses who had been the head pro at Southward Ho for the better part of forty years. According to my sources, Joe, who had started his career as a caddy master, had been summarily dismissed from the club by a faction of Wall Streeters on the governing board who were frustrated by his laid-back manner and his lack of interest in pro shop merchandising. Watching him roam the plastic mats at Oakdale with a beat-up old five iron in hand was like watching Hemingway's fisherman-hero Santiago monger fake minnows at Sea World.

When I pulled Joe aside to introduce myself and explain my dilemma, he curtly informed me that he had not revisited Southward Ho in the eighteen months since his dismissal. "They just came in the pro shop one day, and said, 'You're out,' " he grumbled. "I've been invited back several times, but I have no intention of going."

Luckily, the hard feelings that rankled in Joe's heart seemed to make him even more willing to share several closely held secrets about the course he knew and loved like no one else. "Southward Ho is a typical Tillinghast tract," he began as we sat down between rows of sportswear racks in the Oakdale pro shop. "He designed it a lot like he designed Winged Foot. He wants you to hit the ball straight and keep the golf course in front of you. If you miss a fairway or overshoot a green, you'll get yourself in trouble."

Joe asked for the scorecard I'd kept during my first practice round, turned it over in his hands, and ticked off a list of par fours that bore witness to his claim. "On numbers one, five, six, eight, and fifteen, you should just leave your driver in the bag," he advised. "The fifth is short and tight, the others are doglegs where there's nothing to be gained by trying to cut the corner and plenty of trouble if you miss the fairways. On those holes you should tee off with a three wood or a two iron or whatever club you hit the straightest. Now, I assume you're familiar with fourteen?"

I nodded, frowning. The fourteenth was a bitch of a hole, a 222-yard par three with a deep but narrow green surrounded by clusters of sharply banked bunkers. And it typically played upwind.

"Just try to hit something to the front of the green, get your par, and get out of there," Joe cautioned. "If you leave number fourteen with a three, you'll probably pick up at least a shot on the rest of the field."

After filling me in on a few other fine points of strategy and ball placement, Joe offered to add what he called a "fifteenth club" to my bag. In this case, it was not the ghost of Harvey Penick, who had guided Ben Crenshaw to victory in the Masters, but a veteran Southward Ho caddy named Kenny Collins. According to Joe, Kenny, who had just come back from watching John Daly win the 1995 British Open at St. Andrews, was the only man alive who knew the ins and outs of the course as well as he did. "If I can get Kenny to caddy for you, you'll qualify," Joe assured me.

I left the Oakdale Golf Center slightly teary-eyed and full of newfound hope. Joe Malloy had reminded me of some of the cliché-sounding but truly endearing things that had made me become infatuated with golf as a kid: the instant bond that formed between players who sincerely loved the game, the heartfelt respect for a well-designed course, and in this case, a common contempt for imperious country clubbers like the Wall Streeters at Southward Ho.

I was again reminded of all that—and introduced to an invaluable practice round research technique—on the Sunday afternoon I played Southward Ho with Skip Yutzler. As Skip and I moved from green to green, he pointed out the tiny dabs of orange paint that marked the pin placements for the following day. Rather than putting to the holes that were cut for Sunday's play, he stuck a tee in the orange dabs and urged me to join him in rolling balls at the dabs from at least four sides to gauge the breaks and speeds.

As a journalist, my natural inclination was to write down detailed verbal notes, since the MGA had not published pin sheets in advance and seldom bothered to provide them for even the most important tournaments on its official calendar. But Skip offered to show me a far more concise and artful way of recording this mass of information. Taking a blank scorecard in hand, he used my pen to put a dot in one of the boxes below the hole numbers that were ordinarily used to report a player's score on the hole. The dot's position in the box—high, low, middle, left, or right—represented the pin placement on the hole. Skip then drew tiny arrows on four sides of the dot representing the directions a putt from those angles would break.

"Save you a lot of time and ink if you do it this way," he said. "It'll also save you from having to flip through several pages of notes every time you come up to a green."

I nodded, feeling dumber than a tee-side ball washer. Surprisingly enough, when I employed Skip's dot-and-arrow markings at tournaments in the weeks that followed, I was amazed to find that many of the professionals and top-ranked amateurs I played with were unfamiliar with his efficiently simple system and readily adopted it themselves.

As darkness fell that Sunday evening, I said my grateful goodbyes to Skip and drove to a cheap motel a couple of miles down the Montauk Highway from Southward Ho, where I cleaned my clubs and marked two sleeves of Titleists with big black identifying *H*'s. Then I turned on the TV and dined on a cheeseburger and chocolate Fribble from the local Friendly's. As I was waiting for the weather report, the telephone rang. It was Joe Malloy.

"I just spoke with Kenny Collins," Joe reported. "He said he's sorry, but he's seventy-two years old and he just cannot go thirty-six holes at his age."

Simultaneously burping and whimpering, I thanked Joe for his efforts and advice, then hung up the phone and stared at the TV screen. The weatherman was predicting an influx of arctic air from Canada in the predawn hours. That coupled with the bad news about Kenny Collins sent chills down my spine.

I started fumbling through my clothes bag. A notice from the USGA stipulated that all contestants were required to wear collared shirts. But unlike the PGA Tour, where all players had to wear slacks, the USGA permitted Bermuda shorts in competition. Having expected the summer heat wave to continue, I'd brought along three pairs of shorts and several changes of shirts. Now I cursed myself for not packing a turtleneck and long johns.

I finally dug up the one pair of khakis I'd stuffed into the bag, and I laid them out on a side table next to a wind shirt and two golf shirts I'd purchased at the 1995 U.S. Open Championship at Shinnecock Hills, hoping that the Indian heads on the logos would bring me luck. Then I left two wake-up calls with the motel desk clerk, one for 5:30 A.M. and one for 5:35 A.M., and telephoned my wife to ask her to call me at 5:45 A.M. just in case the desk clerk dozed off.

"Whack 'em good, honey," Alison said once again, adding in what sounded to me like a rather ominous tone, "And remember, I love you no matter what."

I told her that I loved her, too—no matter what—deliberately neglecting to add that the same did not apply to myself. Even though the Amateur qualifier was my first serious golf tournament in a quarter of a century, I could never again look at myself in the mirror if I wound up finishing dead last.

When I arrived at Southward Ho at around 6:30 A.M. on Monday, I felt like I was dead and wished I really were. There must have been some interlude of sleep during the preceding night, but I could not recall when it had occurred. My mind had begun to race as soon as my head hit the pillow, and it never seemed to shut up.

The Southward Ho starter assigned me a tall, goateed caddy from Central Islip who had the same first name and self-destructive aura as the late pop music idol Kurt Cobain. I asked him what he did besides toting golf bags. "I sorta work for the Postal Service as a sorta mail sorter," he replied, smirking at his double entendre. "The rest of the time I reside in Florida."

The experience of playing the first round of the U.S. Amateur qualifier, with Kurt at my side strumming my golf clubs and the flagsticks like imaginary guitars, proved to be something like trying to concentrate on passing a four-hour final exam in nuclear physics at a Nirvana concert. Still mystified by the big muscle motions Eden Foster had taught me, I carried both the pin placement scorecard Skip Yutzler had helped draw and a spiral notebook of three-by-five-inch index cards with the basic principles for every conceivable type of shot jotted next to the usual notations on course yardages. As I mumbled Harvey Penick's mantra about taking "dead aim" under my breath, my stomach growled on the previous night's cheeseburger, my hands shook like a Fribble mixer, and my brain kept belching from an overload of swing thoughts. But my play-by-numbers approach seemed to work. I'd made a few stupid mistakes in round one, including clumsy bogeys on the par five second hole and the tight par four fifteenth. But I'd also rallied with nifty birds on the sixth and the twelfth, as well as the putt-in from off the green on sixteen, and I'd holed more than a few character-building par saves. For whatever reason, I had been in that elusive state of being athletes call "the zone." And as I swatted away on the Southward Ho practice range in preparation for round two, I kept tying to get back into the zone by hook or by slice until a voice over my shoulder snapped me out of my reverie.

"Hey, dude, aren't you paired with Espo and Goldstein?"

I turned to face the loudmouthed guy who had been playing in the threesome behind us in round one.

"Better get your ass over to the tee," he said. "They're ready to go."

I snatched up my driver and sprinted across the parking lot to the tenth tee. As I reached the starter's table, I saw that Goldstein had just teed off and Esposito was preparing to follow him. A Metropolitan Golf Association official in a buttoned-down long-sleeve shirt and regimental-striped tie accosted me with a snarl.

"You just came within an eyeblink of getting yourself a two-stroke penalty, pal," he warned. "You been around long enough to know better than to be late for a tee time."

"Sorry, sir," I wheezed, trying in vain to catch my breath. "Scorekeeper lady said we were running behind schedule. Plees forgimme. This my first tournament in twenty-five years."

The official arched his eyebrows in evident disbelief and snarled at me again.

"Well, welcome back."

What happened next was a painfully predictable tragicomedy of second-round rock-and-rollover. Although I was spared the threatened two-stroke penalty, the sprint to the tenth tee and the untimely confrontation with the MGA official got my heart beating faster than my caddy's imaginary guitar strumming. It also got my dander up and increased my swing tempo almost to the speed of light.

With a rage reminiscent of 1950s-era PGA Tour club tosser

Tommy Bolt, I clobbered my longest drive of the day off the number-ten tee, then turned and glared at the MGA official as I started down the fairway. But like Bolt's infamous outbursts, my anger only hastened my undoing. I followed my drive with a temperamentally topped three wood shot that barely traveled sixty yards and a semishanked three iron that rolled haplessly into the first cut of rough short of the green. Then I poleaxed my pitch some fifteen feet past the hole, leaving myself an almost impossible downhill putt to save par.

My playing partners were graciously sympathetic. "We tried to go get you on the practice tee," Esposito confided as we walked across the tenth green to mark our balls, "but that official wouldn't let us."

"There's two things wrong with the MGA and the USGA," I groused. "Too many rules and too little common sense. They want to bust your ass for being five seconds late for your tee time, but they won't let you fix the damn spike marks other players make when they scrape their fuckin' shoes on the putting surface."

My insult to golf's governing bodies quickly led to injury. As I backed up the green to line up my downhill par putt, I failed to notice that Kurt was standing behind me, and accidentally stomped my right heel down on his left toe. He let out a yelp that resounded across five adjacent fairways.

"Oh, shit," I cried, wheeling around. "Now I've crippled my own caddy. I'm really sorry, man."

"Hey, it's all right, it's all right—my fault, my fault," Kurt replied, wincing. "Shoulda been watchin' where you was walkin'. Just go ahead and make this damn putt now."

Remarkably enough, I did hole my fifteen-foot downhiller to save par on number ten. The feat prompted a round of applause from Esposito, Goldstein, and my injured bag toter.

"Fuck the MGA, the USGA, and their two-stroke penalty," I shouted, punching my right fist in the air like Corey Pavin. "Let's get it on."

That triumphantly defiant gesture set the stage for my inevitable demise. As I realized later, I should have paused to take several very deep breaths, and get my heartbeat down to double digits. Instead, I marched directly to number eleven tee, asking permission from Goldstein and Esposito to reassume the honor of hitting first.

I wanted to bunt a Lee Trevino–type intentional fade to the

wide-open right side of the eleventh fairway, but I was so pumped up I blew through the ball with an uncontrolled excess of hand and arm speed and hooked it into a bunker fifty yards to the left of my targeted landing area. Instead of emulating the Merry Mex, I played the next four shots like the Hexed Tex, butchering my bunker shot, topping a two iron, and skulling a sand wedge. I wound up having to sink a curling twenty-footer just to save bogey on the otherwise birdieable par five.

Prior to teeing off the short par four twelfth, I tried to collect myself by retreating into the adjacent woods to drain my bladder. It occurred to me that given my pounding pulse, I might do better to pretend that I was the quick-tempoed Tom Watson rather than the easygoing Trevino. If I could mimic Watson's style from tee to green, I might really have a chance to salvage my afternoon round after all.

When I returned to the field of battle, I slammed a Watson-esque three wood down the middle of the fairway, then popped my pitching wedge approach to twenty feet. I felt certain of making the kind of routine par sorely needed to settle my nerves when I rolled my first putt to within three feet of the hole. But as I bent over to finish off my turn, my right wrist twitched involuntarily, causing me to push the putt off-line. I gasped as the ball lipped out of the cup, realizing that I had just suffered an attack of the infamous Watson yips.

The mishaps on eleven and twelve foreboded similarly careless errors to come. I got by the treacherous fourteenth with another par, but on the fifteenth, I hooked my three wood tee shot too close to the corner of the dogleg and had to punch out of deep rough. The situation demanded the kind of skillful scrambling for which my former junior golf buddy Ben Crenshaw was famous. But a poor pitch and an even poorer putt led to a bogey five, and the only thing I scrambled was the invisible egg on my face as I went on to bogey both the seventeenth and eighteenth to go six over on the day.

I hitched up my khakis and attempted to mount an Arnold Palmer charge on the second nine of the afternoon round. Except for a few unfortunate rubs of the green and my inability to emulate Palmer's trouble shot skills, I might have pulled it off. After ramming in a bird on the par five second, I drilled an audacious six iron approach shot to seven feet on the par four third. It looked like my birdie putt was heading straight for the center of the cup, but a spike mark bounced it off to the right inches short.

At that point, my heart sank and so did my chances of qualifying. Knowing that I probably needed to birdie most if not all of the remaining holes to make the cut, I reminded myself that Palmer had made four straight birds in the 1960 U.S. Open at Cherry Hills. But after barely salvaging par on the fourth, I pushed an overly aggressive three wood shot into the trees to the right of the fifth fairway, then bashed my next-to-impossible five iron punch into the overhanging branches. The ensuing bogey there, followed by a similarly frustrating five on the next hole and a brain-dead double bogey on the seventh, knocked me completely out of contention. I staggered in with an inglorious afternoon round of 79.

Upon returning to the clubhouse to check out the scoreboard, I discovered that my thirty-six-hole total of 151 put me among the upper third of the finishers but a full eight shots above the score needed to capture one of the five available qualifying slots. I found some minor consolation, however, in the fact that some of my fellow old fogeys had bested most of the long-hitting young flatbellies in the field.

The Southward Ho medalist was none other than my forty-two-year-old former practice round partner Bill Bartels, who fired an impressive three under par 139 that also turned out to be the lowest score tallied at any Amateur qualifying site nationwide. One of the two men tied for runner-up at two under was forty-seven-year-old David Kaplow, a pear-shaped Veterans Administration computer programmer who told me that he played golf after work at a public course in the shadow of the Verrazano Bridge and couldn't hit his driver more than 240 yards. Slots three and four were taken by two veteran amateur circuit competitors, thirty-seven-year-old co-runner-up Ken Bakst and thirty-five-year-old Jon Doppelt, who fired an even par 142.

There had to be a five-way sudden death playoff for the fifth qualifying slot, and it developed into a exhibition of the unique joys and pains of amateur golf. As my erstwhile member friend Skip Yutzler and a contingent of well-wishers led by an Asian beauty in a white miniskirt gathered at greenside, Terry McBride, a roughishly handsome forty-seven-year-old mechanical contractor with prematurely gray hair and extremely supple legs, sunk a ten-foot birdie putt on the first playoff hole, the par five tenth, thereby winning the right to join Bartels, Kaplow, Bakst, and Dopplet at Newport Country Club in Newport, Rhode Island, two weeks later.

After one of the other playoff contestants bogeyed number ten, three par-makers remained in contention for the first alternate spot. The unlikely cast of characters consisted of Adam Decker, a strapping twenty-one-year-old senior at Penn State University; Matt Corrigan, a square-jawed, beer-swilling thirty-nine-year-old fire department chief from Bethpage with his shirttail hanging over his gut; and Malcolm Smith, an early-thirtysomething Huntington-area country clubber with shoulder-length hair who was dressed in black from sun visor to shoe soles.

Smith smugly discombobulated the officials on the scene by announcing that he had no interest in competing for first alternate. Then he picked up his bag and stomped off to the parking lot.

Decker and Corrigan immediately commenced a second sudden death shootout that lasted for six suspenseful holes. The contest resembled a race between tortoise and hare. Corrigan, who had enlisted my former playing partner Matt Esposito as both bartender and caddy, kept bumping his ball back and forth from the fairways to the surrounding roughs, sucking from a bottle of Heineken in between each shot. Decker kept outdriving him by at least fifty yards on every hole, only to falter upon reaching the greens.

On the sixth and final playoff hole, a 419-yard, par four, Corrigan once again yanked his drive into the rough, and carelessly compounded his problems by punching his second shot into an even-deeper clump of grass bordering the left green-side bunker. He then chugged down the rest of his Heineken and staggered off toward a nearby tree, proclaiming, "I'm gonna take me a pee."

"Well, don't wet your pants, old buddy," I advised. "It looks like your opponent is taking an unplayable."

Sure enough, Decker had hit yet another of his resounding 320-yard drives underneath a cone-shaped pine tree that was unreachable from the tee for short knockers such as Corrigan and myself. He lifted his ball, acknowledged that he was taking the requisite one-stroke penalty, and calmly lofted a pitching wedge shot to a seemingly safe spot on the green fifteen feet above the hole.

Corrigan proceeded to chip his third shot a good twenty feet past pin high. Evidently unconcerned, he pulled out his extralong-shafted putter and, quicker than you could say, "Espo, pop open another beer," rolled his ball close enough for a tap-in five.

As Esposito and I huddled next to each other holding our breaths, Decker slid his potentially winning downhiller for par a full six feet past the hole. The kid took his time lining up the come-backer and put a pretty good stroke on it, but his ball skimmed around the edge of the cup, refusing to fall. Corrigan had won the playoff for first alternate with a bogey that bested Decker's double.

"I can't friggin' believe that putt didn't go!" the Bethpage fire chief exclaimed as Esposito slapped his back in congratulation. "But I sure as hell know where I'm goin'. Let's hit the Oyster Bar. This calls for a beer."

needless to say, the cannons of good sportsmanship compelled me to show up at the Oyster Bar on the evening of Matt Corrigan's upset victory in the playoff for first alternate at Southward Ho Country Club, and a jolly good time was had by all, including the otherwise deflated young Adam Decker. But despite the sudden onset of several tournament-induced physical and mental ailments, my conscience likewise compelled me to keep the solemn promise I had made to give thanks for my respectable showing in round one of the U.S. Amateur qualifier. The sport that had long since driven me to drink was now driving me back to religious worship.

The following Sunday, I was pleasantly surprised to find that the Catholic church in Sag Harbor, which I had neither noticed nor set foot in before, happened to be called St. Andrew's just like the tabernacle of golf in Scotland. Appropriately enough, the processional that morning was a hymn titled "Canticle to the Sun." Its refrain featured the lines: "Come dance in the forest, come play in the fields/And sing, sing to the glory of the Lord."

When the church organ sounded the final notes of the hymn, I made the Sign of the Cross and knelt down to pray that the Almighty Lord of the Links would continue to protect my unworthy soul with more Acts of Divine Intervention. Heaven knew, I needed them. For in the next phase of my quest, I would bid farewell to the pure sportsmanship of USGA-sanctioned amateur competition, and prepare to dance in the forests and play in the fields with the mammon-worshiping pagans on the pro golf circuit.

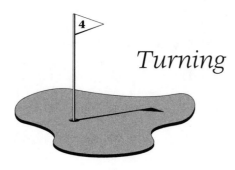

Turning

"**I** turned yesterday, guys."

"Sounds kinda nasty."

"It is."

"Congratulations."

"Thanks. Just wanted you to be the first to know."

I was climbing "Alps," the third hole at the National Golf Links of America, with two other transplanted Texans on the Saturday morning before Labor Day. A mild breeze off Sebonac Bay pushed at our backs, and a couple of high school–age kids were packing our golf bags. But with a ninety-degree sun beating down on our heads and soggy blankets of humidity hugging our legs, all three of us kept slip-sliding, huffing, and wheezing as we searched for our balls on the mountainous hummock guarding the green of this 418-yard, par four.

My member-host for the day was C. Barkley Davis II, a Midland-born financier with a double-digit handicap. Blond-haired, blue-eyed, and broad-minded, Davis had a tongue sharper than the horns of a bucking bull and a pair of arms as strong as any rodeo cowboy's. He had been hobbled by a foot injury, however, which forced him to wear basketball sneakers instead of spikes, and he found himself punching his golf clubs as if they were branding irons.

By contrast, his buddy Bill Weeds was a dark-haired, dark-eyed, fifty-year-old engineer with narrow facial features and a bona fide four handicap. Weeds, who hailed from Fort Worth, had an old-fashioned but very effective buggy whip swing that resembled the motion of his hometown PGA Tour pro Mark Brooks. Weeds was also about as skinny as a buggy whip, and he answered, not always pleasantly, to the nickname "Pencil Dick."

"Haven't you always been a little turned?" Davis asked as we started foraging through the green-side rough in pursuit of my ball.

"Yep," I said, poking at a tightly twisted patch of fescue grass with a pitching wedge. "But nothing like I am now."

Twenty-four hours earlier, I had committed the life-changing act of becoming a professional golfer, known in the trade as "turning pro" or simply "turning." In another twenty-four hours, I was scheduled to fly down to South Carolina, where I would make my pro tournament debut.

"I hear turning pro is a lot like losing your virginity," Weeds said.

Davis choked back a laugh. "What would you know about that, Pencil Dick?"

I allowed that turning pro was actually several strokes easier than getting laid for the first time. You didn't have to get a sex partner to agree to it. You didn't have to wait for an appropriate occasion. You didn't have to find a mood-enhancing aphrodisiac or slip on a condom.

"You don't even have to drop your pants, at least not right away," I added. "All you have to do is declare yourself—orally or in writing—to be in the game for the money."

"I presume you took the oral route?" Davis asked.

"Nope, I did it in writing on Friday morning when I filled out my entry form for PGA Tour Qualifying School. There's this little clause printed in bold-faced type at the bottom that says by signing the application you agree to forfeit your amateur status for a minimum of one year. You send in the application along with your three-grand entry fee, a letter from a PGA pro certifying your golfing ability, and a character reference letter from a nonfamily member, and presto, you've turned."

"Whoa, partner, hold on there," Davis insisted. "Are you saying that forfeiting your amateur status automatically makes you a pro?"

I shook my head, frowning.

"No, that's just what the USGA says. I'm still not sure what it takes to become a real golf pro. Remember when we were growing up in Texas how all the Mercury, Gemini, and Apollo program veterans used to mock the new NASA recruits who tried to call themselves astronauts? Thing was, you couldn't really call yourself an astronaut until you'd been shot off the end of a missile and hurled into outer space. I figure that to call yourself a golf pro, you've got to take that kind of flier. It ain't enough just to forfeit your amateur status and play for money. Any fool willing to ante up an entry fee can do that. As far as I'm concerned, you at least have to win some money. And maybe do something else on top of that."

Weeds looked over at me, smirking.

"See, I told you turning pro was like busting your cherry. You ain't guaranteed to get anything, not even an orgasm. But you sure as shit lose what you had before. You lose your eligibility to play in the U.S. Amateur, the Mid-Am, and the Trans-Miss. You lose your eligibility for the Walker Cup team. You might even lose your eligibility for the Davis-Mason."

Just then I found my ball sunk in a clump of ironweed. Hooding the face of my pitching wedge, I attempted to muscle it onto the green, but the ball squirted over the back edge into some even heavier grass.

"Pardon my ignorance," I said with a perturbed frown. "But what the hell is the Davis-Mason?"

"It's a three-day team tournament Barkley and one of our friends started a few years ago," Weeds informed me. "We play a Ryder Cup format at National, Shinnecock, and Maidstone every fall."

Davis stopped on the apron of the green, pondering the matter. "As a cofounder of the Davis-Mason, it is my considered judgment that Harry has not lost his eligibility to participate," he said at last. "But I reckon he'll probably lose lots of money. Since he's a pro, he's lost his handicap. He'll have to play scratch and spot all of us plenty of strokes."

"Fuck you very much, Barkley," I shot back, baring my teeth.

The Almighty Lord of the Links to whom I had prayed on both preceding Sundays back at St. Andrew's Catholic Church in Sag Harbor apparently decided to punish me for that ungentlemanly rejoinder. Having started the round with auspicious pars on number one and number two, I skied off "Alps" with a double-bogey six. I watched ruefully as Weeds holed a six-footer to save par and Davis two-putted for a bogey.

Moments later, I mounted the grassy ledge behind the green and paused to admire one of the most famous and breathtaking panoramas in the world of sports. The National Golf Links of America is sprawled over a wedge of former waste ground similar in shape but actually smaller in total area than the isthmus of Barcelona Neck. Its lush, immaculately conditioned fairways and pristine roughs encompass just 205 acres bordered on three sides by Bulls Head Bay, Cold Spring Pond, and Sebonac Bay.

In the distance, I could see flocks of gulls, geese, and ducks circling the old wooden windmill adjacent to the second hole, the elegant eaves of the brown stucco clubhouse overlooking number one, and the towering flagpole on the cliff behind the eighteenth green. I'd always harbored intensely mixed feelings about National, but for a brief moment I was struck by what its creator, Charles Blair Macdonald, used to call a "limitable sense of eternity, suggesting contemplation and imagination."

"The first time I saw that windmill, I could see why a lot of people think of this place as old Macdonald's funny farm," Weeds announced, disrupting my silent musings. "But you know, it's really just the pioneering version of Tour 18."

I couldn't help snickering at the intentional irreverence of his allusion. Tour 18 was a newly built course in Houston that claimed to offer players a global golfing adventure in one package; each of the holes at Tour 18 was touted as a near-exact replica of a famous hole at a legendary course such as Pebble Beach. But Macdonald had actually inaugurated the copycat technique back in 1912 by designing National in the image of St. Andrews and other well-established Scottish and British courses.

"You truly are a Philistine, Pencil Dick," Davis said, chucking a golf ball at his head. "For your information, Macdonald's homage to other golf course architects consists of only five holes."

Davis ticked off the names of the holes in question with an identifying comment on each one. He noted that number two was known as "Sahara" because it boasted a vast bunker inspired by Royal St. George's. "Alps," the hole we had just finished, was modeled after the seventeenth at Prestwick. Number four, known as "Redan," was a rendering of the par-three fifteenth at North Berwick. Number seven, "St. Andrews," had a green-side pot bunker

similar to the one on the legendary Road Hole but played as a par
five. Number thirteen, "Eden," was a par three in the spirit of the
eleventh at St. Andrews.

"The other thirteen holes on the course are composites or
uniquely sculptured from the existing terrain," Davis added. "You
may remember Macdonald's famous line that a green is to a golf
course what a face is to a portrait. You'll see exactly what he meant
when we come to the fourteenth, which he called 'Punchbowl.' It's
another of his original designs."

"I stand corrected," Weeds returned. "National isn't Tour 18.
It's only Tour 5."

As we sauntered over to the fourth tee, I listened to Davis and
Weeds continue their verbal sparring over the multifaceted personality and character of C. B. Macdonald. I had read enough of his
memoir, *Golf: Scotland's Gift*, to know that he had been a prideful,
ambitious old coot with all the fervor of a reformed sinner in
woolen knickers and a snap-brimmed cap. As young man, he had
admittedly considered golf "a form of tiddle-de-winks, silly and stupid." But while attending college in Scotland, he had fallen in love
with the royal and ancient game and with the Old Course at St.
Andrews.

Upon returning to the United States, Macdonald had first distinguished himself as a player, though not without the kind of con-
troversy that haunted him throughout his career. In 1894, he
finished second in what was meant to be the first United States
Amateur Championship, only to pronounce the event an unofficial
trial run. In 1895, he helped found the United States Golf Association with fellow linksters from Newport Country Club; Shinnecock
Hills; The Country Club of Brookline; St. Andrews Golf Club in
Yonkers, New York; and the Chicago Golf Club, of which he was
captain. That same year, he won the first USGA-sanctioned U.S.
Amateur at Newport, the site of the 1995 centennial championship.

Macdonald soon went on to make his name as one of America's
leading native-born golf course architects, laying out such famous
tracks as Piping Rock in Locust Valley, Long Island, and the Mid
Ocean Club in Bermuda, as well as National. He often boasted that
"The National," as he called his most beloved brainchild, was the
oldest championship course on eastern Long Island. That claim
arrogantly discounted The Maidstone Club, founded nineteen years
earlier, as being below championship caliber. It likewise insulted
the provenance of Shinnecock Hills, whose original links dated

back to 1892, though its present championship eighteen was not completed until the Roaring Twenties. It was also a claim that, according to Macdonald's many critics, could not be supported by the facts.

"The bottom line on old Macdonald and his funny farm," Weeds maintained as his ongoing debate with Davis reached a climax, "is the story of 'the million-dollar shot.' That was the real clincher on all his pretenses to greatness. And it came straight from the family circle, too."

"Excuse me for butting in," I interjected. "But at the risk of gettting caught in the crossfire, I'd sure like to know what million-dollar shot you guys are talking about."

"It's the famous million-dollar shot," Weeds informed me. "It came out of a wager between Macdonald and Peter Grace, the heir to W. R. Grace and Company, who was also the old man's son-in-law. Grace argued that National didn't meet up to the standards of a championship course because the first hole, which is called 'Valley,' is such a short par four. I think it measures something like three hundred and ten yards from the back tees and only two hundred and ninety from the front. Anyway, Grace bet his father-in-law that he could prove his point by driving number one green with a following wind. Macdonald agreed to give him three tries. Grace came up short and wide on the first two drives. But on his third attempt, he smacked the ball right onto the green."

"Jeez," I said. "So Grace won a million bucks on that one swing?"

"No, he lost a million," Davis corrected. "Macdonald was so pissed off about being embarrassed by his son-in-law that he decided to cut Peter Grace out of his will. The members at National figured that Grace would have inherited about a million bucks, so ever since, they've called that third drive the million-dollar shot. I asked Pencil Dick if he wanted to bet me a million that he could drive number one, but he didn't have the balls."

Weeds started practice swinging with a long iron that sent divots flying at Davis's feet.

"Eat shit, Barkley. This ain't nothing but a glorified miniature golf course, and you know it."

"The only thing miniature is between your legs," Davis countered. "I'll remind you that Bernard Darwin, the greatest golf writer of them all, concluded that 'there is not one single hole that can be called dull' because at National the player is 'perpetually on the rack, always having to play for the flag itself.' If you learned to read without moving your lips, you might look that up some time."

Privately, I had always tended to side with Weeds in the debate over National's championship merits. But I started leaning toward the Davis/Darwin side—and in almost every other conceivable direction—as my ball found a variety of the course's famous swales, dales, clefts, crannies, and hummocks. Bogeys on three of the next six holes gave me a new respect for National and a humbling outward nine of 42.

Not surprisingly, my playing partners were prompted to ask if there was any possibility of my regaining my amateur status in the near future.

"Afraid not," I replied. "You can write to the USGA to request reinstatement once the minimum twelve-month period expires. But as you know, golf is the only sport where an amateur organization sets the rules for all the pros. The USGA doesn't look kindly on guys who turn pro for a lark, especially not if you play in more than one or two events like I plan to do or if you wind up making any money at all. They'd probably make me wait at least a couple of years just to make sure I intended to repent my professional ways."

Davis led the way to a green wooden halfway hut, where we drank a six-pack of Heineken and munched Ritz crackers smothered with peanut butter.

"How much," Weeds asked me between bites and swallows, "you figure it's gonna cost you to play the pro golf circuit?"

"Much more than is wise or healthy."

I told him that friends of mine who had chased the mini-tours and the PGA Tour claimed you could expect to spend $1,000 to $1,500 a week on travel and entry fees. My biggest single expense so far had been the $3,000 entry fee for Q School. But I'd also spent more than twice that on clubs, balls, bags, gloves, golf shoes, clothes, greens fees, and lessons. All told, I figured my comeback quest would cost me at least $25,000 to $30,000 over the coming year, not including normal living expenses and such incidentals as paying my home mortgage.

"Guess you must be counting on your winnings to cover the tab for playing the pro golf circuit, huh?" Davis said, chuckling.

I hung my head, pained by the memory of our just-completed outward nine.

"No way. Most of my expenses are coming out of my book deal

and an article I'm writing about Q School for *Sports Illustrated*. I'm also getting some support from the people at Cobra Golf."

I explained that my coach, The Maidstone Club's pro, Eden Foster, had rush-ordered my set of King Cobra irons prior to the Amateur qualifier but had not asked me to pay for them. Instead, Eden had telephoned Cobra representative Jim Vincent, who immediately recognized the potential public relations value of backing my quest. Vincent, in turn, had put me in touch with publicists Karen Doren and Alison Jenks, who agreed to let me keep the irons and to send me a bag, head covers, and several caps.

For the sake of research, the Cobra people had also told me to contact their PGA Tour traveling representative, a guy by the name of Arnie Cunningham, just to see how he'd treat any other rabbit who called him out of the blue. Cunningham had said that he couldn't do a thing to help me unless I actually qualifed for the PGA Tour, and even then, I'd have to show that I was a real star. He claimed that Cobra had equipment deals with only ten players on the big Tour, most notably Greg Norman, Ben Crenshaw, and Hale Irwin. Beyond that, they supported four Senior Tour players, four Nike Tour players, and three players on the LPGA Tour.

"According to Cunningham, the Cobra Golf philosophy is just the opposite of Ely Callaway's," I reported. "He says the Callaway Golf people are after big overall numbers, that ol' Ely likes to brag about the high percentage of tour pros who use the Big Bertha and the Great Big Bertha. Cobra, on the other hand, supposedly concentrates on signing quote-unquote good players who are consistently winning tournaments. The idea is to get in bed with the big names and use them heavily in the Cobra advertising campaigns. Like I told Cunningham, it's probably gonna be a while before you guys see me in a TV commercial with Norman and Crenshaw."

"How about your balls?" Weeds asked.

Davis spun a Ritz cracker across the table, grinning.

"I trust Harry's still got his pair, Pencil Dick."

"Unfortunately, that's the only two balls I've got for free. I tried to get a bite out of the Titleist people, but they liked to take a bite out of me."

I recalled that a buddy who chased one of the mini-tours had showed me a letter from the Titleist promotions supervisor that said they offered full-time secondary tour players a 25 percent discount on balls, gloves, and shoes for their personal use. So I had telephoned company headquarters to ask about the programs they had for secondary and PGA Tour players, and to see if they might do something with me. The Titleist folks had acted like I was trying to subpoena them for a criminal grand jury. They had not only refused to answer my questions, they had complained to the advertising department at *Sports Illustrated*, where they had a big account, about the fact that I would even dare ask them to discuss their promotional programs.

I added that as soon as my already purchased cache of Titleists ran out, I planned to switch without benefit of discount or corporate enticement to Maxflis, the brand endorsed by Norman, Couples, and Nicklaus.

"Hmm," Davis mused aloud. "Perhaps there's cause to investigate exactly why Titleist is the number-one ball in golf."

I splayed my palms, grunting in affirmation.

"Maybe so, but I'm too busy to screw with that now. In the next six weeks, I'm gonna be playing in tournaments on three different coasts. Stage One of PGA Qualifying School starts October 15. I signed up for the Texas site at the Ranch Country Club in McKinney, which is out there in the sticks north of Dallas. Before that, I'm gonna try to qualify for a Nike Tour tournament in Sonoma, California, as a kind of tune-up for Q School."

"Cool," Weeds declared, peanut buttering another cracker. "What are your chances of qualifying for the Nike Tour tournament?"

"About the same as making it through Stage One of Q School," I conceded. "Which is somewhere between slim and none, and I'd guess that by now old Slim's about ready to hop on the next freight train out of Dallas. But that's still about ten times better than trying to qualify for a full-fledged PGA Tour event."

I explained that the entry fees for both PGA Tour and Nike Tour qualifiers were two hundred bucks a pop. The big difference was that in the Monday qualifiers for the PGA Tour events, you had about two hundred guys competing for only four spots in that week's tournament, which was why they were called "four spotters." The Nike qualifiers usually drew about the same number of players, but they offered up to fourteen spots a week.

Davis guzzled down the rest of his second Heineken, motioning for us to do the same.

"Let's proceed, gentlemen. Shinnecock awaits."

*   *   *

I stepped onto the tenth tee feeling almost as emboldened as Peter Grace. The hole that lay in front of me was a 435-yard par four dubbed "Shinnecock" after the nearby former U.S. Open site, whose clubhouse was visible in the distance behind me. Although I had no hope of driving the green, I was intent on showing my companions that I possessed some modicum of golfing talent, and I silently swore that my second nine of the day would be at least six strokes better than the first.

I blistered my tee shot down the open right side of the tenth fairway, only to see that my ball had barely rolled past Weeds's. My two iron second shot against the wind failed to carry the pot bunker twenty yards short of the putting surface. Once again, I was staring at another bogey in the making.

"This pro golf business sounds more speculative than trading pork bellies on the commodities exchange," Davis observed as we trudged toward the tenth green. "There's no guarantee you're even going to qualify for a single fucking tournament, is there?"

"Only what you'd probably regard as the most fucking tournament," I said. "I convinced the p.r. man at the Hooters restaurant chain corporate office to give me a sponsor's exemption for the Hooters Tour BB&T/Granddaddy Classic next week in Myrtle Beach."

"All right, that's more like it," Davis exclaimed, patting me on the back. "Pencil Dick and I went to a Hooters somewhere in West Palm Beach. Their ribs and chicken wings really suck, but the waitresses have the biggest boobs in the fast-food business. If you've got a sponsor's exemption, that means the fix is in. You're bound to get laid."

I shook my head, inhaling a deep breath.

"Not exactly. As a golf pro pal from Abilene once told me, getting a sponsor's exemption is like getting free admission to a whorehouse. It guarantees you'll make it through the door, but it don't guarantee you'll make whoopee."

My sponsor's exemption merely allowed me to bypass the regularly scheduled Monday qualifier for the BB&T/Granddaddy Classic. I would be exempted to play in the Wednesday pro-am and the opening rounds of the tournament on Thursday and Friday. But after that I was on my own. If I played well enough to make the thirty-six-hole cut, I'd be able to play in the final rounds on Saturday and Sunday and compete for a paycheck just like the real pros. If I failed to make the cut, I'd leave with nothing but the memories.

After bogeying the tenth hole from the bunker, I made yet another misstep on number eleven, known as "Plateau," wincing aloud as a four-footer for par rimmed the cup. My tortured expression moved Weeds to inquire about my physical health.

"Been feeling okay these last few days, but it has been rough," I admitted. "Playing in that Amateur qualifier at Southward Ho reminded me that golf is not a noncontact sport."

I told him that I had awoken the morning after feeling like I'd been in a car wreck and had spent the next week shuttling back and forth from driving ranges to doctors' offices. As it turned out, I'd developed a pinched nerve in the C-6 area of my cervical spine, a hip pointer, and carpel tunnel syndrome in both wrists. My wife had forced me to take a week off to rest, and it appeared that I had recovered from most of my injuries. But I wished aloud that I had started an exercise and stretching program before I had started playing golf again.

"It's never too late to get healthy," Davis pointed out, adding with a simpering smile, "I'm sure the Hooters girls would love to give you a workout."

I tried to ignore the jibe, and focused my attention on the 385-yard, par-four twelfth hole, known as "Sebonac." I hit the kind of drive Davis and Weeds liked to call "a blondie"—their shorthand term for "a fair crack down the middle"—and an even better approach shot. But my twenty-footer for birdie ran five feet past the cup, and I stubbed the comebacker.

"That kind of play won't help you score with the Hooters girls," Davis teased. "I hear they only go for guys who can get it in the hole."

"I believe the term is 'taking it deep'," Weeds said, smirking. "That's Hooter girl talk for shooting under par."

Determined to show my bigmouthed buddies that I could take it deep with the best of them, I started pressing my drives and shooting at sucker pins in the hope of setting up a string of birdies. The result was a series of bogeys and disappointing pars that added up to a seven-over score of 43 on the inward nine. I was supposed to be teeing it up with the pros in three days, but I had once again failed to break 80.

* * *

davis tried to revive my sagging spirits by treating Weeds and me to a traditional National lunch. We draped the mandatory blue blazers over our golf shirts and sat down in a dining room that looked out on number one fairway. The menu featured cold lobster, fish cakes, beet salad, and two bottles of a very expensive Puligny Montrachet. My wife, Alison, dropped by to say hello just as the waiter served the rice cake and syrup dessert.

"Are you really gonna let this wild man loose on the Hooters girls?" Davis asked her.

I wanted to pop him in the nose, but my arms couldn't reach that far.

"Sure am, honey," Alison said, smiling. "And he better not come home with any nicks on his sticks."

Davis almost doubled over, laughing.

"Sounds like your wife can talk golf better than the Hooters girls."

"You betcha," I said, as my cheeks turned redder than the beets we'd just eaten. "In fact, she's the best golf watcher I know. She used to be an actresss and a dancer before she went into the restaurant business, and she can mime any golf swing she sees more than twice. We went up to Newport to watch the final rounds of the U.S. Amateur last weekend. If you ask her nicely, Alison'll give you a better rundown on why Tiger Woods steamrolled the field than all the talking heads on NBC and ESPN combined."

"That I'd like to hear," Davis allowed. "Pray tell, what did you think of the young lad?"

Alison smiled again, then turned quite serious.

"He's a beautiful player. But that horrible man from Maine that he played against in the semifinals—"

"She's talking about Mark Plummer," I said. "What a great character, exact opposite of Tiger Woods. The guy's forty-three years old, red-haired, and bowlegged with a big red handlebar mustache. He tried to make the PGA Tour back in the late seventies, but busted out of Q School. He finally got reinstated by the USGA, and won the Maine amateur something like five times."

"I don't care if he won the Grand Slam, his mustache is hideous," Alison countered. "You could hang Christmas tree ornaments off that thing. Plummer's form is just as hideous. The way he wraps those fat pink hands of his around the end of the club you'd think he was holding onto a monkey wrench. He even swings like a plumber, jerk-jerk-jerk, clank-clank-clank. And he needs to learn some manners. I saw him spit on his club, then wipe it off with a paper towel and hand the towel back to his caddy. Ugh!

"That Tiger Woods, on the other hand, has nice manners," Alison continued. "He may be part black, part Thai, and part who knows what, but he has a lovely, milky-smooth complexion with nice round features. And he doesn't spit on his clubs. He's also got the most gorgeous swing. He takes the club back ever so slowly in a wide, wide arc, and sort of pauses for a split second at the top. Then he whips it through with these ballet dancer hips of his, and the ball takes off so high you think it's going to disappear in the clouds. You should hear the noise his drives make. They don't just go *whack* like my husband's drives. They make this loud whistling sound, like a guided missile going by."

I added that Woods seemed to intimidate the hell out of his opponents before they even teed off. Along with his legendary length (his drive on the tenth against Plummer measured 385 yards, and he was routinely hitting two irons up to 290 yards) he had a legendary swing coach in Claude "Butch" Harmon, Jr., the mentor of Greg Norman and Davis Love III. His caddy was sports psychologist Jay Bruner. The captain of Team Tiger was his father, Earl Woods, a Vietnam veteran who went around telling anyone who would listen that his son was destined to win fourteen major championships. Woods's gallery, estimated at ten thousand strong, was the largest crowd to watch a U.S. Amateur since the halcyon days of Bobby Jones.

The way the Woods mystique had affected my former Southward Ho practice round partner, Bill Bartels, was a perfect case in point. Because he had shot the lowest score in the nationwide regional qualifiers, Bartels had been paired with Woods, the defending champ, in the thirty-six-hole qualifier for match play at Newport and Wanumetonomy country clubs. He had carded uncharacteristically miserable rounds of 79 and 77, missing the match play cut by eleven strokes.

"Bartels told me that the first shot he hit on the very first hole at Wanumetonomy went out of bounds," I reported. "The crowd is already moving down the fairway, and he's announcing that he's going to hit a provisional. His hands are shaking, and he's saying to himself, 'My God, Tiger thinks I'm going to shoot 100.' That one bad swing led to a triple bogey on number one. He claims he didn't strike the ball too badly after that, but he couldn't get anything going with his putter. The next day, he hit sixteen greens at Newport Country Club, and kept missing two- and three-footers for par."

"Well, if you ask me," Alison interjected, "Tiger Woods's father has done a much better job than whoever it was that raised that Mark Plummer."

"Yeah, but Plummer hung in there a lot longer than anybody expected, Tiger included," I reminded her. "Woods only had him one down when they got to the eighteenth. Then he hits his second shot stiff, and Plummer folds."

In the thirty-six-hole final the following day, Woods's opponent was another forty-three-year-old, George "Buddy" Marucci Jr., a dour-faced luxury car dealership executive from Berwyn, Pennsylvania, who had won club championships at Seminole and Pine Valley as well as four home state amateur titles. Marucci had actually had Woods three down after the first twelve holes, only to squander his advantage in the opening holes of the second round. Once again, Woods had arrived at the last hole protecting a one-up lead. Then he had punched an eight iron to within eighteen inches of the cup to seal another two-up victory.

"When the match is over, somebody in the media tent asked Tiger which of his two consecutive U.S. Amateur titles meant the most to him," I recalled. "The kid didn't miss a beat thinking about it. He said, 'This one meant more because it showed how far my game has come. That shot at eighteen—damn! That's the only shot I could hit close, that half shot. I didn't have it last year. I didn't have it at Augusta.' "

Davis ordered a third bottle of wine and announced that in his humble opinion, the jury was still out on Tiger Woods.

"I seem to remember that a doughboy from Ohio named Jack Nicklaus had an amateur career that was just as impressive, if not more so. In fact, if memory serves, I believe Fat Jack finished second to Arnold Palmer in the 1960 U.S. Open at the age of twenty, the summer before he turned pro. Since then, he's won over eighty pro tournaments of which twenty have been major championships. Last time I looked, Woods's best finishes in major league pro events were a tie for forty-first at the 1995 Masters and a tie for sixty-eighth at the 1995 British Open. In seven prior PGA tournament starts, he's never even made a cut."

Alison leaned over and hugged my shoulders.

"Hear that, honey? Barkley sounds like he knows what he's talking about. You'll be better than Tiger Woods some day if you just keep whacking."

"Yeah," I snorted, "same day hell freezes over."

Davis looked around the table, grinning.

"Well, now that we all seem to be nicely lubed, what say we play another eighteen?"

"Great idea," Weeds said with a burp. "I'd like to go head-to-head with this here Hooters Tour pro to see if he's ready to take the heat. He doesn't even have to spot me any strokes."

At that point, Alison wisely excused herself, explaining that she had to go into Southampton to supervise the pitching of a six-pole tent for a charity party she was catering that evening. Against my better judgment and the protests of my bloated belly, I reluctantly agreed to take up Weeds's challenge.

"Good man," Davis cheered, lifting his wineglass. "Here's to whipping Pencil Dick Weeds today and Tiger Woods tomorrow."

all three of us needed two extra mulligans just to get off number one tee. But after that wobbly start, my wine-tuned tempo found a groove, and I began to play almost as well as a bona fide touring pro. I made routine pars on one and two, got past "Alps" with a crisp par-saving chip from the fringe, and birdied the par-five fifth to set up an outward nine of one under. Weeds battled back valiantly, but found himself three down at the turn.

The inward nine became considerably more difficult as the northerly wind whipped up, making National's longest par fours unreachable with anything less than a four wood. But after three scrambling bogeys in a row, I rallied with pars on thirteen, "Eden," and fourteen, "Cape," to remain three up on Weeds with four holes to go.

Even after reconstructing the incident a dozen times over the next two months, I was never able to determine exactly what happened on the fifteenth, known as "Narrows," but whatever it was, it could not have occurred at a worse time. After pushing my drive onto a mound in the right rough, I confronted a 175-yard sidehill shot with my ball lying almost at eye level. Intent on closing out my match with Weeds, I ripped my five iron around and through like a baseball bat. The ball jumped out in a leftward spiral, coming to rest a good 80 yards short of the green. Then I felt a needle-point prickling in the middle of my back.

"Nice try, Mr. Hooters," Weeds shouted across the fairway. "Appreciate you leaving the door open."

Luckily, I slammed the door shut after we halved both "Narrows" and "Punchbowl," the crater-greened sixteenth, with bogeys. The middle of my back burned with every step I took. Whenever I attempted to make a full swing, the flames grew even hotter. It was all I could do to finish the round without bawling like a baby.

When the three of us finally made it back to the locker room, I started rubbing my spine up and down one of the ceiling support poles in the hope of alleviating the pain. At Davis's request, an attendant brought in a tray of rum-spiked Southsides. But the pain still refused to go away.

"Jesus H. Christ," I muttered in between pole rubs. "This is all I need right before my first pro tournament."

"Hey, don't worry," Weeds said as the attendant served another tray of Southsides. "You got your game going again on the second eighteen."

Davis poured the ice from his drink into a locker-room towel, wrapped the towel into a ball, and wedged it between my back and the pole.

"What you need is a good hard massage," he said, grinning as he had during lunch. "And I know just who'll give it to you good and hard."

Davis hoisted his Southside for a toast.

"Here's to those Hooters girls," he cheered. "Looks like Harry's gonna have his hands full—and so are they."

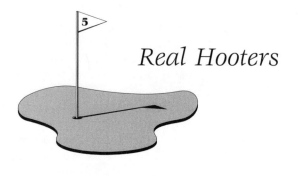

Real Hooters

Isabelle bent over my half-naked body and placed her soft, supple hands around the nape of my neck. As she turned me facedown on the bed table, I heard the tintinnabulations of a New Age mood music tape pierce the cool dry silence of the darkened room. A strange sweet herbal scent began to fill my nostrils, making me yearn for Isabelle to release me from the palpitating ache that seemed to permeate my entire being.

"Just remember, it's okay to moan," she whispered, quickly adding with a giggle, "You can't imagine how many of my clients try not to—like God forbid, they might enjoy this."

Slowly, smoothly, but with steadily increasing firmness, Isabelle began working her way down my spine, fingering, fondling, caressing, affricating each nook and cranny. At last, she reached my most hypersensitive area, touched it just once, then stopped short and gasped.

"Oh, my. It feels like a rope."

I jerked my head around and stared up at her, moaning as if on cue.

Isabelle had an aloe vera–oiled complexion, beguiling brown eyes, and close-cropped brunette hair. She also had the bulging biceps and barrel-chested build of an NFL offensive guard. Physically, professionally, and in almost every other way, she was a far cry—and many, many moans—from the Hooters girls back at the BB&T/Granddaddy Classic.

But frankly, my dear, Isabelle was so good at her job as resident massage therapist at a tourist spa in North Myrtle Beach that I wouldn't have given a damn if she had been uglier than the Wicked Witch of the Intercoastal Waterway. As soon as she began applying her unique personal talents to untying the rope-tight knot that had crucified the middle of my back for the past three days, I was ready to dance her down the Grand Strand and whisk her off to the nearest wedding chapel.

For better or worse, I quickly realized that fantasy just wouldn't be happening at half past seven o'clock on the morning of September 7. Isabelle was happily married to another massage therapist named Marty, and it was much too late for us to dally. In a few short hours, I was supposed to tee off in my first professional golf tournament. I didn't want to embarrass the Hooters Tour officials who had given me a sponsor's exemption—or myself—by not even being able to swing a club.

Isabelle broke the bad news about my condition as gently as she could.

"I'm afraid your psoas muscle is in spasm. I've gotten it to relax a little, but it'll take several more sessions before the knot is going to release completely."

Isabelle noted that I was suffering from the most common occupational hazard of my new profession. She said government research showed that the back was the most vulnerable of all the major body parts, accounting for over 25 percent of the 3.5 million injuries in the American workplace each year. Golfers ran up to twice the risk, with an estimated 50 percent of all on-course injuries involving back problems. It was no wonder than the entourages of successful PGA Tour pros often included a physical trainer, a masseuse, and/or a chiropractor.

The good news was that I didn't have the same types of afflictions that plagued Lee Trevino and Fred Couples. Their problems were located in the lumbar region of the lower back, and reportedly included serious disk or degenerative complications. My problem was basically the result of putting too much stress on a muscle, the psoas, that stretched from my pelvis to my middle back.

"The best thing to do is give it a rest," Isabelle advised, "so you don't subject the muscle to any more strain."

"No can do." I sighed. "Gotta play golf for at least the next two days in a row, and hopefully for two more days after that, if I make the cut."

"Playing golf is probably the worst thing you can do," Isabelle warned. "Most golfers get hurt because they don't do any stretching. How about you?"

I shook my head. "Uh-uh. Don't know how."

Isabelle instructed me to lie down on the bed table again, this time with my face up and both arms pointing out at right angles from my body. She grasped my left heel and eased it across my right knee toward my right shoulder. I could feel and hear a cacophony of crackling in every muscle group. Isabelle returned my left heel to its original position and repeated the crossover contortion with the right leg. Once again, my muscles crackled in protest.

"The only way you're going to get through the next four days," she said, "is by doing this for at least twenty minutes before and after you golf. Otherwise, that psoas is just going to keep tightening up on you."

Isabelle showed me a few variations on the leg crossover, some hamstring stretches, and some neck and shoulder stretches. When our hour-long session was over, she sent me on my way with a mini-lecture on the importance of drinking plenty of liquids.

"You've got to keep lubricating your system," she reminded me, "so the back muscles have a chance to loosen up and start healing."

I kissed her on the cheek and staggered out the door, cursing my recklessly indulgent behavior at the National Golf Links of America.

"Getting lubed on those damn rum Southsides last Saturday is what caused me to screw up my back in the first place."

"Try water this time around," Isabelle suggested.

When I arrived at Pine Lakes International Country Club in Myrtle Beach later that morning, the first thing I wanted to do was dive into an ice-cold mint julep, Isabelle's advice notwithstanding. The impulse came partly from my smarting psoas and partly from the sore sights before my eyes. As I pulled up in front of the white-columned three-story plantation-style clubhouse, I was greeted by a foursome of black retainers dressed up like Scottish clansmen in red tunics, blue tam-o'-shanters, and color-coordinated tartan knickers. Two of them opened the driver's-side door of my rented Grand Am, while the other two rushed around to the trunk, offering to shine my shoes and polish my clubs.

I tipped one of the Afro-American Highlanders five bucks to take my golf bag over to the practice tee.

"I sure do appreciate that, sir," he said. "You're the only man who's given me any money around here. I'm close to God, and I will be prayin' for you."

I thanked him for his help and his prayers, then ducked back into the Grand Am to collect a couple of pens and the notebook in which I had jotted down the historical facts pertaining to Pine Lakes' bizarre multicultural motif.

The day before, one of the grill room's resident barflies had informed me that the place was called "The Granddaddy" because it was the first golf club in Myrtle Beach. The original eighteen holes, of which only the front nine remained, had been built in 1927 under the direction of golf course architect Robert White of St. Andrews, Scotland. The Highlander-style employee uniforms were supposedly intended to honor White's influence. In keeping with its international theme, Pine Lakes also boasted a croquet court with a putting green grass surface and rectangular cast-iron wickets.

"Our other great claim to fame is that *Sports Illustrated* got started right here in 1954," the barfly had added. "A bunch of the top executives from Time-Life Inc. were down here on a kinda retreat, and they came up with the idea for their new magazine. One of 'em wrote the name with a piece of chalk on the oak bar inside the clubhouse. We would of had us a real nice little memorial to the foundin' of *Sports Illustrated* if one of the help hadn't come in the next mornin' and rubbed it off with a washcloth."

I slipped the notebook and pens into my hip pocket and headed across the parking lot toward a silver trailer that served as the Hooters Tour's mobile command post. Both sides of the trailer were emblazoned with the sponsoring restaurant chain's coyly contrived orange-and-brown logo, which sported a wide-eyed hoot owl as its centerpiece.

My heart began to race as a far more eye-catching gaggle of Hooters girls gathered next to the scoreboard behind the trailer.

They were all dressed in orange short-shorts and white tank tops designed to flaunt their bountifully endowed bosoms. As usual, they were chaperoned by a slightly older woman in a blue pantsuit who kept clapping for their attention and calling out shrill instructions like a corporate den mother.

The very presence of the Hooters girls was both an anomaly and a tease. Pro golf seemed to attract proportionately fewer female groupies than tennis or glamorous arena sports such as basketball, and as the flyers for the Hooters Tour's regular Wednesday night Bible study classes indicated, many players were devoutly religious family men. Although I knew that there were also several wild and crazy party animals in the tournament field, I doubted if they or anyone else had much of a chance of scoring with one of the Hooters girls, given the presence of their chaperone.

Ironically, the closer I got to the Hooters girls, the less appealing most of them looked. At least five of the six in my line of sight had dishwater-dull faces layered with too much makeup and teased-up hairdos that were fraying amid the day's double-80 heat and humidity. The one notable exception was a tall blonde who had emerald-green eyes, lightly freckled skin, and breasts the size of beach balls. As I rounded the far end of the trailer, I kept staring at her, and for a passing instant, I thought I saw her staring back.

Inside the Hooters Tour trailer, I met tournament director Cliff Calvert, a lean and frenetic fellow with the freshly scrubbed look of a Boy Scout, and Lee Moore, a veteran publicist with silvery hair and a sonorous voice. Calvert handed me a pairings sheet for the first two rounds of the tournament, while Moore tried to dig up the latest edition of the Hooters Tour media guide. I asked them what had possessed a fast-food chain to sponsor a professional golf tour.

"Market research," Moore replied. "The Hooters Corporation took a survey of our customers and found that 60 percent of them play golf. About that same percentage of customers are also stock car fans. So we decided to peg our image to two kinds of sporting events, NASCAR races and the Hooters Tour."

Moore explained that the idea for the Hooters Tour—officially titled the Hooters Jordan Tour—had come from the Florida mini-tour circuit that had sprung up in the middle 1980s. If the PGA Tour was the major league and its offshoot, the Nike Tour, the equivalent of AAA, the mini-tours were like AA and A farm teams. Most of the mini-tours, including one organized by a golf promoter named Rick Jordan, were localized around a single headquarters city, and they tended to change names and sponsors so frequently that the pros referred to them as the "alphabet tours." Hooters saw a way to mine the potential of minor-league golf as a marketing tool by sponsoring the first "national" mini-tour.

"Ours is a tour that emulates the PGA Tour," Moore informed me. "We put on approximately twenty-four tournaments per year, primarily in the central, south, and southeastern parts of the country, where most of our restaurants are located, and we broadcast final-round television coverage hosted by Jim Simpson, Larry Cirillo, and myself over the Prime Sports Network. All of our tournaments are seventy-two holes, not just one- or two-day events like most of the mini-tour tournaments. We have Hooters Tour qualifying school tournaments before our season starts, and we have Monday qualifiers for each week's event. We offer a purse of at least $100,000 per tournament, half of what the Nike Tour offers."

Moore claimed that most of the other mini-tours were "a form of legalized gambling" because the players were basically competing for a percentage of the entry fees, with about a third of the pot going to the organizers. A little over 85 percent of Hooters Tour purses came from entry fees; the rest was provided by the Hooters corporation and local sponsors with nothing taken out for themselves. The top money winner typically made close to $80,000 a season, with a chance to win a $100,000 points system bonus funded by Naturally Fresh Foods.

Moore estimated that over 2,500 players had competed in Hooters/Jordan tournaments since the tour's inception in 1988. He claimed that at the end of any given season, as many as thirty Hooters Tour players moved up in the professional golfing ranks by winning PGA Tour cards, Nike Tour cards, or conditional status on the Nike Tour. He then ticked off the names of some of the Hooters Tour's most prominent alumni: Jeff Maggert, Brian Henninger, Dave Stockton Jr., Mike Standly, 1993 U.S. Open champion Lee Janzen, 1995 Ryder Cupper and future British Open champ Tom Lehman, and John Daly, winner of the 1992 PGA Championship and the 1995 British Open.

"Must have been entertaining to have Long John around," I said, alluding to Daly's highly publicized alcohol and marital problems.

"John was John," Moore recalled. "He joined the Hooters Tour in the 1988 season and won about $20,000. You could tell he was a good player with a lot of ability. He not only could hit it a long way, he could chip and putt. Everybody liked him. But he did love to drink, and he was barely getting by financially. Sometimes he slept in his car because he couldn't afford a motel, and occasionally he'd have to get the other players to loan him his entry fees."

At that point, Moore had to take a phone call from somebody at BB&T, the local bank co-sponsoring the BB&T/Granddaddy Classic. I excused myself from the trailer and walked over to the locker room to strap on an elastic rib brace I'd picked up at a corner drugstore on my way back from Isabelle's massage.

Just as I finished bracing myself, *Sports Illustrated* photographer Jim Gund came into the locker room lugging a pair of zoom lenses about the size of a golf cart's tires. Gund was a nicely tanned, very laid back thirty-two-year-old bachelor from Atlanta, which happened to be the Hooters corporate headquarters.

"You ought to go take another look at the scoreboard," he said as we started back out the locker-room door. "The girls misspelled your name. Instead of 'H-U-R-T,' they wrote 'H-U-N-T-T.' I got a shot of it for posterity."

Moments later, I heard someone calling at me from across the parking lot. It was the Highlander who had taken my golf bag out of the car.

"Mr. Huntt, Mr. Huntt, I got a caddy for you, sir," he said. "He goes by the name West, Johnny West. He's the best man out here, and he ain't been taken by nobody yet. Like I told you, Mr. Huntt, I've been prayin' for you."

The Highlander insisted on escorting Gund and me to the practice tee, where he introduced us to Johnny West. This highly recommended bag toter turned out to be a slim, slightly hunched over golf course maintainence man with indigo skin, a gold-capped front tooth, a pair of copper-framed aviator glasses, and a fake silver Rolex. He appeared to be anywhere between thirty-eight and fifty-eight years old, depending on whether he was standing under a shade tree or out in the sun.

"I predict we gonna do all right," Johnny said as we shook hands. "I want you to know that I caddied for Greg Norman over at the Dunes when he first come out on tour back in the 1980s. I hear you just comin' out on tour right now, so I predict we gonna do just about the same. You know, you look like him some, too—the hair and the shoulders."

Gund laughed so hard he almost dropped his zoom lenses.

"Let's hope Mr. Huntt here plays like Greg Norman," he said, struggling to maintain his camera grips. "Then we'll all be in Fat City."

Shortly after one that afternoon, I surveyed the first hole at Pine Lakes with a Maxfli-size lump in my throat and a chronic heat rash burning my butt. In an effort to increase the difficulty of the relatively short 6,609 yard, par 71 course, Hooters Tour officials had made it a par 70 by converting the 493-yard, par five eighteenth hole into a par four without any reduction in length. They had also switched the order of the outward and inward nines. The new front nine, which was not part of the original eighteen holes designed by Robert White, was shorter than the new back nine and more tricked up than a traveling circus.

My assigned starting hole, the new number one, called for the golfing equivalent of a tightrope walk. It was a par four that measured just 344 yards long, but the landing area looked to be no bigger than a trampoline. Thick stands of moss-limbed pines barricaded the right flank of the hole; a T-shaped pond on the left flank cut across the entire width of the fairway about 250 yards off the tee. The green was protected by a parade of elephant-back bumps covered with bands of monkey grass, and two hippopotamus-size bunkers.

I quickly discovered that my playing partners for rounds one and two were as idiosyncratic in their own separate ways as the golf course architecture. Like most of the other young players, they were carrying ultralightweight bags with pop-out stands to save caddy expenses, and they had the seemingly generic names Jim Johnson and Steve Jones. But they were cut from very different molds.

Johnson was 6'5", a lean, lanky, extremely long hitter with a pleasantly plain face. A California native in his late twenties, he had just returned from a year on the South African tour, where he had finished among the top fifty money winners. Jones was a twenty-three-year-old former junior college quarterback from Washington State, 6'3", with a brawny muscle tone and a sullen scowl. He later confided that he had been playing golf for only two years, a fact that would become starkly apparent and mutually frustrating well before the day was done.

Prior to teeing off, I tried to put Johnson and Jones at ease by explaining why a *Sports Illustrated* photographer was going to be following us around the golf course. "I made the guy promise to stay way back so he won't distract us," I told them, quickly adding, "but I figure having him around will be good practice, since we'll all be playing in front of thirty-five thousand people at the U.S. Open one day."

Johnson simply smiled and nodded, but Jones declared that the presence of the photographer would probably help his game. "I play better in front of a lot of people," he informed us.

I somehow channeled my first tee stage fright into the business end of the King Cobra two iron I'd chosen to lay up with. The sound of my tee shot echoed against the surrounding trees as I watched it fly straight down the fairway and bound to a stop comfortably short of the pond. To my relief, Johnson and Jones then hit safely down the middle as well.

"I predict we got about a hundred and fifty-five yards to the pin," Johnny West announced when he reached my ball. "Feels like we going into a little bit of a breeze, so I predict you need to hit a nice smooth six iron."

I tossed up a handful of loose grass to confirm his wind reading, and silently reminded myself to swing easy. Then I bored one of the best six iron shots of my life into the breeze with a slight draw. The ball cleared the left bunker and dropped onto the green about eight feet below the pin. Johnny signaled his approval by asking me to break out my tin of Schimmelpennick miniature cigars.

"I like to be smokin' a cigar," he said with a wink, "whenever a birdie presents itself."

I knew from my two previous practice rounds and the pro-am event the day before that the lumpy Bermuda greens at Pine Lakes were slower than the Labor Day weekend traffic on Kings Highway. As I lined up my eight-footer, Johnny reminded me to give the ball a good firm rap. I nodded, and rammed it over the back lip.

"Tough luck." Johnson sighed. "You were robbed on that one."

My caddy wasn't quite so sympathetic. "We come out here to get us some dinner," Johnny lectured as we walked to the next tee. "Ain't no use huntin' for pars. All we want to eat is birdies and eagles."

I promised to do better the next time a birdie presented itself, but that proved to be long in coming. After scrambling to save par on number two, I pulled out my hook-prone three wood and attempted to lay up short of the monkey grass–covered bumps that had been inserted across the middle of the fairway on the 495-yard, par-five third hole. Ben Hogan once remarked that a fade, for all its obvious faults, was a shot that you could control; a hook, he declared, was like having a rattlesnake in your pocket. I understood what he meant when my tee shot snapped to the left. The next thing I knew, I was serpentining my way out of and back into the woods en route to a double-bogey 7.

I bumbled through the next five holes in a stress-induced daze as my aching psoas muscle wreaked havoc on my tempo and my heat rash compelled me to stop every half dozen steps to paw at my itching butt. Each time I swung my driver, I either forced my follow through to overcome my back pain or failed to complete my follow through because of the pain. The result was what the pros called "army golf." My shots went left, right, left, right.

Upon reaching the ninth hole, a 370-yard dogleg-right par four, I was four over on the day and ready to jump in the lake guarding the green. But at Johnny's behest, I agreed to hit a three iron off the tee, and put my ball in the fairway for the first time in half a dozen holes. I then hit a six iron to five feet, and sunk the putt for my first birdie in professional competition. Johnny immediately demanded a Schimmelpennick to celebrate.

"We back in the hunt now," he proclaimed, exhaling a thick puff of cigar smoke. "Let's go on and get some more of them things with wings."

Up to this point, I had been so completely focused on getting through the round that I had forgotten all about the Hooters girls who were operating the refreshment wagons at various strategic points on the course. But as our threesome was making the turn, the freckle-skinned blonde with the beach ball–size breasts I had ogled on my way to the Hooters Tour trailer earlier that day approached from the parking lot. She offered me a can of Poweraide with one hand, while pointing at Gund and his camera lenses with the other.

"I kinda feel funny about doing this," she said, "but that photographer asked me to give you this drink and tell you to quit scratching your ass."

My face turned brighter than the blonde's orange short-shorts.

"I feel funny about it," she repeated. "No one's ever asked me to do something like this before."

"Me either," I said. "You see, I'm sort of the booby pro in this event."

The blonde cringed at my unfortunate choice of words as I tried to explain that I was writing a book about chasing the professional golf circuit.

"Well, good luck, Mr. Booby," she said, rolling her emerald-green eyes and turning back toward the parking lot. "I hope you hit a bestseller."

My temporary embarrassment quickly turned to seething annoyance on the 563-yard, par-five tenth. A weakly faded tee shot followed by another duck-hooked three wood left me scrambling to save par. But my efforts were made all the more trying by the mini-spectacle Jones created. After whalloping a drive down the middle of the fairway, he topped a long iron shot that stopped a good 140 yards short of the putting surface. He then uncorked a screaming eight iron that carried all the way over the hurricane fence behind the green.

Johnson and I watched wordlessly as Jones turned his golf cap around so that the bill was pointing at the back of his neck and marched to the fence in search of his ball, humming an off-key rendition of some rock-and-roll tune. After determining that his ball had indeed gone out of bounds, he marched back to the spot from which he had struck his errant approach, dropped another ball, and skulled it into the right green-side bunker. By the time he finally holed out, I had lost count of the number of strokes he had taken, but since I was keeping his scorecard, I had to ask.

"You know what I made," Jones snapped, throwing his golf bag down next to the eleventh tee. "I made a fucking snowman. I drove twenty-five hundred miles in three days just to make a fucking eight on a par five."

As the round wore on, both Johnson and I tried to keep concentrating on our own games, but our playing partner proved to be more of a distraction than my *Sports Illustrated* photographer and all the Hooters girls in the tri-county area combined. With each hole, Jones's shotmaking got worse and his infantile outbursts and off-key humming got louder. He reminded me of some of the club-breaking brats I'd played against in junior golf, save for the fact that he did not destroy any of his equipment.

I made my second birdie on the 367-yard, par-four seventeenth hole, but it was too little and too late to offset bogeys on eleven and thirteen, and a hapless homecoming bogey on eighteen. Johnson also faltered on the same back nine holes. At the end of the day, our tall boy threesome turned in numbers that sounded like basketball scores. Johnson and I shot 73 and 75, respectively. Jones was high man with an 86.

I felt the Maxfli-size lump in my throat plummet to the pit of my stomach when I checked out the scoreboard. It showed that sixty other players had shot 69 or better, which meant that the projected cut line would be at least one under par. The low score of the day was a course record 63 carded by Brett Quigley, a lantern-jawed twenty-five-year-old former New England Open champion who hailed from an accomplished Rhode Island golfing family.

I crept off to find a beer, consoling myself with the notion that I had two reasons not to commit suicide on the spot. First and foremost, I had avoided the shame of finishing last in the 168 man field thanks to Jones and half a dozen other players who did not break 80. Second, but almost as important, I had also bettered my previous day's pro-am score, which had inspired one of my fellow pros to brand me with a rather dubious nickname.

"**H**ey, lookee here," cried a high-pitched voice the moment I entered the clubhouse bar. "It's Wayne Gretsky, a.k.a. the Great One."

I turned around to see veteran Hooters Tour prankster Robert "Spike" McRoy crouching over one of the tables. As his own nickname implies, Spike has the wiry physique of a golf cleat accentuated by a pointed brown goatee and a razor-sharp tongue.

"You shoot hockey sticks on this dog track again today?" he asked.

I shook my head from side to side, forcing a smile. The term "hockey sticks" was not a reference to my clubs, but golfing shorthand for an eponymously figured 77, my score in the pro-am.

"Made it around in two under," I reported.

"Sheet," Spike wheezed. "You shot a damn 68?"

"No, I shot two under hockey sticks. How about you?"

"Sixty-nine," Spike replied. "My favorite fucking number."

I plopped down at one of the tables with a beer in hand and sized up the postround crowd of pros in the room. It seemed that most of the guys chasing the Hooters Tour could be divided into three categories. There were the aging has-beens on the way down who had spent previous seasons sliding from the PGA Tour to the Nike Tour and the mini-tours. There were the young wanna-bes on the way up who were attempting to get their games into tournament-hardened condition for a run at PGA Tour Qualifying School. And then there were various drawn or faded journeymen who appeared to be stuck in a kind of mini-tour rut.

My newfound friendly nemesis Spike McRoy fell into category number three. He had shown flashes of brilliance as the number-one player on the University of Alabama team, but had never quite managed to contend for the individual scoring title in the NCAA championships. Now age twenty-seven, he had distinguished himself as one of the most consistent players on the 1995 Hooters Tour by making twelve cuts in nineteeen tournament starts. Even so, he expected his gross winnings for the year to amount to only $40,000, which meant that he would barely clear enough to cover his traveling and living expenses.

The young wanna-bes gearing up for Q School often seemed to look like and swing like the former Hooters Tour players they dreamed of emulating. At one end of the range, you had the short and straight knocking Brian Henninger types, such as twenty-five-year-old Jack O'Keefe, a former four-time All American at the University of Arkansas who had been named the 1994 Australian Open Player of the Year. At the opposite end, you had the long and lanky Lee Janzen-like jocks such as 6'4" Mike Swartz, another Arkansas alum who had played in two U.S. Opens and listed boxing and bungee jumping among his hobbies. In sharp contrast to the baby-faced O'Keefe, the thirty-one-year-old Swartz had a singularly stone-faced demeanor that had earned him the nickname "Lurch."

O'Keefe and Swartz were currently locked in a very close race for first place in the $100,000 Naturally Fresh Foods bonus points championship. But the two ex-Razorbacks did not let their competition interefere with their friendship or vice versa. In fact, they traveled together in a purple Ford minivan and shared a common dislike for the touring pro's occupational hazard of living life on the road. "I get really sick of having to eat out all the time," O'Keefe complained. "It seems like the service is always bad wherever we go." Swartz nodded in semistoic agreement, adding, "And it seems like you're constantly packing."

Packing had also become a habit for the Jeff Maggert-like fairway to middling types who had sound all-around games but limited mini-tour experience. Among the more remarkable of the lot was thirty-one-year-old Eric Epperson, a blond-haired former landscape contractor from Dallas known for his deadly accurate iron shots.

Epperson had been playing golf only since his early twenties, but over the past year he had made up for a lot of lost time by driving cross-country in his red Ford pickup to play Nike Tour events in California, Lone Star Tour events in Texas, and Hooters Tour events on the East Coast. Several of his buddies had tabbed him as a dark horse candidate to make it all the way through PGA Tour Qualifying School in the fall.

Unlike most local mini-tours, the Hooters Tour also boasted a colorful contingent of foreign-born players, including several hard-swinging South Africans. But the most inspirational ball striker in the bunch was thirty-six-year-old Javier Sanchez, the son of an impoverished corn farmer from Michoacan, Mexico. At the age of twenty, Sanchez had illegally immigrated to Palo Alto, California, where he started teaching himself to play golf between shifts as a dishwasher. After turning pro in 1991, he had qualified for three U.S. Opens, become a U.S. citizen, and married an American Airlines flight attendant with whom he had produced an infant son. Although he was still struggling to emerge from the minor leagues, Sanchez retained a wonderous appreciation of how far he had come since leaving Mexico.

"I brought my parents up to show them what I was doing not too long ago," he told me. "When I took them out to the golf course, they just did not understand at all. I might as well have taken them to the moon."

Despite their diverse backgrounds, all these Hooters Tour pros shared something. This might have been AA ball rather than the major leagues of the PGA Tour, and Pine Lakes might have been a pitch-and-putt compared to Shinnecock Hills, but you almost always needed to shoot four rounds in the high 60s, and often a round or two in the low 60s, to win a Hooters Tour tournament. Brett Quigley's course record opening round of 63 was just the latest evidence that the competiton I was facing could "take it deep."

Over the next twenty-four hours, I would find out how deep.

"**Y**ou suck!"

"You swallow!"

I staggered into Yesterday's on Friday night following round two of the BB&T/Granddaddy Classic just as the regularly scheduled pep rally was reaching an off-color crescendo. Close to five hundred people had jammed themselves around the elevated dance floor in the main room. A frenetic deejay wearing baggy Bermuda shorts and a green tam-o'-shanter with a golf ball dangling from a cord attached to the crown kept exhorting the patrons on one side of the room to jeer at the patrons on the opposite side of the room.

"What do we have to say to that side?" the deejay asked.

"You suck!" the stage left crowd repeated.

The deejay pranced back over to stage right while pointing stage left.

"Tell me one more time what we have to say to that side."

"You swallow!" the stage right crowd answered.

I tried to spot some familiar Hooters Tour faces among the side that allegedly swallowed, only to realize that virtually every male in the room looked, dressed, and acted like a golfer. That was no mere coincidence. Myrtle Beach proudly advertised itself as "the golf capital of the world." There were over eighty golf courses in the metropolitan area, including one called Wicked Stick designed by John Daly and one that could only be reached by a ski lift–style gondola. At night, visiting hookers and slicers could choose between entertainments ranging from Dolly Parton's Dixie Stampede to the Euro Circus, the Hard Rock Cafe, Thee Dolls House strip show, and the discos on Kings Highway of which Yesterday's was the newest and most popular.

I finally found my own group of pro golfing buddies huddled around a table close to one of the bars. Two of them, Spike McRoy and Eric Epperson, now had something in common with me. That afternoon, we had all missed the thirty-six-hole cut of 139. The only guy at the table to make the cut, Spike's on-the-road roommate, David Bishop, a twentysomething Hooters Tour rookie from Florida, was celebrating his success by buying rounds of pink and greenish blue colored drinks in tall glass vials.

"Lemme get you a Sex on the Beach," Bishop offered as I sat down on a nearby bar stool. "Unless you'd rather have a Kamikaze."

"Looks like the Great One is in a hari-kari mode," Spike observed. "Sex on the Beach would just be wasted. Better go with the Kamikaze."

After downing a couple of quick shots at Bishop's expense, I felt a warm glow on my cheeks that blotted out any thoughts of suicide. Then Spike, who had missed the cut by two strokes after a second-round 72, began needling me about my own dismal performance.

"I saw where you only missed by eighteen shots," he said. "Did somebody make you play an extra nine holes?"

"No." I sighed, gesturing at him with the middle finger of my nondrinking hand. "But they should have let me play nine holes less on account of the guys they paired me with."

I told Spike that Steve Jones had showed up for round two singing rock-and-roll tunes with his golf cap flipped around backward. Jim Johnson had brought along his father, Jim Sr., who turned out to be a domineering little know-it-all. While Jones was humming "Stairway to Heaven" and Johnson's old man was making practice swings with a golf umbrella, I lipped out a very makable eight-footer for birdie on our first hole, the par-five tenth. I had almost equally good chances for birdies on eleven and fourteen, but ended up three-putting both.

"As we're coming to fifteen tee, I see this TV camera crew setting up in the tower, so I decide I'm gonna put on a show—and boy, howdy, do I." I recalled. "First, I yank my drive in the left rough. Then I chunk a five iron into one of the green-side bunkers. Then I blade my sand shot over the green, stub two chip shots coming back, and drain a ten-footer for a routine double."

I paused to guzzle down a Kamikaze.

"At this point, you might as well stick a fork in me because I'm just about done, but I figure what the hell, let's just keep shooting at pins and see what happens. Naturally, I wind up with fried egg lies in the traps on sixteen, seventeen, and eighteen, thank you very much, and bogey those three holes to go twelve over for the tournament. Then all of a sudden, I start getting it together again as soon as we make the turn. I lip out birdies on one, two, and three, and knock it ten feet on number four. That's when old man Johnson gets in the act."

Just as I had been drawing back my putter to run at a bird on number four, I heard what sounded like pocket change jangling over by the corner of the green where old man Johnson was standing. I had flinched in mid-stroke, and pushed the putt a good four feet off-line.

"Now I'm pissed, and the old I-don't-give-a-shit light is going on in my head," I continued. "Just as we start walking to the next tee, old man Johnson comes up to me with this sucky little grin on his face, and he says, 'Are you sure you're not a twenty-twohandicapper?' I look the fucker in the eye and say, 'Are you sure you ain't Mr. Bojangles?' I then proceed to slash through the last five holes like a mass murderer on the rampage. I try to cut the corner of doglegs I couldn't carry with a bazooka. I bang thirty-footers right at the cup without even bothering to read the break. By the time it's all over, I've racked up two more bogeys and a triple for a big fat 81, which just happens to be the worst score I've shot in a tournament since age twelve."

"That's why you're known as the Great One," Spike said, shrugging, as he and Bishop ordered more drinks.

The only one of my tablemates to express the slightest sympathy for my travails was fellow Texan Eric Epperson, who had fired a pair of 73s to miss the cut by seven shots.

"Keep hanging in there," Eric urged. "One week you miss the cut, the next week you may be in contention to win."

"Lookee here, Mr. Great One," Spike interrupted, poking me in the ribs. "I think we just might be watching some real pros."

He pointed at three long-legged women on the dance floor, two blondes and a redhead. They were gyrating à trois around one of the gold-plated support poles, smiling and licking their lips like stripteasers. Just as they appeared to be on the verge of taking their show one step over the line, the deejay with the green tam-o'-shanter recaptured the crowd's attention.

"Hey, yo," the deejay shouted into his microphone. "Anybody in here about to get married?"

A mousey young woman in a turquoise sundress raised her hand.

"What's your name, honey?" the deejay asked.

"Vicki."

"Tell me something, Vicki—can you give a good blow job?"

"Sure can," Vicki replied, giggling.

"Well, come on up here."

The deejay escorted Vicki onto the stage. Then he pulled up a chair, sat down, and propped a Kamikaze vial between his legs. Vicki leaned over, placed her lips around the Kamikaze vial, and drained it in one long slurp.

"All right, let's hear it for Vicki!" the deejay cheered. "She not only sucks, she swallows!"

Spike poked me in the ribs again, laughing.

"There's one more thing you have to learn about being a golf pro," he said. "If you've gotta miss a cut, the best place to do it is in Myrtle Beach."

.
I got a crash course in what it was like to make the cut at a Hooters Tour tournament—and what it took to contend and win—when I returned to Pine Lakes to watch the final round of the BB&T/ Granddaddy Classic on Sunday afternoon. As I crossed the parking lot, I spied my Afro-American Highlander friend and my prediction-prone former caddy, Johnny West, staring at the scoreboard in shock.

"Mr. Huntt, I sure did pray for you this week," the Highlander said. "But it looks like we need to get a whole lot closer to God."

"I predict you ain't never seen numbers like this," Johnny added.

The scoreboard showed that Brett Quigley still held the lead after fifty-four holes at fifteen under par. But there were eight other players within five shots of Quigley, including local favorite Steven Larick of nearby Blytheswood, South Carolina, at fourteen under. My drink-buying buddy, David Bishop, had fired a rather remarkable third-round 68, which left him several shots out of the lead but in good position to collect a decent paycheck. Even more astonishingly, Quigley's opening-round course record 63 had been broken the day before, not once but twice, as Lan Gooch of Houston, Mississippi, and Eddie Carmichael of Knoxville, Tennessee, fired new course record scores of 62.

"Pretty hot stuff, huh?" called a familiar voice.

I saw my former playing partner, Steve Jones, whom I expected to have vanished by now, standing on the practice tee with sweat pouring off his forehead. Jones beckoned for me to come over and offered a sort of begrudging apology for his behavior during rounds one and two.

"It was basically just my ego," he confessed, poking at the divot-dented mudpack with a three iron. "I was always a great athlete in high school and junior college, and I felt like I could do anything. Even though I've only been playing golf for two years, I went from shooting 95 to shooting 75 so fast that I felt like I could go on to shooting 65 just as fast. It's killed me to have to try to grind it out on every hole just to make pars. But my head is what kills me the most. I'm such a fucking dreamer. I drive to all these tournaments, and I sleep in my car and stay up reading golf books all night. I used to just step up and hit. Now I have all these swing thoughts going through my head all the time."

But Jones claimed that he had no intention of quitting.

"I think the way you learn is by getting beat," he said. "So many players don't ever give themselves a chance to see if they can make it or not. They think they don't have anything to prove because they can shoot under par at some fancy country club. My father is a truck driver, and I don't have a country club to fall back on. Until the other day, I was one of those guys who thought that all they had to be able to do is make a couple of birdies every round and they'd be playing for a check on the weekend. I just didn't know how good you have to be."

I found myself encouraging Jones to hang in there, just as Eric Epperson had counseled me at Yesterday's two nights before. Then I headed off to find Quigley's threesome.

As I rounded the clubhouse, the relative quietude of the golf course was shattered by a series of dull roars that sounded like a convoy of tractor trailers barreling down an interstate highway. An enormous hot air balloon bearing the Hooters Tour logo was being inflated in an open space near the eighteenth green. The dull roars were not coming from the gallery, which numbered less than seventy-five people, including the half dozen Hooters girls working the scoreboard, but from the heating irons the balloonists were using to keep their craft aloft.

"We're having some fun now," grumbled one of the pros lingering in the parking lot. "I sure hope the golf tournament doesn't get in the way of the circus."

One of his buddies spat at the asphalt in disgust.

"The Hooters Tour doesn't give a rat's ass about golf or about us. I watched their so-called broadcast of the third round yesterday on TV. In fifteen minutes, I only saw three golf swings. I actually counted 'em. The rest was commercials for Hooters restaurants."

I arrived at the corner of the dogleg on number eighteen just as Quigley lumbered down the fairway carrying his golf bag on his back with a knapsack-style strap. The scoreboard showed he had gotten himself to sixteen under, but he was now clinging to a mere one-stroke lead. He had to make a four on the 493-yard former par five to avoid a playoff. Where I had been unable to reach the green with anything less than a four iron, he was pulling out a seven iron for his approach. As it turned out, Quigley could have used a little more club himself. His ball took off on line with the flagstick but checked up about forty feet short.

A few minutes later, as Quigley stood on the green and drew his putter back to strike his first putt, I heard yet another eardrum-pounding roar coming from the hot air balloon. I watched his ball snake up an incline and stop some four feet below the cup. Had I been in Quigley's position, I would have demanded that the damn balloon be deflated until I finished putting out. But Quigley took only a few seconds to line up his four-footer, then calmly tapped it in.

Lee Moore climbed down from the Prime Sports Network television tower to preside over the awards ceremony. As the entire company of Afro-American Highlanders gathered in a semicircular pose on the eighteenth green alongside a covey of BB&T bank officers, Moore picked up a microphone and a giant cardboard check for $15,000.

"How was that heart pumping on eighteen?" he asked Quigley. "I saw that putt you left yourself—it was not a done deal."

"I was really nervous the last three holes," Quigley admitted with a modest shrug. "But I got it in the barn."

A battery of still cameras flashed as Moore handed over the cardboard check. I gave Quigley a quick thumbs-up and left for the parking lot.

Johnny West intercepted me when I opened the door to the Grand Am.

"Mr. Harry, hold on just a minute," he insisted. "There's something I want to talk with you about before you go."

"What's that?" I asked. "We all square on the caddy fees, aren't we?"

"Yessir, you took good care of me." Johnny nodded. "But I just want you to know we ain't got nothing to be sorry about because of the way we played. I also want to tell you that from watching the way you was hitting balls on the practice tee, and knowin' you only been back at it for three months, I predict in another three months, you gonna be right up there with 'em."

"Thanks, Johnny," I said, patting him on the back. "The only problem is, Q School's just one month away."

Johnny stroked his chin thoughtfully.

"Well, Mr. Harry," he allowed, "I predict you gonna have to keep on playin' for two more months after that."

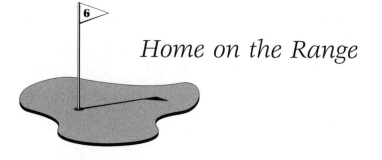

Home on the Range

dick Harmon, the legendary swing doctor to the stars of the PGA Tour, leaned against a bag rack in the back corner of the practice range at River Oaks Country Club and took dead aim at me with his video camera. It was a seasonably sticky September morning in Houston, the birthplace of my golf swing and myself. The dewy grass seemed to simmer and steam in the sun, and the air smelled like chicken-fried cotton balls. I could see bayous of perspiration streaming down Dick's forehead as he prepared to deliver his diagnosis.

"You don't need major surgery," he declared. "In fact, your backswing is almost perfect. It's your downswing we need to work on."

I hit another half-heeled drive into the boiling haze, wincing with pain as the ball died off to the right and gobs of Tiger Balm oozed from my badly inflamed psoas.

"Let's get a second opinion on the major surgery," I said. "My backswing might look okay, but my back feels like it's been run over by an oil tanker."

Dick wiped the condensation off his video camera, nodding and smiling. He was a sunburned tree stump–shaped fellow about 5'9" and 180 pounds with rapidly receding sand-splashed hair. He was wearing a pair of baggy tan Dockers and a white golf shirt bearing the Titleist logo, and as he walked toward me, he seemed to sway from side to side like a sailor listing on a flotilla of Footjoys.

"I know you must've heard this before," he allowed, "but you sure do remind me of your father."

"Look who's talking."

Dick's father was Claude Harmon Sr., the late patriarch of a family as renowned in the pantheon of professional golf instruction as the Kennedy clan in politics. Dick promptly cited one of the old man's dictums as he set about correcting the flaws in my hitting motion.

"People like my father and his friend George Fazio used to say you should hit the ball 'down the line.' But the golf swing isn't a line—it's a circle. You need to visualize that circular path as you strike the ball."

I watched Dick hit a few five iron shots to demonstrate what he meant. Then I tried it myself. My first attempt resulted in a shank, as did the second.

"Looks like this is going to take some time to get used to."

"Yeah," Dick replied. "About an hour."

He dropped a handful of range balls on the plastic mat beneath my feet and arranged them in an arc that led from the point of impact around to the follow-through position. Then he told me to lay down my driver and hit five irons until my downswing mirrored the path marked by the range balls.

In less than forty-five minutes, I was nailing shot after shot as if I had swung that way my entire life. My only complaint was that the balls seemed to fly toward the target green with a slight fade rather than the draw I preferred. Dick scolded me for nitpicking.

"Now you're getting caught up in the same obsession as every pro on the Tour," he said. "I call it The Search for the Perfect Golf Swing. I've seen it happen to dozens of guys over the years, Curtis Strange and Lanny Wadkins to name just a couple. No matter how good they're hitting the ball, they're never satisfied. I remember after Curtis won the U.S. Open in 1988, he came to me wanting to fix up his swing. At the time, he was fading the ball, but he felt like he needed to learn to hit draws again. With Lanny it was the other way around. But the thing all of them had in common was this constant quest for the perfect swing."

Dick glanced at his wristwatch, and told me to keep working

on the semicircle drill until the next day, when we had a second lesson scheduled. As I watched him walk down to the other end of the range to attend to one of the club members, I was once again reminded of the Harmon family's almost mythic legacy.

Claude Harmon Sr. had pioneered the teaching profession with a self-taught style and a gift for plainspoken storytelling that endeared him to peers and pupils alike. He had been born in Savannah, Georgia, in 1916, and reared in Orlando, Florida, the son of a once-wealthy real estate developer who went bankrupt in the Depression. The Harmons typically vacationed at oceanside beaches, but young Claude had an ear ailment that prohibited him from going in the water. Instead of learning to swim, he started caddying at a local country club and learned to play golf, rejoining the family beach outings only to practice his sand shots. At age eighteen, he turned pro.

Short, stocky, and cocky as a bantam rooster, Claude Sr. went on to establish his Hall of Fame coaching credentials at Seminole Golf Club in North Palm Beach, Florida, and Winged Foot Golf Club in Mamaroneck, New York, where he helped launch the playing careers of Dave Marr, Mike Souchak, Jackie Burke Jr., and many others. But he was also a first-rate competitor in his own right. In 1948, he won the Masters by five strokes over a field that included Ben Hogan and Sam Snead, distinguishing himself as the only club professional to triumph over the touring pros at Augusta National in the postwar era.

Like Joe Kennedy Sr., Claude Sr. also fathered four sons, each of whom eventually hacked his way out of the Oedipal shadows and into a prestigious teaching professional post. Dick's oldest brother, Claude "Butch" Harmon Jr., age fifty-two, was director of golf at Houston's all-male Lochinvar Golf Club, where he had won international acclaim for coaching Greg Norman, Davis Love III, and Tiger Woods. Craig Harmon, age fifty, was head pro at Oak Hill Country Club in Rochester, New York, site of the 1995 Ryder Cup and the 1956, 1968, and 1989 U.S. Open Championships. Baby brother Billy Harmon, age forty-six, was head pro at Newport Country Club in Newport, Rhode Island, site of the 1895 inaugural and 1995 centennial U.S. Amateur Championships.

As director of golf at River Oaks, Dick Harmon, age forty-eight, was following in his father's footsteps. Claude Sr. had served an interim tenure at River Oaks during World War II following the death of Jack Burke Sr., the club's first resident pro. But despite bearing striking similarities to his father in physical appearance and teaching philosophies, Dick was as different from the old man as he was from his three equally accomplished siblings.

During their youth, Dick and his brothers had literally lived on a golf course, sharing their parents' duplex near the maintainence barn at Seminole in the winters. In the summers, they shuttled back to the family homestead in New Rochelle but spent most of their waking hours working in and around their father's pro shop or playing the Tillinghast-designed track at Winged Foot. Although Dick had won the Winged Foot club championship at age nineteen, he was the only one of the Harmon boys to rule out a run at the PGA Tour.

"When people ask me 'Why don't you play?' I tell them I tried," Dick had confided before our lesson began. "In 1964, I played in the U.S. Junior Amateur Championship in Eugene, Oregon. I shot 73 the first day and thought that was pretty good until I saw that a kid from California named Johnny Miller had shot a 67. Miller ended up lapping the field. It comes down to a matter of talent. I think it's God-given. Either you're born with it or you're not. Johnny Miller has it. Ben Crenshaw and Bruce Lietzke have it. I don't have it."

Dick had briefly considered a career that had nothing to do with golf, graduating from San Diego State with a finance degree and apprenticing on Wall Street. But upon getting married at age twenty-one, he returned to the game in a kind of semidesperate panic. (As he recalled, "Teaching golf was the only thing I really knew how to do.") He began as supervisor of the golf cart fleet at Cottonwood Country Club in San Diego, then moved up to an assistant's post at Waverly Country Club in Portland, Oregon, the home course of a promising junior golfer named Peter Jacobsen.

At the age of twenty-seven, Dick was recruited for the head professional job at River Oaks. Perennially ranked on the list of America's top one hundred teaching pros compiled by *Golf Magazine*, he had coached the likes of Fred Couples and Steve Elkington, as well as Strange and Wadkins. And while he had inherited his father's natural instinct for swing analysis, he had a more affable manner of dealing with fancy-pants country clubbers.

Claude Harmon Sr. had left River Oaks after less than six months, complaining that the members treated him like hired help. Dick, who took his meals in the men's grill with the sons of many of those same members, was about to celebrate his twentieth year on the job. In addition to operating a lucrative pro shop business, he charged $150 an hour for lessons and had quarterly or annual consulting contracts with various touring pros that provided him with an income greater than many of the bluebloods he taught on the practice range. I had chosen to come to him following my poor performance at the Hooters Tour tournament in Myrtle Beach both because of his reputation for rehabilitating golf swings and because he now presided over my former home on the range, where I hoped to find some sorely needed spiritual renewal.

In the event, River Oaks, founded circa 1923, had changed rather dramatically in the half century since Claude Sr.'s stormy departure and in the quarter century since my youth. The cozy Spanish Mediterranean tile-roofed clubhouse designed by local architect John Staub had been torn down and replaced with a Georgian brick structure larger than many airport terminals. Likewise, the original eighteen-hole track laid out by famed Scottish-born architect Donald Ross had been redesigned and lengthened more times than the basic four-door family car. The membership had undergone an even greater transformation and expansion, as the arch-conservative chartering families whose fortunes were based on oil, cattle, and real estate ceded hegemony to an urbane new generation of golf-crazy doctors, lawyers, investment bankers, and high-tech wizards.

My late father, a wildcatting independent oilman and former World War II test pilot born in 1899, had carried the torch for the establishment on and off the golf course. Although he did not come from a wealthy background himself, he had hobnobbed with the nation's leading industrialists and financiers as a member of River Oaks Country Club, Houston Country Club, the New York Racquet Club, The Brook, and Seminole Golf Club. In 1960, he had won the annual Latham R. Reed Amateur-Professional Tournament at Seminole in partnership with Dave Ragan Sr., whose son Dave Jr. later worked as an assistant to Dick Harmon at River Oaks.

Old enough to have been my grandfather, my dad had spent the last three decades of his life orbiting between our home, his downtown office, and ROCC. He had never tossed footballs or baseballs with me. He didn't like fishing or boating or hunting. And by the time my younger brother and I came along, he had sold his twin-engine Beechcraft to help pay for our private school educations. Golf was the one sport he played, the sole recreation he enjoyed, and it had provided the only venue for bonding with his sons.

My old man had come to the game with several handicaps not registered in any USGA computer. In his youth, his left arm was permanently warped by a fracture incurred when he fell off a horse in the middle of what was now downtown Houston; as a result, it was impossible for him to straighten and fully extend it on his backswing. He had incurable hearing and balance problems due to an ear injury suffered in the crash landing of a navy test plane in World War II. And he had less patience than a rear admiral scrambling fighter squadrons off an aircraft carrier.

But the Hurt family patriarch had also possessed two gifts invaluable to the pursuit of the perfect golf swing or any other goal, self-discipline and perseverance. While he disparaged "country club bums," he found nothing contradictory in hacking away for hours on the practice range at ROCC, sweating like a roustabout on a drilling rig as he tried to master the latest tip he had read about in some golf magazine. For all his efforts, his best score was a 73, and he had shot it only twice: first in a Saturday morning round with friends at ROCC and then in winning the pro-am at Seminole in 1960.

Harry Hurt Jr. had died of complications related to Parkinson's disease in 1988, one year before the passing of Claude Harmon Sr. Along with living through the evolution of golf from the hickory shaft era to the age of graphite, he had witnessed River Oaks' evolution from a sleepy small-town club with a couple of hundred members to an exclusive modern golfing mecca whose 1,500 members and their guests played up to 35,000 rounds annually. Given his oft-repeated admonitions against becoming a "country club bum," I wondered what he would have thought about the fact that his eldest son had decided in midlife to become a touring pro—and whether he would have seen any appreciable difference in the two pursuits.

When I ventured into the locker room after my practice session, I noticed that my father's name was still posted on the locker my younger brother had inherited, a green metal cabinet centrally located beneath the cathedral ceiling in front of the wide-screen television and only a few steps from the bar and the showers. The crew of African-American attendants I'd known as a kid had long since been replaced by a more politically correct mix of whites, Hispanics, and blacks, but most of the locker-room staffers had been on the job long enough to have known my old man.

As soon as I sat down on the bench in front of his former locker, Danny, the red-bearded young chief attendant, rushed over to offer me drinks, shoe shines, and general assistance as if I were a full-fledged member rather than a guest visiting from out of town.

"Welcome home, Mr. Hurt," he said, grinning. "It's been too long."

I stared up at my father's nameplate again, grimacing.

"Yes, it has. And my back's feeling like it, too."

"I believe Doc Harper is on his way over," Danny replied. "Must be something he can do to help you out."

Sure enough, my old friend Dana Harper wandered into the locker room a few minutes later carrying a putter and a tennis racket. He was a lithe and muscular former landscape contractor turned chiropractor with a handsome, high-cheekboned face that made him a dead ringer for the actor Michael York. Although we were exactly the same age, he was much better preserved and much better coordinated. Back in high school, he had been a three-sport letterman, and he still held several unbroken track and field records. The only game I could ever beat him at was golf.

"Congratulations, I hear you've turned pro," Doc Harper said with a chuckle as we shook hands. "It's about time you got back out on the circuit. We're gonna be old enough for the Senior Tour before too long."

"My back feels like it's ready for the Wheelchair Tour. Any chance you might be able to crack or pop it back in shape, Doc?"

"Let's take a look."

Doc Harper led me to a fully equipped exercise studio adjacent to the locker room and instructed me to take off my shirt and lie down on one of the mats. As he bent over and began feeling his way down my spine, I told him that the pain had started in the middle of my back but now seemed to be spreading to both sides.

"Oh, man." He sighed. "Your psoas is still in major spasm, and so are the intercostal muscles between your ribs. Stand up for me."

When I got on my feet, Doc Harper grasped me from behind in a kind of variation on the half-nelson hold used by wrestlers and ordered me to lean back on him. He administered two quick jerks that seemed to reverberate throughout my entire skeletal structure and up into my cranium. For a split second, I hurt like hell all over. Then I felt a slightly dizzying warmth.

"Jesus Christ, you're tight," Doc Harper muttered. "My advice is to lay off the golf completely for at least a week or two and give your back a chance to get better."

I nodded my bleary head.

"You're singing exactly the same song I heard from the masseuse in Myrtle Beach last week, Doc. Unfortunately, I can't lay off, not right now. I've got to play in a Nike Tour qualifier in California week after next. Then I have to start Q School two weeks after that."

"Oh, man," Dana said, sighing again. "In that case, my advice is to do a lot more stretching before and after you play. But make sure you warm up before you stretch. Jog around or just walk fast for a couple of minutes to get the blood flowing. Otherwise, you're only gonna injure yourself worse."

Dana showed me several floor exercises to add to the regimen Isabelle had prescribed, and suggested that I seek out a good chiropractor at each of my upcoming tournament stops. I asked if taking whirlpools was a good idea.

"A good hot soaking couldn't hurt." He nodded. Then he added with a mischievous grin, "But if worse comes to worst, we might have to saw a few grooves in the spinal column. Adjusting your back was like trying to adjust a two-by-four."

$t$he following morning, I arrived for my second lesson with Dick Harmon eager to show off the progress I'd made overnight. A series of whirlpools, saunas, and massages had made my back more like plywood than the proverbial two-by-four Doc Harper had tried to adjust. A dinner of Tex-Mex food and several Cuervo and Cointreau margaritas had emboldened my hopes of keeping up with the flatbellies I would face in Q School. As images of the long hitters back on the Hooters Tour flashed through my mind, I endeavored to swing harder and harder, only to find my drives traveling shorter and shorter distances.

Dick timed my motion with his video camera, and frowned disapprovingly.

"The Tour average on the backswing is point ninety-five seconds, and you're at point sixty-five," he reported. "I think maybe we ought to at least slow you down to a blur."

"I'm just trying to generate some club head speed. If I can't drive the ball two seventy-five or two eighty, I'm screwed. Those kids will be hitting eight irons to the long par fours, and I'll have to hit three irons and four irons."

"Are you planning on hitting the ball with your backswing?"

Dick's question made me flush.

"Well, how the hell do I slow down and not lose any distance?"

"Come on," he returned, chuckling. "I'll show you."

Dick took me inside the pro shop, where he fed an archival tape of Steve Elkington's swing into the video player. The first sequences were dated March 1988, and they showed a puffy-faced Australian fresh out of the University of Houston flailing at the ball with overly extended arms and lightning-fast wrists.

Dick pressed the fast forward button until he came to a sequence dated January 1995. It showed the reigning PGA champion hitting drivers from a much more compact and upright posture with a tempo slower than the swing speed I typically used on a pitching wedge.

"As you can tell from the pictures, Elk's been lifting weights," Dick noted. "That's helped him add twenty yards to his drive. But the key to his ball striking is that tempo. He's always had a silky smooth rhythm with his arms. When he first came to me back in '88, he had gotten too reachy and too wristy, and it was destroying his timing."

"So what do I do—pretend I'm the new improved Steve Elkington?"

"Exactly," Dick replied. "After we're done on the range, I want you to come in here and watch this tape. Play it over and over as many times as you like. Get an image of Elk's tempo imprinted on your mind, and take it with you out on the golf course. Whenever you start to swing fast, remember that tempo is the key and try to match Elk's tempo."

"That's it?" I asked incredulously.

"That's part of it. I'm also gonna show you a couple of drills to help slow down that backswing. You might not like them at first because you're gonna lose a little distance. But in the long run, you'll start striking the ball more solidly and the distance will come."

I followed Dick back out to the practice range feeling more

skeptical and distraught than ever. He teed up a ball for me and told me to hit my driver to the 150-yard flag with a full swing. I nodded, and banged the ball about 200 yards.

"That's too far," Dick said. "I only want you to hit it one-fifty. Try again."

My second attempt traveled about 185 yards.

"You're still going at it too hard," Dick informed me. "Be soft. And slow it down. Feel like you're holding back with your hands and arms when you start the downswing. Keep holding back until the club gets past your right knee. Then you can be quicker if you want."

It took a dozen more balls and an equal number of pointed reminders before I finally managed to start tapping my drives to the 150-yard flag. I felt like I was swinging in slow motion, but I also began to notice that my club head seemed to be making increasingly more solid contact with the ball.

"Okay, step back a second," Dick said at last. He pointed to a tree at the far end of the driving range, about 260 yards away. "Now deliver the ball to that target. No swing thoughts. Just visualize the shot and hit it."

I took a deep breath and swung as instructed. The ball jumped off the club face on a line that appeared to me to be slightly left of the target, then slid directly toward the tree and bounded across the right-side roots.

"How'd that feel?" Dick asked.

"Amazing. I felt like I barely touched the sucker. There's only one problem—I'm still hitting a little fade."

Dick rolled his eyes.

"Here we go with that perfect swing shit again. The shot you just hit wasn't a fade. It went straight. And it had plenty of distance."

"I know a draw will go farther."

"Golf isn't a driving contest. It's about putting the ball in play."

"Fair enough," I conceded. "But what happens on doglegs that call for a draw or a fade?"

"Just visualize the shot and make a couple of minor adjustments," Dick advised. "If you need to hook the ball, drop your right foot back slightly so you can take the club back more inside and swing a little faster with your arms. If you need to hit a fade, visualize Lee Trevino's swing. Open your stance and turn your hips a little faster."

I spent the next fifteen minutes grappling with the subtleties of these so-called minor adjustments. But after finally managing to hit three intentional draws and three intentional fades in sequence, I started hitting the ball dead straight again regardless of how I tried to change my stance or tempo.

Dick shrugged off my continuing frustration.

"Better get used to it," he said, "because that's the shot you're going to have to play with—if you're lucky. There's a lot worse things you can do than hitting it straight. My father used to say, 'If you want a guy to quit hitting it straight, just get him to play for money.' "

I pointed out that the entry fee for Q School was a cool three grand, which was plenty of money relative to my checkbook balance.

"Give me a call after you get through Stage One," Dick suggested with a knowing smile, "and tell me how straight you hit it."

I thanked him for his help and promised to file a full report.

Then I got into my rental car and drove out to the airport to catch a flight back to the East Coast, where I had arranged to meet with two other golf gurus whose specialties were the short game and the mind game.

two days after my lessons with Dick Harmon, I found myself working up a shirt-soaking sweat on yet another practice range at the Robert Trent Jones Golf Club in Manassas, Virginia. The weather was every bit as sultry as it had been in Houston, but instead of being coached on how to hit drivers and five irons, I was being tutored in the arcane art of controlling wedge shots by Tom Jenkins, a former PGA Tour pro who had become one of the country's leading short game experts.

"You've got to learn to get the hit out of it," Tom told me as I whacked my 52-degree Mizuno gap wedge toward one of the nearby flags. "The idea is to let the big muscles do the work and keep the small muscles quiet."

Tom had a big-boned, thick-bodied build that belied his refined sense of touch and feel. At the age of forty-eight, he looked like he might have been a former major league baseball player, not a short-stop or a centerfielder—he carried a mite too much bulk for those positions—but a starting pitcher or an ace reliever, the closer who put the game away with an unhittable curveball.

"Don't square up your stance for these kinds of shots, keep it nice and open," Tom advised. "Openness allows the big muscles to accelerate through the ball. Squareness restricts the movement of the big muscles and forces the small muscles in your wrists to get into the act, which can be deadly."

A native of my own hometown, Tom had attended the University of Houston, where he had roomed with Jim McLean, the future teaching pro at the Doral Golf Resort and Spa, and played on the same team with future PGA champion John Mahaffey. In 1975, he had won the Philadelphia Golf Classic, his only victory in thirteen years on the Tour, using a pronged putter borrowed from a former NASA engineer named Dave Pelz. After a series of injuries sidelined him in the mid-1980s, he had spent six years as the top instructor in Pelz's rapidly expanding chain of short game schools. In early 1995, he had decided to start his own independent outfit.

Now based in Austin, Tom had come to RTJ to conduct a short game seminar for a foursome of club members, one of whom was a mutual friend from Houston. He prided in taking a hands-on approach. Students at the Dave Pelz Schools typically paid anywhere from $1,800 to $2,700 to participate in three-day programs with a group of up to fifteen other golfers who rotated from station to station under the supervision of four Pelz assistants. The Tom Jenkins School offered two-day seminars limited to four students who paid $625 each and received personal instruction from Tom himself.

Like being back at River Oaks, my encounter with Tom Jenkins at RTJ smacked of a nostalgic sense of déjà vu. Although he was five years older, we had competed in different age brackets in many of the same junior golf tournaments in Houston, and I had always idolized him as a big brother figure. He had graciously agreed to give me a two-hour private lesson free of charge.

To paraphrase a well-worn cliché, I knew that being able to play the short game for dough, not driving for show, was what truly separated the pros from the amateurs. This was hardly a big secret. In recent years, innumerable golf magazine articles and instruction manuals had underscored the importance of the short game by citing a single telling statistic: at least 60 percent of the shots in a round of golf, including putts, were played within 100 yards of the hole. But those publications seldom did an effective job of explaining how to master the short game arts or how to practice them. Tom's method of instruction provided the essential personal element.

"The best way to control the distance of your wedge shots under pressure is by calibrating the radius of your backswing like the hour hand of a clock," he said. "Basically, you make a longer backswing for longer shots and a shorter backswing for shorter shots. But the key is to keep your swing speed the same on all shots. When you're out there playing under pressure, the troops aren't ready for half-speed swings."

Tom told me to hit three shots in sequence: the first with a full backswing, the second with a "nine o'clock" or half backswing, and the third with a "seven-thirty" or one-quarter backswing.

"Now let's mark the precise spot where each of those shots landed," he said when I had completed the assignment. "We're only interested in finding out how far the balls carried, not where they finally ended up. You can't control the bounce or the roll of a shot, but you can control how far they travel on the fly."

The RTJ happened to be perfectly suited for such an exercise.The $30 million centerpiece of a luxury real estate development built by the Bishop Estate of Hawaii in 1990, the club was a state-of-the-art golf facility whose members included former vice president Dan Quayle and Supreme Court Justice Sandra Day O'Connor. Along with boasting a 7,238 yard, par 72 course designed by the famous architect for which it was named, RTJ had a three-tiered range whose laser-measured flagstick distances were listed on a special page in the yardage book.

Tom and I could tell without even leaving our hitting post that my full swing, nine o'clock swing, and seven-thirty swing with the 52-degree Mizuno wedge had carried 100 yards, 85 yards, and 50 yards, respectively. He directed me to repeat the same sequence of swings with my sand wedge, the antique 58 degree Spalding Dynamiter I'd inherited from my late father. My shots with the Dynamiter flew 80 yards, 68 yards, and 40 yards.

"Those are your distances," Tom noted in a rather cryptic tone. "Remember them, because we'll be coming back to those numbers a little later."

He then led me to the practice bunker, where we spent the next half hour working on the basic sand shots. He recommended that I use the Dynamiter only for distances of ten yards and under; for longer distances, he said, the 52 degree was a better choice. In either case, the same familiar principles applied when hitting out of a normal lie in the trap: I should employ an open stance, a quick wrist break on the backswing, and an accelerating downswing that cut across the ball to impart spin. The only departure from my own standard routine involved the grip and club face setup. Rather than gripping the club and then opening the face, Tom urged me to open the face first, then grip the club.

"And when I say open the face, I mean really open it up so that it looks like you're gonna strike the sand with the hosel," he added. "That's gonna feel funny at first, but it's crucial if you need to get the ball up and land it softly on the green with plenty of backspin."

After I'd hit a dozen good shots from normal lies, Tom demonstrated his "cock and pop" method for excavating a ball from a buried or fried egg lie in the sand trap. As the term implied, the procedure called for a very sharp wrist cock on the backswing, followed by a hard downward pop into the sand behind the ball on the way through. The crucial difference between executing this shot and a shot from a normal lie was that you closed rather than opened the face of the wedge to enable the club to cut through the greater amount of sand surrounding a ball in a buried lie. Since a "cock and pop" shot would not and could not stop quickly, you had to aim for the widest section of the green and plan on the fact that the ball would run.

We spent another fifteen minutes on chipping, for which I had always been blessed with an instinctive feel. Tom helped codify my instincts into useful typologies. He noted that there were basically two kinds of chips: high soft shots, and low hard shots. High soft shots demanded soft hands, a high backswing, and high finish. The delicate, seemingly magical flop shots for which Phil Mickelson was famous were basically a variation on this theme. To hit a flop shot that climbed high above your head but carried only a few short yards and stopped, you simply put most of your weight on your back foot, lowered the position of your hands at address, and swung "high to high" on the backswing and follow-through.

Low hard shots required firm wrists and a "low to low" swing pattern. The single most significant difference between Tom's methods and the chipping tips I often saw in golf magazines was that he did not regard a low running chip with a club such as a five iron or a seven iron as a "lofted putt." In contrast to the standard putting stroke in which the arms never turn over, he maintained that the best way to hit a low running chip was to allow the left forearm to rotate toward and a little past the target line. This arm rotation supplied just enough force to make the ball leave the club face with a modicum of spin, thereby enhancing distance control.

"By the way, how is your putting?" Tom asked when we had finished our chipping drills.

"Fine," I replied. "At least from inside two feet."

Realizing that our scheduled two-hour lesson was almost over, I asked Tom to elaborate on his earlier comment about my fairway wedge shots.

"What did you mean when you said those are my distances?"

"I was referring to any situation that calls for you to lay up," Tom replied. "Let's say you're setting up your approach shot on a par five or you've hit your tee shot on a par four into the rough or into a fairway bunker. You don't want to hit just any old layup shot. And a lot of times you don't even want to try to hit the ball as close to the green as you can because there might be more trouble waiting around the green, more bunkers or more heavy rough, maybe a water hazard. You want to lay up to the spot from which you're most comfortable in controlling the ball flight and the distance of your approach shot.

"I noticed, for example, that you're pretty consistent in hitting that fifty-two-degree wedge a hundred yards with a full swing, but not too consistent with the seven-thirty swing that goes fifty yards," he continued. "That full swing that goes a hundred yards is your preferred distance for that club. So if you're trying to decide what kind of second shot to play on a par five and you know you can't reach the green in two, you might not want to hit a three wood if it'll put you fifty yards from the green. Instead, you might want to lay up with a three iron that'll leave you a hundred-yard shot. You'll have a much higher percentage of getting the ball close to the hole and making birdie."

Tom ended our session with a few tips on the proper way to practice controlling my wedge shots in preparation for Q School. He told me to break down the various practice ranges I would be using in much the same way as I would break down an unfamiliar golf course. I should take the time to step off the yardages on the practice ranges, paying heed to prevailing wind and weather conditions, so I would know the exact distances to my wedge shot targets. Finally, he urged me to spend at least as much if not more time working on my short game as I spent working on my full swing.

"You're probably not going to be able to outdrive most of the kids you'll be playing against in Q School," he predicted. "But if you get your short game in shape, you can sure as hell outscore them."

the following evening, I sat down on a soft, pillowed couch inside a basement in Charlottesville, Virginia, that served as the office and visiting client residence of the preeminent sports psychologist in professional golf. His name was Dr. Bob Rotella, and he was a professor at the nearby University of Virginia who had recently published a bestselling book titled *Golf Is Not a Game of Perfect*. Far more impressive from my point of view, he had counseled a long list of PGA Tour stars including Tom Kite, Davis Love III, and Lee Janzen, each of whom had praised him for helping raise their mental games to a higher level.

"We've got to get your head into being a player, not just a writer," he declared, plopping down on a well-worn brown leather lounge chair. "When you get to Q School, you absolutely cannot feel like you're in a strange world where you don't belong. Don't be self-conscious about who you are, and don't go around telling the other guys you're just a writer. You've played a lot of golf over the years, even if you have laid off for a long time. You played with great players when you were younger. You played with Ben Crenshaw, who's won the Masters twice. He's cheering for you. He thinks you belong. He wants you to make it."

As I listened to Doc Rotella's pep talk, I was struck by the fact that he looked and sounded much more like a thirtysomething head coach than a fiftyish headshrinker. Lean, lithe, and deeply tanned, he had razor-cropped hair that grazed the tops of his ears and he half slumped in his lounge chair with one heel resting on the seat cushion. He told me that he had been an All American club lacrosse player in college and, later, a lacrosse coach at the University of Connecticut, where he had earned his doctorate in education. A former recreational tennis player, he had been playing golf in serious amateur competitions for only about twelve years, but he had transformed himself from a hacker who could not break 90 into a two-time Fairfield Country Club champion and the reigning city champion of Charlottesville.

"Everybody comes into Q School thinking, 'I've got to shoot 65 every day or I'm not going to make it,' but that's a myth," he declared. "You've just got to shoot par or better on a regular basis. You don't have to shoot zero every day. You've got to say to yourself, 'With my short game and my attitude, I can only hit four fairways in eighteeen holes and I'll still shoot par or better.' "

According to Rotella, the keys to success were trust and patience.

"You've got to say to yourself, 'Nothing's going to upset me,' and you've got to make sure that nothing does. You've got to trust your key clubs, your driver, wedge, and putter. And you've got to trust your three wood or your one iron or whatever club you use when you have to be sure to put the ball in the fairway. We don't care how a round starts because there's lots of holes to play and we're going to be patient. But if you find that you're four over after five holes, you've got to be prepared to find a way to play better. By the same token, make sure your brain is comfortable with being five under after five holes. We don't want to be five under and put on the brakes."

Rotella went on to offer some very specific advice about how I should organize my preparations for Q School. Step one was making a scouting expedition to my Stage One site at The Ranch Country Club in McKinney, Texas.

"I want you to get there fairly soon, do your scouting, then go back to Houston or someplace else and stay far removed from The Ranch. Don't go back there more than two days before the tournament. What happens is, it ends up being an environment with one hundred highly anxious people, and you don't need to be exposed to that. Go now and see the golf course. Get your yardages, pick your targets off the tees, find out about the typical winds, find out what the sand's like in the bunkers, break down the holes you'll want to lay up on and the holes where you don't want to shoot for the pin.

"On your scouting expedition, I want you to find a convenient motel, but I don't want you to stay where all the other guys are staying," Rotella continued. "I want you far removed from them. I don't want you constantly exposed to all their anxiety, all their talk about what it's going to take to qualify. Make sure you find a motel that has the things you want, a good shower, good air-conditioning, a good TV. Make sure you decide where you want to stay in the motel. You don't want to be in a place where trucks are going by all night and you can't get any sleep. Also make sure to bring something along to keep your mind off golf when you're not playing, a book or some movie tapes, for example. I don't want you to go back to your motel room and think about golf all night."

Rotella told me to return from my scouting expedition with a well-paced, systematic plan for the final week before Q School. I should practice the kind of shots The Ranch C.C. demanded most, be they long irons, fairway woods, or whatever, and spend plenty of time working on my short game without wearing myself out. Just as important, I should also do exercises to enhance my mental game.

"I want you to spend a good twenty minutes every night with the phone off the hook thinking about playing great in Stage One," he advised. "You should say to yourself, 'I'm going to have fun seeing how great I can play.' And get your mind totally wired for playing to win. The worst thing you can do is start playing to qualify. You'll either make it on the number or miss it by a shot."

I interrupted Rotella's spiel to mention that my long layoff from competitive golf seemed to have made me particularly susceptible to attacks of stage fright on the first tee in opening rounds of a tournament. He noted that that was, pun intended, par for the course.

"You've got to totally prepare yourself for having the butterflies. But look at it as excitement and enjoy it. Say to yourself, 'That's why I got into competition, to feel that way.' If you're feeling a lot of butterflies, do these two things: one, be more conservative with your strategy, but, two, stay aggressive with your swing. Stick your expectations in your pocket and just play golf. Don't add up your score on the golf course."

As our counseling session reached a climax, Rotella surprised me with a kind of strategic reversal of field. Having begun our two hours together by urging me to think of myself as a player, he now suggested that my unique status as a writer-golfer was something to be exploited.

"You've got a big advantage over everybody else because you're not really there, even though you are," he noted. "I'd milk that. You have to remember that even if you don't have more experience in playing golf than most of the other guys, you have more experience at being a human being. You can't possibly embarrass yourself because nobody expects you to do anything out there. You can't lose. You can write a good book even if you don't make it through Q School. People will want to read about it because it's interesting and they've dreamed about trying it themselves. If you do make it, then you've really got an amazing story to write."

"Hold on a second," I said, squirming in my seat on the couch. "At the risk of sounding pedantic, I studied psychology for four years in college, mostly Freud and Jung, and what you've just said seems kind of contradictory. I'm supposed to be a player, not a writer, but then again, I'm really a writer after all, so it doesn't matter how I play."

Rotella smiled back at me and shrugged his shoulders.

"You can focus on being consistent or you can focus on being successful," he said. "The choice is up to you. A good coach is someone who teaches you how to win. Freud liked to sit around blaming everything on Mom and Dad, which to my mind is just finding an excuse for not being successful. I can't help it if you didn't have a happy childhood or if your coach in fourth grade didn't like you. I'm concerned with teaching you how to be successful in the present. Other psychologists would describe me as a cognitivist or a behaviorist. I believe the tenets of William James are more valuable than pyschotherapy in what I do. James said the keys to success are personal responsibility, discipline, and will-power."

With that, Rotella rose from his lounge chair and gave me a quick guided tour of his basement office. The floor plan consisted of two small bedrooms and a bathroom adjacent to the main room, where we had been sitting. The walls were covered with newspaper clippings, plaques, and various mementos he had received from famous golfers and clients. As I stared at a flag from the eighteenth hole at Pebble Beach autographed by Kite, Janzen, and Jack Nicklaus, he offered some final words of advice.

"I still believe that you'll be better off if you go into Q School thinking of yourself primarily as a player who can shoot as low a score as any of the other guys in the field," he said. Then he added with a wink, "But if you do wind up shooting a 65, I think you should go ahead and tell them you're a writer."

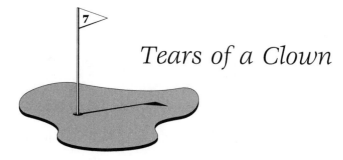

Tears of a Clown

i squinted into the steadily sinking northern California sun, cringing with pain and impatience. It was well past two o'clock on the afternoon of Monday, September 23, and I was finally about to tee off at the Santa Rosa Golf and Country Club in an eighteen-hole qualifying round for the Nike Sonoma Open. When the starter called my name, I raised my driver against the twenty-five-mile-per-hour wind that was chapping my lips and forced a smile. Then I turned around to look at the discouraging scene behind my back.

The Santa Rosa clubhouse complex consisted of a series of dirty white army barracks–style buildings huddled amid a middle-class subdivision on the outskirts of the wine country. There were now less than a dozen golfers left on the putting green in front of the clubhouse, but given the agonizingly slow pace of play, it was by no means certain that they or the rest of the two hundred-man field would be able to get in eighteen holes before sunset. Off in the distance, the baked brown range of the Macombre Mountains seemed to glower with disdain.

"What part of California is Sag Harbor located in?" the starter asked.

He was a rotund, rumple-shirted volunteer official with a bald head and a gratingly talkative disposition.

"It's on the far, far right side," I replied. "The part they call New York State."

"Oh," he said, nodding. "I thought it might be somewhere on the coast down south."

"By the time we make the turn, it probably will be. Just need a couple of real good earthquakes."

The starter handed me a scorecard and a pin sheet, clucking his tongue.

"Are you a golf pro or a comedian?"

I shrugged my shoulders, forcing another smile and then frowning again.

The question would be duly answered by my performance on the holes ahead. Having spent the last few weeks flying back and forth across the country for intensive coaching sessions, I felt like a college student cramming for the most important test of his life. If the PGA Tour Qualifying School tournament three weeks hence was the equivalent of a final exam, this Nike Tour qualifier was like a pop quiz that would measure the progress I'd made since my Hooters Tour debut.

Oddly, my golf game seemed to be improving at the same pace that my physical and psychological health were deteriorating. As per Dick Harmon's instructions, I had slowed down my tempo to at least a half blur, and I had begun to finish my downswing in a more circular pattern. Thanks to the tips provided by Tom Jenkins, I was gaining much greater control of my wedge shots and bunker shots. Upon arriving in Santa Rosa, I had followed Doc Rotella's prescription for pretournament preparation, finding a motel far removed from the maddening crowd of fellow would-be Nike Tour qualifiers and spending twenty minutes at night thinking about how great I was going to play.

But rather than attaining a modicum of inner peace, I was in a state of panic. My distress traced directly to the unrelenting aches that had spread across my back. I had failed to complete my Sunday afternoon practice round before dark even with the aid of a golf cart. My psoas muscle hurt so much every time I attempted a full swing that I needed almost twice the normal amount of time to play each hole. It required a major effort just to bend over to get my ball out of the cup, an experience that had rarely occurred in the regulation number of strokes since I had barely managed to break 40 on the front nine.

Although the Nike Tour rules permitted contestants to ride in golf carts in the qualifier, I had no idea how I would make it through the opening rounds of the Sonoma Open even if I did win one of the fourteen available qualifying spots. Motorized vehicles were prohibited in regular tournament play, and I could have used a minivan just to transport my load of medical supplies and miscellaneous equipment. In addition to balls, gloves, club brushes, yardage books, and ball markers, the inventory included two bottles of Evian water, two bottles of Advil, a box of small Band-Aids, a box of large Band-Aids, two rolls of first aid tape, a jar of Mineral Ice, a tube of Ben-Gay, an ankle brace, a rib brace, a spare set of contact lenses, a pair of untinted prescription glasses, a pair of wraparound Bolle sunglasses, two tins of Schimmelpennick cigars, and two lighters.

My mental anguish had been twisted up several more notches on Monday morning when I had sought treatment from Dr. Will Parker, a twenty-nine-year-old chiropractor who also happened to be a single-digit-handicapper at the Santa Rosa Golf and Country Club. "You're badly out of balance, and your condition appears to be chronic," he had told me. "You can lay off golf for a couple of weeks and let your back heal, but the pain's going to return as soon as you start playing again." He had then added to my psychic distress by discovering a previously undiagnosed physical ailment— the onset of bursitis in my left elbow.

Dr. Parker had provided some marginal relief to my psoas with hot wraps, but he hadn't attempted the kind of crack-and-pop adjustments I'd gotten from Doc Harper because he worried that they would make me too sore to play. Instead, he suggested that I try to keep my back from becoming even more out of balance by alternating left-handed swings with my right-handed swings on the practice range. For the bursitis, he had prescribed ice and massage lotion.

"I'm sorry your back's in such rough shape, but I wish I was in a position to do what you're doing," Dr. Parker had confided as he peeled off the hot wraps. "I thought about trying to qualify for the Nike tournament this year, but I've been working too hard. And I'd love to be going to Q School; that's everybody's dream. I just hope you don't hurt too much to enjoy it. Golf is an amazing game. You see people's souls."

*   *   *

I saw much less prosaic visions flash across my mind's eye on the first tee at Santa Rosa when the starter called my name for the second and final time. Twenty-four hours earlier, the United States had lost the 1995 Ryder Cup matches to Europe at Oak Hill Country Club in Rochester, New York, by a score of $14^{1}/_{2}$ to $13^{1}/_{2}$. The evening news had shown a clip of U.S. team member Brad Faxon, who had lost his final day singles match one down, crying over the defeat like an orphaned child. Somehow I sensed that Faxon's tears might be a harbinger of things to come.

"You know, it's funny," the starter said as I teed up my ball, "you wouldn't think that those trees on the right come into play very often, but they sure do seem to today."

I took another hard look at the fairway in front of me. The first hole was a tight little 378-yard dogleg-right par four playing into wind quartering from the right. The left side was guarded by a pair of traps that started about 220 yards off the tee and extended another fifty yards toward the green. The trees to which the starter had referred, a stand of thick-leafed oaks, marked the right corner of the dogleg, about 225 yards out.

I glanced over to the side of the tee box to size up my assigned playing partners. One of them was a short, stocky Japanese-American named Curtis Matsuno, who was head pro at a golf center near San Jose. He had black hair, a black shirt, and a black metal-headed driver with a forty-eight-inch shaft, and he looked like he probably had a black belt in judo, as well. The other member of our threesome was a tall, broad-shouldered twenty-four-year-old kid out of Sacramento State College. His name was Kriss Casselman, and he had a sweetly smiling puppy dog face that poked out from under a grass-smudged baseball cap.

I could tell from the way Curtis and Kriss were whispering to their caddies that they, too, had heard more than enough out of the starter. As I had drawn the honor of hitting first, I decided to speak for the group.

"Thanks a lot for reminding us about the trees, pal. Never would have noticed them without your help."

"No problem," the starter replied.

When I finally got ready to assume my stance, I tried to shut out any thoughts of the oaks on the right. My game plan was to take them out of play by hitting a gentle draw at the far corner of the second trap on the left. But the instant I began my downswing, the starter's gratuitous remarks flooded back into my consciousness. I knew even before I finished my follow-through exactly where my drive would be heading.

"See what I mean?" the starter said after my ball collided with one of the oak branches and dropped straight down. "Those trees are brutal."

I watched Curtis Matsuno cut-fade an almost identical shot that got caught up in the trees and kicked hard right. Then Kriss Casselman found the fairway with a crackling line drive that carried a good thirty yards past my own ball.

"That's more like it," the starter declared. "Good luck, gentlemen."

"Yeah, thanks a lot," I muttered, flooring the accelerator of my golf cart. "Keep the porch light on for us."

My mood grew even surlier when I pulled up beside my ball. I desperately wanted to get off to a good start by making a routine two-putt par on the first hole, but my tee shot had come to rest right behind a tree that blocked the direct route to the green. Resigned to the fact that I would now have to scramble to make a four, I took a deep breath and punched a five iron underneath the tree limbs toward a clearing about twenty yards short of a greenside bunker.

My third shot immediately put the lessons I'd learned from Tom Jenkins to an acid test. The pin was tucked in the front left corner of the green no more than fifteen feet beyond the bunker. My only hope of getting the ball close was to hit a flop shot à la Phil Mickelson. I silently ticked off the key elements of the setup during my preshot routine—ball forward, weight back, hands low— and reminded myself to swing "high to high." To my delight, I spun the ball to within twelve feet of the pin.

Now came the real knee-knocking part of the program. Tom and I hadn't had time to work on my putting stroke, and I had never putted on poa annua grass prior to my Sunday practice round. Unlike the silky bent grass greens back east, poa annua was lumpier than an old mattress; even the most smoothly stroked ball typically began to bounce and shimmy when it left the putter face. As far as I was concerned, poa annua was also harder to read than the rosetta stone. Unlike the Bermuda grass down in Houston, it was not governed by subtle grain patterns, but it was more resistant to slopes and undulations. That meant any given putt was likely to break less than you might think. The problem was figuring out how much less.

At first blush, it appeared that my twelve-footer for par would break about two inches to the left. I decided to divide that figure in half and play about an inch of break. I should have halved the break once more. Although my ball rolled rather nicely off the putter face, it refused to turn more than a centimeter to the left and slid by the high side of the cup. I grunted and tapped in for a bogey five. Then I retreated to the apron while Curtis salvaged his par and Kriss narrowly missed a birdie putt.

We had to wait for nearly twenty minutes on the tee of the second hole, a very reachable 490-yard, par five playing slightly downwind, because the two groups ahead of our threesome had been stacked up by the groups ahead of them. When I got my turn at long last, I hit a Greg Norman–style high sailing draw that belied the increasing tightness of my torso. My ball came to rest 225 yards from the green, which was protected by a bunker that looked like a quarter section of the Mohave Desert. Intent on making up for my opening bogey, I went for it with a three wood, only to look up and top the ball about 170 yards.

Once again, the Tom Jenkins tips came to the rescue. I rallied from my foozled second shot with a neat little gap wedge pitch that stopped ten feet from the cup. Mindful of my missed par putt on number one, I halved the break I read, then halved it again. Evidently, I needed either a math tutorial or more local knowledge of poa annua greens. This time, the ball missed the hole by an inch on the low side, forcing me to settle for a par.

I vowed to keep my cool at all costs, remembering that Ben Hogan had double-bogeyed the first hole at the Colonial Invitational in Fort Worth one year and still finished with a one-under-par 69. Despite botching two very makable putts, I was just one over. I also remembered Dr. Parker's mentioning that an even par round had qualified for the Nike Sonoma Open the previous year. Santa Rosa's par 72 course was a very moderate 6,598 yards, and there were plenty of short par fours on the back nine that offered birdie opportunities. All I needed to do was get by the tough par fours on the front and I'd be fine.

From that point forward, however, a golfing nightmare descended upon me in much the same manner that F. Scott Fitzgerald described the onset of financial bankruptcy—gradually, and then all of a sudden and without relief. Number three, which measured 439 yards, was the longest of the front nine par fours, and it demanded a long and straight drive. But as I prepared to hit my tee shot, I felt like someone had clamped my torso in a steel corset perforated with pointed screws; each practice swing seemed to make the screws pierce deeper into my psoas muscle. Before I knew it, I was on my way to making another bogey thanks to another weakly faded drive and an anorexic two iron approach shot, both of which were co-produced by the screw teeth in my back.

On the tee of the 194-yard, par-three fourth hole, which was playing into the ever-strengthening wind, I began to understand what the great Bobby Jones meant when he observed that in golf, "one always feels that he is running from something without knowing exactly what nor where it is." I tried to hit an easy three wood to the middle of the green but hooked it onto a patch of hardpan next to the cart path. I chili-dipped my second shot into a clump of heavy grass. Then I bladed my third shot fifteen feet beyond the pin. I put a pretty good stroke on my par putt, but it missed the cup on the high side again and rolled four feet by. Instead of marking my ball, I informed my playing partners that I'd go ahead and finish. I then knocked my four-footer four more feet past the cup, missed the comebacker by an inch, and tapped in for a quadruple-bogey 7.

The rush of embarrassment and despair that overwhelmed me at that moment was more excruciating than any physical or mental pain I had ever suffered on a golf course or anywhere else. I had come to California buoyed by Doc Rotella's optimism about my chances of making it as a pro. Now I plunged into a spiritual water hazard full of self-hatred and hopelessness. The invisible screws in my back penetrated all the way to my heart. My eyes welled up with tears, and my head felt like it was going to explode. As I slunk back to my golf cart, I muttered the same sorrowful words over and over.

"I have no business being out here. . . . I just don't belong. . . . I want to go somewhere and hide. . . ."

Incredibly, the worst was yet to come. On the par-five fifth hole, I sliced my tee shot into a real water hazard a good half acre to the right of my intended landing area. Then I flubbed a series of elementary approach shots, and three-putted for a triple-bogey 8, the first snowman in the short history of my golfing comeback. At the 174-yard sixth, I hit a five iron to the front fringe and chipped to within eight inches of the cup. On any other day, I would have happily bet my house that I could make that putt. But on this horrific afternoon, I missed the eight-incher. The error was so completely unbelievable, I felt compelled to scream for confirmation of its occurrence.

"Did I just miss a fucking eight-inch putt?"

Kriss Casselman's caddy nodded solemnly.

"That'll get you talking to yourself," he said.

My self-talk quickly degenerated to inane babble, as I began mumbling the dictum of the legendary turn-of-the-century champion Harry Vardon, "No matter what happens, keep on hitting the ball." On number seven, a 400-yard dogleg-left par four, I followed his advice a little too close to the letter. After reaching the front apron of the green in two shots, I bumped a nine iron chip to within five inches of the hole. While my playing partners lined up their birdie putts, I announced that I would hole out. And guess what? I muffed the five-incher. Not missed it, mind you, muffed it by accidentally nudging the ball as I stood over it. I doubted that either Kriss or Curtis had noticed the nudge, but I had too much respect for the game of golf, if not for myself, to stoop to cheating. I called the stroke on myself, and tapped in the remaining 4.9-incher for a bogey.

At this point, I did not know whether to laugh, cry, or just impale myself on the putter shaft. Looking back on it, I'd have saved myself more misery by choosing the third option. I hit another Norman-style high sailing drive down the left side of the eighth fairway and stuck my five iron approach about twenty-five feet from the pin, only to three-putt for another bogey. I played the ninth hole even more like Norman from tee to green, depositing my drive in the center of the short grass and punching a wedge right at the flagstick. But the poa annua lumped up and tripped me into missing a ten-footer for birdie.

as we made the turn, I was seriously thinking about quitting. The leaderboard next to the tenth tee showed that there were already eight players in the clubhouse with scores of one under par or better, and I was twelve over for the day. Even if I birdied every par four and par five on the back nine and made hole-in-ones on both par threes, I could only get it back to one over. My watch showed that it was almost half past five, and with the sun slipping lower over the horizon, there was a real possibility that night would fall before we could complete the inward nine.

I decided to keep playing, however, because I dreaded getting a reputation as a quitter as much as I abhorred the idea of being branded a cheater. My resolve to continue was further reinforced when Curtis Matsuno, who had bogeyed number nine to go six over on the day, asked Kriss Casselman to hand over his scorecard, then tore it into pieces and walked off. That put both Kriss and me in an awkward position. Kriss was only one over, and still had a legitimate chance of qualifying. But in order to turn in a bona fide round, he needed another contestant on hand to certify his score, and the only other contestant remaining in our threesome was me.

I determined to do everything I could do within the rules to help Kriss make a charge on the back nine. On the 367-yard, par-four tenth, both of us reached the green in two and faced birdie putts of approximately the same length from the same side of the cup. I insisted on putting first, hoping to provide Kriss with a read on the break and speed. Well-intended as it may have been, the gesture did not do much good. I almost holed my birdie attempt, but Kriss wound up three-putting for bogey.

Our fortunes then underwent a mellow dramatic reversal. I started to strike the ball better and better despite all my aches and pains, while Kriss's shot making grew ever more erratic. I lipped out birdie putts of fifteen feet or less on the eleventh, the thirteenth, the fourteenth, and the sixteenth, and made skillful scrambling pars on number twelve and number fifteen. Kriss made another sloppy bogey on eleven, countered with a snaking bird on twelve, then stubbed a par save on fourteen.

I gleaned from our small talk between shots that we had more in common than the frustrations of this particular round. Kriss had also quit golf and was making a comeback, though his hiatus had lasted just two years instead of twenty-five. He told me that he had been introduced to the game at the age of twelve by a teaching pro who had continued to coach him for the next decade. Each year, the coaching sessions had grown more intense and the expectations for Kriss's performance on the golf course had gotten higher. According to Kriss, his coach had an extremely mechanical approach to teaching, offering a dozen swing thoughts for every type of shot.

"I had never taken lessons from anyone else, so I thought all teaching pros were like that," Kriss confided. "It got to where I had so many things running through my head that I started freezing over the ball. Finally, I just had to give it a rest. Now that I'm back, I've decided I'm going to find my own way to play."

I kept hoping Kriss would find that way before we ran out of holes. Upon reaching number seventeen, a 186-yard par three, I calculated that he needed to finish birdie-eagle to have any hope of qualifying. Having held the honor for the last two holes, I was due to hit first again. By this time the sun had disappeared behind the low hills to the west and the wind was gusting and swirling. The rules prohibited Kriss from asking me what club I was hitting, but they did not bar me from telling him if I chose to do so. I stepped onto the seventeenth tee holding both a four iron and a three iron, then tossed the shorter club to the side.

"Oh, lookee here," I said as we watched my tee shot fly to the back fringe, "Kriss and his caddy are undecided about what club to hit until they secretly overhear Uncle Harry blurt out, 'Gee, I guess this three iron was just too much club. Should've hit the damn four iron.' "

Kriss laughed so hard he nearly busted his gut. Then he asked his caddy for a four iron and knocked his tee shot six feet from the cup. But my umpteenth well-intended gesture of the back nine did no more good than the first. I got up and down from the fringe, and Kriss failed to convert his birdie attempt.

When we stepped onto the eighteenth tee, a tournament official drove up in a golf cart and asked if either of us had a chance of finishing at two under par or better. Kriss and I shook our heads. The official turned his cart back toward the clubhouse and disappeared into the gloaming twilight. That speechless act was enough to let us know that we no longer had any chance of qualifying. But with only one hole left, we still wanted to complete the round, if only to avoid the dishonor of having the initials "NC" (for "no card") posted beside our names.

As I pulled out my driver, I realized that a minor miracle was taking place. Starting at the ninth hole, I had run off a string of nine consecutive pars. The eighteenth was a narrow 498-yard par five with out of bounds on the left and trees on the right. If I could put my tee shot far enough down the fairway, I might have a chance of getting home in two. An eagle or birdie finish would partially compensate for my performance on the first eight holes and make it much easier to resume my Q School preparations with a positive attitude the next day.

"To hell with my damn back," I said, taking my stance. "I've been hitting nothing but weak fades all day long. I'm gonna stay behind one long enough to hit a hard running draw."

True to my word, I did stay behind my final drive of the evening, a little too far behind, in fact. The ball took off down the middle of the fairway, then snap-hooked over the out of bounds stakes on the left. I heaved a sigh and teed up another ball. Like a replay of my front nine drives, this one cut-faded into the right rough. Kriss then unleashed a boomer that literally carried out of sight.

Playing our approaches to the eighteenth green gave new meaning to the term "blind shot." It was now too dark to see more than a hundred yards, but Kriss and I kept whacking away with perverse joy, traipsing after our balls with the instincts of Seeing Eye dogs. Kriss ultimately managed to make a two-putt par that gave him a 75. I wound up three-putting for my second snowman and a rotund 86, the worst score in the brief history of my golfing comeback.

I thought that was going to be all she wrote for me and the Santa Rosa Golf and Country Club until I drove my golf cart past the scorer's table. The leaderboard showed that there were two players in at 67, three at 68, and six at 69, accounting for eleven of the fourteen qualifying spots. There were eight others tied at 70, which meant that there had to be a playoff to decide which of them would win one of the last three spots in the Nike Sonoma Open.

Although the course was now pitch-black, I could see by the light of a roof lamp on the clubhouse that a dozen men were standing around the ninth green. I got out of the golf cart, slung my golf bag on the ground, and walked over. As I reached the edge of the green, I heard voices calling back and forth in the darkness.

"Where are you, Dale?"

"Right here."

"That you, Arlen?"

"Uh-huh."

"Move to the left a little. Your shadow is blocking the light."

"I can't fucking believe you guys are letting shadows bother you now."

I quickly realized that the playoff for the last three qualifying spots was being conducted in what was effectively the dead of night. With the help of the clubhouse light, I discerned that there were now only five players left in the running. I watched a heavy-set fellow whose face was shrouded in shadows three-putt for what had to have been at least a bogey. Then I saw the other four tap their balls into the hole and leave the green shaking their heads.

"Jesus, that was ridiculous," one of them complained. "I had to fire up a whole pack of matches just to see the yardage markers on the last hole, and I still couldn't tell where the hell the green was."

"I just aimed for the light on top of the clubhouse," said another.

"Guess we're going to have to go at it again tomorrow morning."

"Not necessarily. I've got a proposition for you guys."

All four men gathered under one of the clubhouse awnings where I could see their faces and confirm from their conversation that they were the only ones left in contention for the last three qualifying spots. I recognized two of them from preround encounters on the practice range: Dale Abraham, a wiry twenty-five-year-old amateur from Walnut Creek, California, who had told me he intended to turn pro if he qualified; and Arlen Frew, a tall and muscular twenty-six-year-old pro from Pacific Grove who had rowed on the crew team at Berkeley. I later identified the other two men as locally based pros Brad Bell and Dana Benke.

"Here's the deal, guys," Benke said. "If each of you give me seventy dollars right now to cover my entry fee, I'll just declare that I'm first alternate, and we won't have to come back and playoff tomorrow. What do you say?"

"I don't know," Bell replied. "That sounds kind of unethical."

"No, it's not," Benke insisted. "I've been in similar situations plenty of times before. One time we decided spots by playing liar's poker in the clubhouse. If we do it this way, I'll be whole, you guys'll be in the tournament, and the Northern California PGA section will save some money by not having to reserve the course for us tomorrow."

The group debated Benke's offer for a few more minutes, then shook hands all around. I never saw any money actually change hands, but I could tell from the smile on Benke's face as he headed for the parking lot that the deal was done.

*   *   *

When I got back to my chosen TraveLodge in one of the seedier sections of downtown Santa Rosa, I was still musing over the after-dark playoff and subsequent payoff proposal I'd just witnessed. The sheer absurdity of the situation made me temporarily forget about my own pitiful predicament. Then I remembered to call my wife. The phone rang before I could dial out.

"Hi, sweetest one," Alison said. "It's getting late, and you haven't called. I was getting worried. How'd it go out there today?"

Something inside my brain clicked at the sound of her voice. I felt the invisible corset around my torso squeeze my ribs so hard I could hardly breathe. Then the pointed screws in the corset began to grind their way toward my heart again. A demonic being roared from my loins.

"Well, you can quit your fucking worrying, damn it. I was just about to pick up the goddamn phone and call you. How did it go out there today? Well, I'll tell you. It was just about the worst god-damn day of my stupid-ass life. I shot an eighty-fucking-six. That's all. An eighty-fucking-six. You could shoot a better score than that, and you don't even play golf. Can you believe that shit?"

There was silence on the other end of the line.

Then Alison began to cry.

"Now what the hell's the matter?" I demanded.

There was more silence, then more crying.

"How can you talk to me that way?" Alison sobbed. "I've been so supportive of what you're doing, and when I call to ask how you're doing, you just growl at me and bite my head off. That's just not fair."

Now I really felt like a piece of shit. I lit up a Schimmelpennick, took a deep drag, and told myself I'd better apologize that second— and make it good, too.

"I'm really, really sorry, honey." I sighed. "You love me so much, and I love you so much, too. There's no excuse for me to blow my top at you this way. I could say I don't know what came over me, but I do know. I'm just at the end of my rope. I haven't played this bad since I was a goddamn beginner. My back is killing me, and it just gets worse every day. But I'll make it up to you, honey, I swear. We'll do something fun together, just the two of us, real soon."

As it turned out, I agreed to atone for my sins sooner than expected. Alison reminded me that she had been wanting to make a trip to the California wine country to sample some new vintages that might appeal to her restaurant customers. I told her to catch the next plane to San Francisco. I'd spend the next few days hanging around the Nike Sonoma Open to see if I could learn something and give my back a chance to get better. At night, we could go wine and restaurant tasting.

"Just remember, honey, everything happens for the best," Alison said as we finalized the details of her travel plans. "No matter how bad things get, don't let them beat you."

I told her again that I loved her. Then I hung up the phone and cried until I fell asleep.

The following morning, I made a refreshing change of scene. The venue for the Sonoma Open was the Windsor Golf Club, an unusually well-kept municipal course several miles north of Santa Rosa. In contrast to the cramped and dowdy site of the Monday qualifier, Windsor sprawled over a vista of gently rolling former farmland still dotted with grain silos and barns. Although the 6,650-yard, par-72 golf course had the poa annua greens I despised, it also featured a cute little blue-and-white clapboard-sided clubhouse and several similarly stylish outbuildings connected by an artfully designed network of meandering cart paths.

The Nike Tour tournament had all the trappings of the big time, thanks mainly to the fact that it was run by the PGA Tour as a kind of AAA version of the major-league circuit. Sonoma was one of thirty events on an annual calendar that included stops in Philadelphia, Cleveland, and Monterrey, Mexico, as well as in such minor-league metropoli as Boise, Shreveport, and Pensacola. The Nike Tour offered purses in excess of $200,000 per event and first-place checks of $36,000. As a result, Nike Tour contests drew stronger fields, larger crowds, and richer sponsors than the hand-to-mouth mini-tours.

The first thing I saw when I walked out of the parking lot at Windsor was a six-pole hospitality tent surrounded by a fleet of brand-new display-model Buicks, some of which doubled as player transportation vehicles. Alongside the eighteen-wheel Nike Tour tractor trailer that housed the administrative staff, there was a medical tent, a sponsors tent, various conveniently located concession stands (including one with an outdoor barbecue grill), and a registration trailer where tournament contestants received two dozen Titleists and a gift bag stuffed with discount coupons and bottles of California wine.

The expansive bent grass practice range also had a decidedly more bustling and upscale look than the mudpack back at Pine Lakes International in Myrtle Beach. The Nike Tour players tended to be in their late twenties and early thirties, marginally older, if not much wiser, than the kids chasing the Hooters Tour. They also had much better financial backing. Instead of toting lightweight nylon golf bags with pop-out stands, most of them had heavyweight leather bags emblazoned with commercial sponsors' logos, and they always had caddies carrying the load out on the golf course. As they beat buckets of range balls toward the target flags, they were watched over by a small company of swing coaches, chiropractors, sports shrinks, equipment company reps, agents, managers, and even a few comely female camp followers.

I cornered a management company executive named Glenn Karp inside the hospitality tent. Karp was a balding, smooth-talking thirty-six-year-old former college baseball player whose clients included PGA Tour journeymen Lennie Clements and Brian Kamm, and Nike Tour veteran Larry Silviera. I was hoping that Karp might provide some insights on what distinguished Nike players from the other mini-tour rabbits, and a little inside dope on the sports management business. But after touching on those subjects with diplomatic brevity, he began questioning my fitness for entering PGA Tour Qualifying School.

"The thing that concerns me is the effect you're going to have on the players you get paired with," Karp declared. "There are going to be guys out there who are going through Q School for the third, fourth, and fifth time. Some of them will even be there for the ninth or tenth time. This is the most important tournament of their entire year. They're going to want to stay completely focused on grinding for pars and making enough birdies to make the cut. If you're shooting scores in the 80s and getting in their way, that's going to drag down their games, too. You could end up being a big distraction."

I guzzled a Diet Coke and stared down at the table.

"Look, my friend, I appreciate your concern," I said at last. "The fact of the matter is that I have just as much right to be out there as anybody else. I've paid my three grand entry fee, and I'm prepared to take my chances. I ain't gonna be trying to interview people out on the golf course or bugging them about what they need to shoot to make the cut. Sure, I've laid off from competition for a long time, but I've also played with plenty of great golfers. You can ask Ben Crenshaw or Bruce Lietzke if I ever got in their way."

I thanked Karp for his time and said I'd see him around the campus. Then I bolted out of the hospitality tent, silently vowing to improve my chances at Q School by learning everything I could from watching the way the average Nike Tour pro performed under pressure.

Over the next four days, I saw plenty of average performances but no average players per se. One of the few things the majority of Nike Tour pros had in common was a fondness for wearing copper bracelets, which left green rings around their wrists and supposedly prevented arthritis and rheumatism. But they came in all sizes and swing types. There were big bruisers with fat bellies and flat arcs. There were tall skinny guys with upright motions. There were short stocky guys who tried to muscle the ball. And there were short cocky guys with hot putters.

Five-time Nike Tour tournament winner Sean Murphy happened to fall in the latter category. A native of New Mexico, he also happened to be a childhood friend of Eden Foster, who had asked me to look him up. Like the rest of his Nike Tour peers, Murphy yearned to move up to the PGA Tour, but so far he was having a tough go. The top ten money winners on the Nike Tour in a given year automatically earned PGA Tour cards for the following year. Murphy, who had been on and off the major-league circuit for the past couple of seasons, ranked number eleven at the time of the Sonoma Open, the next-to-last tournament on the Nike schedule. And yet he seemed to be brimming with confidence, as I discovered when I asked if he thought the poa annua greens were as tough to putt as I had found them to be.

"Nope," he chirped. "Not when you hit the ball as close to the hole as I do."

I encountered a different brand of confidence when I sought out two Nike Tour rookies who were over two decades apart in age. The younger of the two also hailed from New Mexico. His name was Notah Begay III, and he was a twenty-two-year-old half Navajo, half Pueblo who had just graduated from Stanford, where he had helped lead the golf team to first- and second-place finishes in the 1994 and 1995 NCAA championships. The media often identified him somewhat condescendingly as the former roommate of freshman prodigy Tiger Woods.

"Everyone's dubbing Tiger the next great player, but he's not much better than me, if at all," Begay complained after shooting a first-round 68. "All spring, he only beat me twice."

In fact, Begay had won the 1995 Northeast Amateur and had top-ten finishes in the Porter Cup, the Sunnyhanna, and the Rice Planters tournaments. Although he had been eliminated from the 1995 U.S. Amateur at Newport Country Club in the second round of match play, he had been named along with Woods to the United States Walker Cup team. But where Woods seemed like an almost-too-perfect computer-modeled golfing machine, his former roommate exuded a rough-hewn, self-styled élan.

Dark-haired, wide-bodied, and coffee-skinned, Begay sauntered down the fairway with a bowlegged gait, swaying slightly from side to side. He wore diamond-shaped sunglasses, and he had a gold ring in his left ear and streaks of clay on his cheeks. ("The clay is a Native American religious rite," he confided. "I wear it to acknowledge the challenge of the game.") He told me that he had been introduced to golf at the age of seven by his father, who worked for a U.S. government health services unit and played in a New Mexico businessman's league. Although he had come up the hard way, saving nickels and dimes as a kid to pay for $2.50 buckets of range balls, he did not seem to have a chip on his shoulder or a naive faith in the American dream.

"Native Americans are always overlooked," he allowed. "But the game of golf doesn't have a cultural bias. Golf doesn't know who you are or where you came from."

The most distinctive feature of Begay's game was his ambidexterous putting technique. He putted right-handed on one hole, then left-handed on another, using a specially designed Bulls Eye blade. His choice was not random or whimsical; he made it according to the direction of the break. Begay told me that a golfer/investor team had done a study at Stanford in 1993 that confirmed that right-breaking putts were the toughest for right-handers, and left-breakers for left-handers, with the degree of difficulty increasing exponentially as the slope and speed of the green increased. I asked Begay how long it had taken him to get comfortable with switching back and forth.

"I'll call you," he replied with a wink, "as soon as I know myself."

Coming into the last three holes of round two, Begay had gotten to eight under par for the tournament. I saw him look over at a scoreboard beside the fairway that showed that he was tied for the lead, and told myself that trouble was in the offing. Sure enough, he bogeyed the sixteenth, a 217-yard uphill par three. On seventeen, a 368-yard dogleg-right par four with a pond protecting the right side of the fairway and the front of the green, he discarded the notion of laying up with an iron and hit a towering drive into position A. Then he went for the pin with a knock-down wedge shot, only to watch his ball spin into the water hazard. After taking the requisite penalty stroke, he hit his fourth shot over the green, chipped poorly, and two-putted for a triple-bogey 7.

Begay went for the green in two on the 546-yard eighteenth, missed, but wound up having to settle for a par because of sloppy short game play. Instead of carding his second straight 68, he came in with a 72, low enough to make the cut but too high to remain in contention for the lead. And yet, Begay expressed no second thoughts about his bold and costly gambles on the inward holes.

"I'm always playing to win," he told me. "And I never give up. Even if things look bleak and I'm shooting 80, I try to shoot 79. The first thing on my agenda after this tournament is Q School, and playing here is the best way to find out what shape my game is in. I'm not going into Stage One just to qualify for Stage Two, I'm going to play to win Stage One."

I later met Begay's rookie alter ego on the Nike Tour, forty-seven-year-old Allen Doyle. Tall, rawboned, and gray-templed, Doyle lumbered down the fairways like a farmer on his way to market, but he was no mere hick. In April, he had won the Nike Mississippi Gulf Coast Classic in a playoff after shooting fifteen under for the four tournament rounds. In August, he had won the Nike Texarkana Open with a nineteen-under-par total. By the start of the Sonoma Open, he ranked sixth on the Nike Tour money list with $129,702. He also ranked second behind Sean Murphy in scoring with an average of 69.7 strokes per round.

Doyle had a story that was uniquely inspirational for fellow over-forty types like me. He had attended Norwich College in Northfield, Vermont, on a hockey scholarship, playing on his college golf team only as a sideline. But he was still good enough to make it to the finals of the Massachusetts State amateur at age nineteen. He had later served a two-year Army hitch in Korea, then moved down to Georgia to work for a textile firm. Between 1976 and 1981, he had more or less given up golf. Then he had read that the Walker Cup matches would be held in Atlanta in 1989, and decided to start playing seriously again.

In addition to qualifying for the '89 Walker Cup squad, Doyle had compiled one of the most outstanding records in the annals of American amateur golf. His achievements just happened to be overshadowed by the presence of several other hotshots, most notably Jay Sigel, Phil Mickelson, Justin Leonard, and Tiger Woods. In 1994, he had confirmed his first-class status by winning the Sunnyhanna, Southeastern, Rice Planters, Cardinal, and Dogwood championships.

By that time, Doyle was supporting his family by operating a driving range in La Grange, Georgia. The oldest of his two daughters was nearing college age, and he reckoned that playing pro golf might be a better way to finance her education than selling range balls. ("I figured the worst-case scenario was that I'd turn pro and end up just giving lessons at my driving range," he recalled.) But thanks to his remarkable rookie season on the Nike Tour, Doyle was now certain of finishing among the top ten money winners and becoming the oldest rookie on the PGA Tour in 1996.

I asked him to pinpoint the keys to his success.

"You've got to have the three *H*'s—your hands, your head, and your heart," he said. "You can be stronger in one of them than in the others. Most people are. But you need all three to be working for you. Things can get pretty tough out here otherwise. There were times this year when I felt like I was in a wind tunnel. I'd be shooting three under par, and I'd look at the leaderboard and see someone else was eleven under."

I asked him what advice he would give to amateurs in our age bracket who dreamed of trying to follow in his footsteps.

" 'Don't,' is what I'd tell them," Doyle replied. "I know that might kill a few dreams, but it's the reality. Some people think they can just quit their jobs and practice a little and then come out here and make it. They can't. Unless you're dominating the amateur level where you're at, you can't move up and be successful."

The final results of the Nike Sonoma Open testified to the truth of Doyle's cautionary words. The winning score was a nineteen-under-par total of 269, shot by Stuart Appleby. Notah Begay tied for eighteenth place with rounds of 68-72-73-66, which put him at nine under. Doyle wound up tied for twenty-first place at eight under, along with a long hitting kid from Minnesota named Tim Herron. All those scores were pretty dazzling from my point of view since the four lowest rounds I'd shot at Barcelona Neck back in Sag Harbor added up to just sixteen under. If the Nike Tour pros were only playing AAA ball, I shuddered at the thought of what the major leaguers from the PGA Tour might have shot.

Even so, I left northern California feeling recharged and more optimistic about my chances for making it through Q School, the doubtful comments of Glenn Karp notwithstanding. Only two of the fourteen qualifiers from Santa Rosa had made the cut at 144, or even par, after the first two rounds. Four of them had failed to break 80 in the first round; playoff survivor Arlen Frew hadn't cracked the egg either day. In round two, I'd seen Notah Begay make the same kind of rookie mistakes I'd made in the Monday qualifier. I'd also seen the superconfident Sean Murphy shoot 76-72 to miss the cut by four strokes. In short, I realized that all these talented young players were susceptible to human error, just like me.

Alison had also done her part to improve my outlook on golf and life. Having been on the road for the better part of the previous four weeks, I had gotten a classic case of the touring pro blues. If I'd seen one more broken motel bathroom sink or visited one more fast-food franchise, I might have puked. But Alison had arranged for us to stay at the Michel Schlumberger winery, where the accommodations were luxurious and the food and drink delectable.

The only glitch in this heavenly interlude occurred on the last night of our stay. We had packed our suitcases and gone to bed early to rest up for our flight to my Q School site in Texas the following morning. I was totally exhausted from tramping around the Windsor Golf Club course and the invisible screws were once again tormenting my back. But just as I was dozing off, Alison got up and staggered toward the closet.

"What the hell's the matter now?" I shrieked. "It's too late for this shit."

Alison acted as if she hadn't heard me. She opened the closet door and peered inside, muttering under her breath.

"Oh, sweetest, I thought someone was stealing your golf clubs."

I suddenly realized that Alison was sleepwalking, and called her back to bed, kissing her on the lips as tears streamed down my cheeks.

"Don't worry, little one," I sobbed. "My golf clubs are still here and so am I."

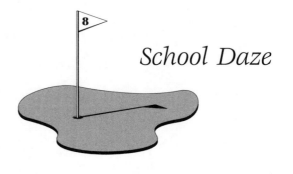

School Daze

Shortly before high noon on Tuesday, October 10, I whipped out my Big Bertha driver and began to pace back and forth across the sun-scorched sixteenth tee box at The Ranch Country Club in McKinney, Texas. A subtornadic southwestern wind was ripsnorting the flagsticks, and airborne particles of ragweed kept slipping behind the fenders of my wraparound Bolles, burning my eyes and singeing my sinuses. My back felt like it was stiffening into a fence post with barbed-wire bangles.

But in spite of all my discomfort, I was happier than a saddle-sore cowpoke doing the two-step with the belle of the rodeo ball. It was early in round one of Stage One of the 1995 PGA Tour Qualifying School, and I had just won the honor for the first time on this sweltering morning, a distinction I hadn't achieved in a full-fledged four-day tournament in over twenty-five years.

My performance so far had pleasantly surprised my younger but far more seasoned Q School playing partners, both of whom had been born the year I'd quit college golf. After three-putting for bogey on number ten, our opening hole of the round, I had rallied for soild pars on eleven, twelve, and thirteen. An errant drive had led to a second bogey on the long par-four fourteenth, but I had then birdied the fifteenth by whacking a wholehearted five iron to ten feet and slamming my sidehill putt into the back of the cup.

That put me at only one over on the day with three potential birdie holes left on the back nine, a position roughly similar to the one I had found myself in during the first round of the U.S. Amateur qualifier back in August. Number sixteen was the trickiest, but also the most tantalizing, of the incoming holes. A dogleg-right par five flanked by a man-made lake that ran from tee to green, it was listed at 549 yards on the scorecard, but you could easily reach the green in two if you were brave enough to slide your drive to the corner. In my Sunday afternoon practice round, I'd gotten home with a two iron, and I was planning to attack the hole in exactly the same way to get to even par.

Unfortunately, I had plenty of time to second-guess my strategy. One of the members of the threesome ahead of ours suffered from a peculiar ophthalmic disability that required him to flop down on his belly to line up any putt over three inches in length. As a result, he and his group were quite literally playing at a snail's pace. But the threesome in front of them was even slower, and the belly flopper could not hit his second shot until the sixteenth green was cleared.

My playing partners remained unfazed. Shane Bertsch, a sallow-complexioned twenty-five-year-old Nike Tour rookie out of Texas A&M, sporting Swoosh-stamped shoes, shirt, and cap, was accustomed to five-and-a-half-hour tournament rounds. He merely flipped his Oakleys up and down, and chortled.

Ren Budde, a long hitting twenty-four-year-old Texas Christian University graduate with light brown hair, tan slacks, and an earth-toned edge that came from banging around the Texas barbecue circuit, shook his head and rolled his eyes each time the belly flopper missed a putt.

"I just wish he'd make a few," Ren said with a sigh, "so we don't have to stay out here until dark."

I gulped down a couple of Advil and gazed at the perimeters of the surrounding Stonebridge Ranch development. The property encompassed 6,700 acres and featured two golf courses—The Ranch, a 7,087-yard, par-72, designed by Arthur Hills; and the even longer and more challenging Stonebridge Country Club, designed by Pete Dye. In the interest of providing maximum fairway-view frontage for homesites, both tracks had been divided into three-, six-, and twelve-hole clusters connected by stone-tunneled concrete

paths that made golf carts mandatory for anyone who didn't want
to grind their spikes into paper clips every round.

The oddest feature of Stonebridge Ranch, however, was the
absence of a human presence commensurate with its sprawling
dimensions. There must have been more than three hundred
brand-new two-story brick houses overlooking the golf courses;
their backyards displayed accoutrements ranging from outdoor
grills and volleyball nets to swing sets and jungle gyms. But on
both weekend and weekday evenings alike, the majority of the
houses were lightless, and I rarely saw anyone entering, leaving,
or occupying them. In fact, the only consistently visible signs of
life were swarms of loose-boweled blackbirds that swirled in kalei-
doscopic roller coasters above the lonesome stands of banyan trees
dotting the former prairie land.

The existential eeriness of Stonebridge Ranch provided a perfect backdrop for Q School, the most inappropriately named contest
in all of sports. Though sometimes described as the PGA's version
of the bar exam, it bore no resemblance to a conventional educa-
tional institution like a law school or a university. It was more like
a country club–hopping outdoor insane asylum overrun with in-
mates who paid entry fees of $3,000 a head in the hope that they
could get in, get out, and never be forced to return by winning and
retaining their PGA Tour player's cards. According to PGA records,
the oldest man to make it all the way through Q School on his first
try was then-forty-five-year-old Jimmy Powell, who accomplished
the feat way back in 1980, when the tournament was still held twice
per year. In the one-chance-per-annum modern era, very few guys
made it through Q School on their first try, and most of them had
either been college phenoms or seasoned mini-tour pros.

Stage One of this three-phase golfing torture test was simultaneously being conducted at The Ranch and eight other sites around
the country, with approximately 1,000 men playing seventy-two
holes over four days. Those who made the cut at the end of Stage
One would move on to one of six Stage Two sites, where they
would play another seventy-two holes in mid-November. The six-
day-long Final Stage was scheduled for Bear Lakes Country Club in
West Palm Beach, Florida, from November 29 through December
4. The 190-man Final Stage field would consist of survivors of the
first two stages and players who had earned exemptions based on
their prior pro golfing records. But only the forty low scorers and

ties would win PGA Tour cards for 1996, with the rest receiving full or conditional Nike Tour cards.

Theoretically, the odds of making the cut at the end of Stage One were about one in three at each of the nine sites. In reality, I figured my chances of finishing among the low thirty-three scorers in the highly competitive 96-man field at The Ranch were about like those of hitting a one iron through the eye of a needle. But as our threesome continued to wait for the belly flopper's group to move along, I reflected on the new perspectives I had gained on performing under pressure, praying that they might somehow enable me to make the cut after all.

I had arrived at Dallas's Love Field airport the Sunday before Q School, looking like an escapee from some out-of-state hospital. Casual passersby were probably wondering whether I had fled the intensive care unit or the mental ward. Although the outside temperature was in the high eighties, I was wearing a woolen sweater vest, and I was clutching a wad of five-dollar bills with one hand while waving for skycaps with the other.

Both my unseasonable attire and my frantic behavior were measures to protect my back. Just as Dr. Will Parker had predicted, the respite I had taken following the qualifier for the Nike Sonoma Open had provided only minimal relief. Once I had started practicing again, I could not even carry my book bag, much less my equipment-stuffed golf bag, without yelping in pain. All told, it had cost me $30 in tips just to make it down the concourse, past the bronze statue of the Texas Ranger in the main terminal lobby, and out to the rental car lot.

I had squeezed myself into a white Chevy Lumina and driven up Interstate 45, bucking and bouncing like a drunk on a mechanical bull at some country western joint. My instincts kept warning me to jump off before I got thrown to the floor, but my conscience kept advising me that I was morally and financially obliged to hang on until the bell rang.

Earlier in the week, I had made my pre–Q School scouting trip to Stonebridge Ranch in accordance with Bob Rotella's prescription. Although my practice round at The Ranch had been washed out by a thunderstorm before I finished nine holes, I had convinced the ladies at the information center to arrange for me to rent one of the blue clapboard guest cottages next to the driving range at Stonebridge C.C. My unit was called St. Andrews, and like its mate, Turnberry, it beat the hell out of the Comfort Inn where many of the other Q School contestants were staying. The most notable amenities were a stone fireplace, cable TV, a VCR, maid service, and access to all the club facilities, including the giant whirlpool in the men's locker room.

The only drawback was that foliage around the guest cottages happened to be a favorite nesting place for the area's resident population of loose-boweled blackbirds. Upon returning to Stonebridge C.C. on Sunday morning, I found the parking lot and walkways adjacent to my unit ankle-deep in blackbird poop, a substance that proved to be as slippery as banana peels and considerably less fragrant.

Later that afternoon, I ventured back to The Ranch to get in a full eighteen-hole practice round. The experience was more encouraging than expected. The fairways had long since dried out from the thunderstorm, and my drives got enough roll to make the course play much shorter than its 7,087-yard length suggested. I even managed to reach a couple of the par fives in two, and came fairly close to shooting 72 with the benefit of a mulligan or three.

My sole cause for concern, apart from my ailing back, was the realization that I had not progressed beyond the play-by-numbers method I had used in every previous tournament. I had recently read an article about Hale Irwin in which the three-time U.S. Open champion was quoted as saying that he liked to think about nothing but his intended target when he stood over a golf ball. Unlike Irwin, I still felt that I had to review a written checklist before attempting all but the most elementary shots.

A couple of tune-up sessions with Dick Harmon down in Houston following my scouting trip to The Ranch had only swelled the list of swing thoughts in my pocket notebook. Under the heading "DRIVER," for example, I had inscribed such reminders as "swing in a circle, not in a line," "don't aim too far right," "turn shoulders back," "clear hips," "watch ball," "keep tempo smooth," and "complete finish, just don't add." Focusing on my intended target somehow seemed to get lost in the page shuffle.

I returned from my Sunday afternoon practice round at The Ranch believing that what I really needed was a little more last-minute advice, not on swing mechanics per se but on the bigger picture. In desperation, I picked up the phone in the guest cottage and called Jackson Bradley, the former head pro at River Oaks Country Club who had coached me throughout my junior and college golf years.

Dave Marr, the Houston-born former PGA champion turned television commentator, had once described Jackson Bradley, who was now in his mid-seventies, as "the David Leadbetter of his time." Unlike Leadbetter, however, Mr. Bradley, as I had once and always would address him, had been an outstanding competitor as well as one of the nation's top teaching pros. Born in Indiana, he had started his career in southern California and Chicago. Between 1947 and 1962, he played in sixteen consecutive PGA championships and ten U.S. Opens. Before a series of foot problems ended his competitive career, he established himself as one of the most consistent players on the PGA Tour and won no less than half a dozen South Texas PGA championships.

When the membership committee asked Mr. Bradley to become head pro at River Oaks in 1953, Claude Harmon Sr. advised him to turn down the job, warning that he would be treated like a servant. But Mr. Bradley had surprised everyone by transforming what had been a sleepy Southern cardplayers' club into a real golf club. He had upgraded the pro shop, established a regular tournament program, and opened the golf course and the practice range to future touring pros from the University of Houston and Rice. He had later co-invented an innovative line of golf clubs molded from a plastic composite whose design would help inspire the lightweight metal woods of the present day.

Along the way, Mr. Bradley had advocated progressive social and employment policies in an era still dominated by archconservatism and racism. He had vastly improved working conditions for the caddies by installing showers and cooling units in the caddy shack and arranging for them to play the golf course on Mondays when the club was officially closed. He had also been one of the first in Texas to hire a female assistant pro, a move that opened the way for one of his own four daughters to become a golf pro decades later. An avid reader and articulate speaker, he had served nine years as the players' spokesman on the predecessor of the PGA Tour tournament policy board.

To me, Mr. Bradley had been a surrogate father figure, role model, and moral sounding board. A devout Catholic, he had sponsored me at Confirmation when I was twelve years old, reprimanded me for my temperamental outbursts of club tossing at age fifteen, and stood by me when the old dinosaurs of River Oaks attacked me for wearing sideburns and fraternizing with blacks at age seventeen. "In life, everything is a learning process," he used to say. "You should try to devote every day to doing things for the honor and glory of God and Harry Hurt III."

I had not seen or spoken to Mr. Bradley in the twenty-five years since I had quit golf, but when he answered the phone at his current home in Austin, he greeted me like a long-lost son and let me know that he had heard about my quest to make a comeback. After filling him in on what I had been doing all this time, I got right to the point: I needed to ask his advice on how to get through Stage One of Q School. He intuitively sensed the swing thought quandary I was in and got right to the point himself.

"Keep it simple," he told me. "The imperative is just to hit the ball. Don't think your way through the golf swing or you'll go nuts."

I replied that I was trying to keep it simple, but that my ball striking was complicated by the fact that my back hurt every time I swung the club.

"Well, all I can say is that something you're doing must not be quite right," he allowed. "It's not supposed to hurt."

Then he wished me luck, adding, "There's a lot of sacrifice involved in trying to play on the Tour. Most people don't realize that until it's too late."

By week's end, I would appreciate the elegantly straightforward wisdom of what Mr. Bradley had told me on the phone. But at the time, his advice left me feeling a little empty and even more befuddled. I decided that I needed to talk to someone a little closer to my own age, a guy who had more recently faced the kind of competition I would contend with at Q School. So I called Bobby Walzel, the former University of Houston player who had traveled the amateur circuit with me back in 1969.

Like Mr. Bradley, Bobby had been something of an icon, if not exactly a full-fledged role model, during my junior golf days. I'd first met him and his younger brother, John, who was my age, at a tournament at Golfcrest Country Club, their home course, on the other side of the tracks from River Oaks. I was only ten years old and Bobby was just twelve, but he probably had more natural talent than any golfer I'd seen before or since. Long-legged and skinny, he was nicknamed "Weed," and although his backswing tempo was smoother than new-mowed grass, he blew through the impact zone in a hip-spinning swoosh. He could drive the ball a mile and rifle irons that literally dented the pins. At the age of fourteen, he was already shooting in the 60s, and by the time he reached his late teens, he was routinely winning men's amateur championships in the Houston area.

But Bobby had never quite lived up to his true potential. In college, he had bounced on and off the U of H team led by John Mahaffey following the untimely death of his mother, who had passed away the day before we were scheduled to play in the Porter Cup in the fateful summer of '69. He had won his PGA Tour card on his first attempt at Q School in the fall of 1973, but he had often seemed to wilt under the pressure of first-class competition. His only victory on the major-league circuit was at the 1979 Magnolia State Classic (now known as the Deposit Guaranty Classic) in Madison, Mississippi, held during the week when the big-name pros were playing in the Masters. By the time he had lost his card in 1981, his total winnings amounted to less than $200,000. Bobby blamed his disappointing Tour record on a mysterious inability to handle chip shots. Like his brother, I always thought that his problems had to do with some mental block.

Bobby had quit golf completely for a couple of years, then reincarnated himself as a kind of traveling pro for hire. He had gone on to found a company called Golf Quest, which organized corporate outings at famous courses across the country. In 1992, he had shot an astonishing course record 60 at the Jack Nicklaus–designed Lochinvar Golf Club course, north of Houston, prompting rumors that he was preparing for another run at the PGA Tour. But when I reached him at his Golf Quest office, I was surprised to learn that our career paths were recrossing in diametrically different directions.

"This is just tonic for our asses," he chuckled, using one of his favorite expresssions of old. "You're going pro and I'm going the other way."

Bobby explained that he had decided to apply to the USGA to have his amateur status reinstated because he believed that it would enhance his business prospects. "I'm kind of excited about being an amateur again," he said. "I can make a lot more contacts playing in four-ball and member-guest tournaments than I ever made out on the Tour."

Bobby delivered the real shocker, however, when I asked after his brother John. The two of them had always been exact opposites and intensely competitive sibling rivals. Flamboyantly personable and perpetually blubbery, John had grown up with the nickname "Fat Cat." By the age of fifteen, he was 6'2" and tipped the scales at something like 240 pounds. He liked to wear expensive alligator golf shoes and brightly colored clothes, and he completed the follow-through of his swing with an arm-twisting flourish copied from Arnold Palmer. Although he had qualified for the 1968 U.S. Junior Championship at age sixteen and won his share of local tournaments, he had never shown Bobby's shotmaking brilliance or scoring acumen. Instead of turning pro, he had carried on and expanded their father's one-shop jewelry business.

I had bumped into John a few times over the past several years, and I knew that he had been married and divorced and that he had a teenage daughter. I'd also heard that he had recently admitted to friends and business associates that he was gay and that he had a live-in boyfriend. What I didn't know was that he had contracted HIV.

"Fat Cat is down to a hundred and thirty-five pounds," Bobby informed me. "His doctor just put him on a special intravenous nutrition program, and he's gained back a little weight lately. We're all hoping for the best, but we're afraid it's just a matter of time until . . ."

As Bobby's voice trailed off, my heart sank. I could hardly believe the words I had just heard. All of a sudden, my own petty problems snapped into proper perspective. Here I was worrying about Q School and my wounded back while one of my oldest friends in the world was fighting for his life. When I asked Bobby if there was anything I could do, he told me that John was presently too sick to receive visitors, but he urged me to give him a call in a few days, when he was expected to get out of the hospital.

"I'll let Johnny know that you're going to be at Q School," Bobby said before we hung up. "He'll be pulling for you to tear 'em up."

I arrived at The Ranch for my final practice round on Monday with a win one for the Gipper mentality and shot a bona fide, mulligan-free 73. In light of what John "Fat Cat" Walzel was up against, the competition I faced no longer seemed so intimidating. There was the perennial crop of flatbellied flashes fresh out of college, and a score of guys in their mid to late twenties who had tuned up on local mini-tours like the Lone Star circuit. There was a handful of Hooters Tour hopefuls, including my Myrtle Beach drinking buddy Eric Epperson, a few Nike Tour vets, a threesome of Argentinians, and a contingent of South Africans led by Deane Pappas, who had played college golf and learned to spit tobacco at the University of Arkansas.

There were also several weather-beaten repeaters, including Ty Armstrong, a short, stocky, freckle-faced journeyman pro in his early thirties with a wife and two young children back in Eden Prairie, Minnesota. Armstrong, who had won but failed to keep his Tour card in 1993-1994, was making his eleventh appearance at Q School.

"It just gets harder every time," Armstrong informed me following my practice round. "These kids today have no fear. They figure if they don't make it through Stage One, they'll go play the mini-tours and scrape by until they get another chance. If I don't make the cut, then I feel like I've wasted my whole year and let my family down."

That, of course, was just the kind of angst-ridden rap Doc Rotella had admonished me to avoid. I fled The Ranch and sped back over to my guest cottage at Stonebridge C.C., where I tried to immerse myself in last-minute ritual chores. First, I yanked my golf bag out of the trunk and lugged it inside the guest cottage, dodging blackbird poop with every step. ("I've heard too many horror stories about guys getting their sticks stolen the night before a big tournament," Rotella had said.) I scrubbed my clubs in one of the double-sink marble vanities, dug out my spikes, and retightened the screws. Then I marked two sleeves of Maxflis with an identifying black *H* and emptied my bag of all other ball types.

Next, I laid out my attire for round one, a solemn rite in which naive superstitions and sponsorship considerations dictated the selection of every article. I ultimately settled on a black-and-gold King Cobra sun visor, a pair of paper-thin white cotton slacks a cheapy-cheap Chinese tailor had copied from a fancy designer pattern, and, after much agonizing over the blessings and curses of various country club logos, the 1995 U.S. Open shirt emblazoned with the profile of a Shinnecock Indian that I had worn in the U.S. Amateur qualifier.

I draped my ensemble over an armchair and sprinkled it with a handful of nickels, the coins I believed to be my lucky ball marks. Then I set all three of the alarm clocks I'd brought along on specific instructions from Rotella. "You can't just rely on a wake-up call or one alarm," he had cautioned. "What if they forget to call you or your alarm doesn't go off? In some other sport, a coach would take care of these things for you. But in golf, you're on your own."

The infernal ticking of the alarm clocks triggered a wave of Q School performance fears. Unlike many of my competitors, I wasn't banking my whole year and family income on making the cut. But in addition to being disadvantaged by my long layoff and relative inexperience, I faced other pressures they didn't. *Sports Illustrated* photographer Jim Gund was once again going to be following me around to shoot my golfing exploits for publication. I didn't want to mess up in front of the camera. But perhaps even more important, I didn't want Gund to distract the other members of my threesome. ("We send a photographer to Q School every year, and the players always freak out," my coldly unsympathetic editor would inform me later. "Just think of the anecdotes you'd have if they were at your throat.")

I pulled out the notes I'd taken during my pep talk with Rotella and tried to slip into a better emotional zone by visualizing my opening round as per his instructions. My threesome would be teeing off on number ten, a nasty little 390-yard par four, uphill and almost invariably upwind, with the illusion of a slight dogleg created by a semi-burned-out Bermuda fairway that tilted right to left. A kidney-shaped sand trap guarded the high side of the landing area. A furry grass bunker and a set of out of bounds loomed on the low side. I saw myself hitting a low draw off the corner of the trap, followed by a four iron to the middle of the knifeblade-narrow bent grass green. I got down in two putts and happily escaped with a par.

The next five holes tested my imaginary shotmaking to the max. The eleventh was a deceptively dangerous par three with a barbell-shaped green slick as steel. The 385-yard twelfth was tricked up with a chute of trees and a terraced green. Number thirteen, an unreachable (at least for me) 582-yard par five, and number fourteen, a 464-yard par four, were bunkered with sand pits the size of Galveston Beach and buffeted by crosswinds. The par three fifteenth could be anything from a six iron to a three wood depending on the pin placement and the wind. But I found that merely by drawing on a montage of good strokes I had already played in my practice rounds, I was able to make it through without a bogey.

That brought me to number sixteen, the lake-lined par five, where I was struck by a strategic epiphany. I realized that I didn't even have to reach the putting surface in two to make birdie. In fact, it was wise to lay up short because of the inherent treacheries of the humpbacked, heart-shaped green. All I needed was another gentle draw off the tee that would keep my drive on dry land, then a smooth three or four iron to the patch of fairway beyond the water. That would allow me to play a routine pitch to any pin placement.

I got my dream round rolling full steam by sinking an eight-foot downhiller for a bird on sixteen. Then, thanks to a brisk following wind, I drove all the way to the fringe of the green on seventeen, a 328-yard par four, and nearly chipped in for eagle. I stayed conservative on eighteen by hitting a high fade down the right side and playing a no-nonsense seven iron to the middle of the green. Two putts later, I turned the nine in two under—and opened my eyes.

My threesome of alarm clocks showed that it was getting on eleven P.M. I had to be up by half past six since it took a good two hours just to do all the stretching needed to limber up my prearthritic joints. I clicked out the light, pledging to complete my dream tour of the front nine in the morning. As I dozed off, I kept mumbling Doc Rotella's mnemonic mantra, spelling out the most important thing I had to do to turn my golfing fantasies into reality.

"You've got to get into your own little world—and stay there."

by the time the belly flopper's threesome finally moved on toward the sixteenth green the following morning, the Advil had quieted my back pain, but my own little world had become a mighty nerve-wracking place. I kept worrying if I'd be able to pick up or even maintain my scoring on the holes ahead. And I kept fretting over the whereabouts of *S.I.* photographer Gund, who was crouched in the rough, wondering whether his very presence was distracting my playing partners half as much as it was disturbing me.

I reached into my right pocket to finger my lucky nickels, reminding myself that I was only one shot off the pace I had set for myself in the previous night's dream round. Myself didn't seem reassured. In the course of my protracted tee box pacing, my throat had gotten as parched as the cart paths, and my hands had started shimmying like the wind-flogged flagsticks.

I tried to focus on my preselected target—the gaping garage door hole of a two-story brick house under construction about 400 yards down the left side of the fairway—but I kept catching glimpses of the lake on the right.

"Okay, nice and smooth," I whispered, taking my driver stance and exhaling a deep breath as the dictums of Dick Harmon, Tom Jenkins, Eden Foster, and Doc Rotella simultaneously rushed through my consciousness. "Just turn your shoulders, bring it inside, and remember, the golf swing's not a line—it's a circle."

Amid this last-second flood of swing thoughts, I somehow neglected to watch the club head come through at impact. I cried out in abject horror as my tee shot started out on line with the garage door, then veered in a banana curve toward the lake on the right.

"Oh, Lord! Is that where I think it is?"

"Yep," one of my companions confirmed. "You're wet."

I might as well have played the rest of the round in scuba gear and flippers. Instead of stealing an easy birdie on sixteen, I took a hard-to-swallow double bogey. As the day wore on, my confidence steadily evaporated. I commited errors frighteningly reminiscent of the ones I had made in my nightmarish qualifying round for the Nike Sonoma Open, chili-dipping wedges, smothering middle irons, and, in obvious overreaction to my errant tee shot on sixteen, pulling drives I intended to fade.

I was snowballing—building up bigger and rounder numbers with every roll of my Maxflis—and I ended up, appropriately enough, shooting 81, a snowman with staff. That put me at nine over par, a seemingly insurmountable seventeen strokes behind the first round leader, who had carded a course record 64.

Eric Epperson, who had fired a two-under-par 70, tried to console me by noting that he'd shot 76 in round one the year before and still survived the cut. "There are lots of holes left," he reminded. "Don't kill yourself." Instead, I decided to do the next closest thing by driving straight to the Dairy Queen in McKinney, where I gobbled downed a bacon cheeseburger, fries, and a large chocolate shake.

When I awoke the next morning, I wanted to crawl back under the covers and hide for the rest of the week. But I returned to The Ranch out of pride and a complusion to get my money's worth out of Q School. The only thing worse than shooting a big number was being branded with a "WD" for "withdrew" or a "DQ" for "disqualified." Mine was by no means the worst score of day one: there was another 81, two 84s and a pair of 89s.

I also owed it to myself and the other thousand men competing at Stage One sites around the country to salvage something from my three-grand entry fee. The PGA Tour was making out like a bandit on Q School. The Tour's gross receipts from entry fees were about $3 million, and even after deducting a generous figure for course rentals and administrative expenses, I figured it would net as much as $2 million. That being the case, I aimed to play all four of my $750-a-day tournament rounds.

I wound up getting an education at Q School after all, but not before paying an additional physical and psychological price. Round two quickly degenerated into a replay of round one, at least for the first sixteen holes. Each time I was in a position to improve my score over the preceding day, I foozled a key approach shot or jacked a makable putt. I then capped off the catastrophe by duck-hooking my tee shot out of bounds on the short par-four seventeenth. That inflated my final tally to 83, two strokes worse than my score in round one.

Having watched Shane Bertsch and Ren Budde, who had suffered but converted their share of ups and downs, cruise around in 71-70 and 69-70, respectively, I began to realize the difference between real pros and the rest of us, them and me. Early on, I'd had two of the elements in Lee Trevino's formula for success: youthful ambition and a couple of timely putts. It was good health—mostly of the mental variety—that eluded me. I wasn't physically incapable of hitting the necessary shots even with my aching back. I had lost it because my Type O blood and Type A personality had boiled over in the heat of Q School.

I also learned that Shane Bertsch was the kind of fellow who might turn out to be a true friend as well as a potential PGA star. In many ways, he was also my own younger alter ego. His father, who owned a Mexican restaurant, and his mother, a former American Airlines flight attendant, had come of age in the same countercultural generation as me and now made their home in the Rocky Mountain paradise of Evergreen, Colorado. Once a promising tennis player, Shane had taken up golf at the age of twelve after losing to Andre Agassi 6-1, 6-0 in a regional junior tournament. He told me that one of the reasons he grew to love golf more than tennis was that "every tennis court is basically the same, but a golf course is going to be different every time you play it."

Like me, Shane was 6"2", on the tall side for a golfer, and he walked with the same big-stepping gait. Unlike me, however, he had an extremely compact backswing, and barely allowed the club to get to the perpendicular position, much less past parallel. Prior to winning a scholarship to Texas A&M, he had attended New Mexico Junior College, where he was coached by Jesse Blackwelder, the same man who had once coached my mentor Eden Foster with less sanguine results. In 1994, he had made the Final Stage of Q School but had failed to score well enough to win his PGA Tour card. He had gone on to chase the Nike Tour for most of 1995, winning a total of only $26,099, which put him in seventy-second place on the money list. Prior to arriving at The Ranch, he had also played in the Nike Sonoma Open, missing the cut with scores of 76-72.

Shane's unflappable display of cool during rounds one and two amounted to a clinic in sports psychology that would have won the praise of Doc Rotella. Both of us had bogeyed the first hole of our opening round on Tuesday morning. But where I had fallen apart after my double bogey on the par-five sixteenth hole, Shane had kept grinding away, making par after par until he got the two birdie opportunities that enabled him to lower his first round score to one under. Though he had far more at stake careerwise in Q School than I did, he never seemed to let one bad shot upset him enough to start snowballing into a whole sequence of bad shots. "I don't know if I looked confident to you," he confided on Wednesday afternoon, "but I felt more and more confident with each hole."

On Thursday and Friday, I was paired with three other players who had also shot high scores the first two days, but I tried to utilize the lessons I had learned from Shane by observation and osmosis. I started round three with a double bogey on number ten, the nasty little uphill, upwind, 390-yard par four. Instead of collapsing on the spot, however, I played the next seventeen holes in only three over par, finishing the day with a 77. While that could hardly be called shooting lights out, it marked a significant improvement over my first two rounds. My final round proved to be something of a relapse as fatigue and spasmodic mental errors combined with my ever-increasing back pain to push my score back up to 80. But I could just as easily have ballooned to another 83 or even a 90 if I had freaked out over my mistakes on the opening holes as I had in round one.

Before the sun set, I was treated to a few more eye-openers at

Q School. What most surprised me and my fellow competitors was how low the low scores were, and that they kept dropping rather than rising on Friday, also known as "Choke Day." Deane Pappas won medalist honors with an eighteen-under-par total of 270. Thirty-one other players started round four at four under or better, but it took six under to stay comfortably above the cut. Shane Bertsch and Ren Budde made the grade with identical scores of minus seven. Kyle Coody, the thirty-one-year-old son of former Masters champion Charles Coody, shot five under and had to win a three-way playoff to snag the final qualifying spot. Perennial repeater Ty Armstrong finished one under, missing out by four strokes. In 1994, the cut line in Stage One at The Ranch had been even par.

Almost equally astonishing was how high the high scores were. More than forty percent of the field failed to break par. My astronomical total left me thirty-seven strokes from qualifying, but I still tied or beat eight other entrants. The last-place score was turned in by a fellow in a black akubra hat who dressed exactly like Greg Norman but racked up numbers more like Greg Louganis, with a four-day total of fifty-two over.

While spared the embarrassment of being high man in the tournament, I was still feeling pretty lowdown. I'd spent over four months and upward of $15,000 on my attempt to qualify for the PGA Tour, and had nothing to show for it except a good tan, a bad back, and a golf bag and set of irons provided by my friends at Cobra Golf. Then I ran into Dean Sessions, a silvery-haired forty-five-year-old former college baseball star from Broomfield, Colorado, who had busted out of his eighth Q School at nineteen over.

Our encounter was a little like the man with no shoes meeting the man with no feet. Sessions confided that in the seven years since he had turned pro at age thirty-eight, he had played in 120 professional qualifying tournaments and had spent $180,000 in entry fees and travel expenses. But he had qualified for only two Nike Tour tournaments and one PGA tournament, the 1991 St. Jude Classic in Memphis. He had shot 81-81 in the opening rounds at the St. Jude, missing the cut by a double-digit figure.

Not counting some small change picked up in a few mini-tour events, Sessions's total winnings as a pro golfer were zero. A stockbroker by training, he owned a small private capital firm whose earnings were also close to zero. During his quest to make the PGA Tour, he had sold his house, purchased a motor home, then sold the motor home and moved into a tiny apartment. His credit cards were long since borrowed upon to their limits, and he would not have been able to come to The Ranch but for the generosity of a friend who offered to pay his travel expenses. Even so, he was already planning to enter yet another series of Monday qualifiers in the coming year.

"When you've done this literally over a hundred times, people start to think you're crazy," Sessions admitted. "But I'm not giving up. I'm going to keep doing what I have to do to be competitive. The first thing my wife said when I walked in the door the other night was, 'We're on a five-year plan now to work toward the Senior Tour. You've been playing against twenty- and thirty-year-olds. When you get out on the Senior Tour, things are going to be reversed physically.' "

Hearing that, I immediately knew how I was going to spend the next five months of my own life. Busting out of Q School in Stage One was not going to be the end of my comeback trail. There was still at least one other route I could take to the PGA Tour without waiting for Q School to come around again in the fall of 1996. I could keep entering the Monday qualifiers for PGA Tour tournaments until I shot a great round and finished among the low four scorers. Unlike my soulmate Dean Sessions, I did not have the financial resources to make one hundred attempts, but I could sure try two or three.

In the meantime, I needed to rest up, regroup, and assimilate what had happened so far. I had not fully appreciated the difficulty of the golfing quest I had undertaken. As my childhood mentor Jackson Bradley had tried to warn, I had failed to realize the kind of sacrifices required to qualify for the PGA Tour. I had underestimated the unrelenting demands it would make on my body, my brain, and my soul. I had listened to so many different coaches and consulted so many doctors, I didn't know who to believe or what to think, much less how to get a golf ball into the hole.

Now that I was all the wiser, I vowed that I was really going to do it right. As I packed up to depart The Ranch, I remembered what Allen Doyle, the forty-seven-year-old Nike Tour star, had said about the all-important triumverate of the heart, the head, and the hands. My heart was still committed to the dream of chasing the PGA Tour. It was my head and my hands that needed rehabilitation and refinement into first-class competitive shape. But instead of merely running back to my hastily assembled team of golf gurus for more of the same, I decided I would start afresh and rebuild from the ground up. I would take my cue from the similarly titled hit song by Frank Sinatra and Jack Nicklaus's first bestselling golf book.

This time around, I would do it my way.

Golf My Way

barcelona Neck beckoned me back home with a bawdy ruckus of colors and a chorus of beery, ruffian cheers. It was a lucent late afternoon in mid-November, windless and unusually warm, with a soft summer hangover lingering in the air. The fairways were still browned out from the August drought, but the cedars and pines prickled a verdurous green, and the oaks flourished hues of scarlet, saffron, amber, orange, and ocher with occasional dashes of violet and magenta.

A threesome of deer froze on the edge of the asphalt entrance road as I slalomed through the S-curve in front of the old Russell family cemetery next to number-four tee. Then a gaggle of Canadian geese passed overhead, honking and flapping their speckled wings, and the deer scampered into the underbrush, as if they were more afraid of the birds than of my big black Jeep.

I parked on the far side of the clubhouse between a pair of battered gray pickup trucks loaded with construction supplies, whiffing the aroma of grilled sausage emanating from somewhere behind the ninth green. When I walked around to the porch side, I saw a score of men in blue jeans, overalls, and khaki work pants sitting at the tables beneath the awning, smoking cigarettes, and guzzling long-necked bottles of Bud and Bud Light.

"Well, look what the cat drug in!" one of them shouted. "It's the Hooters pro from Sag Harbor."

The others quickly joined in with good-natured guffawing.

"Hey, bub, ain't you supposed to be out on the PGA Tour?"

"I heard you was gettin' ready to kick Greg Norman's ass."

"Yeah, me, too. We thought we'd be seein' you on the TV by now."

I hopped up the porch steps, nodding at each of them in turn. There was Frankie the barber, Val the volunteer fireman, and Jack Somers, the former baseball player known as Jack the Rat. Construction foreman Whitey King and Paul Bailey, the former state trooper turned arbitration judge. Little John, the short, squat aluminum can collector with the voice box who was also known as Cheech, and Jimmy Schiavoni, the bighearted plumber with the sewer-pipe-size arms.

Several other Sag Harbor Golf Club regulars hovered around a grill just off the porch, poking at a rack of sausages: Bob Kiselak, the portly high-handicapper who was a dead ringer for Rodney Dangerfield. Charlie Collins, an even more portly higher-handicapper who looked like a white-haired Buddy Hackett. Marshall Garypie Jr., a gray-haired schoolteacher who had served on the Sag Harbor village council. And a couple of younger guys in sweatshirts and golf caps whose names I hadn't learned yet.

"Sorry, fellas," I said, retreating inside the clubhouse to grab a beer. "I'm afraid the only way you're gonna see me on TV is if I get arrested, which is a very distinct possibility the way my luck's been going."

I heard a round of knowing mumbles and bottle clinking.

"So what the hell happened out there, Mr. Hurt?" asked Jimmy Schiavoni when I returned to the porch.

"I got beat up, then I got beat down. I fucked up my back right before I turned pro, and it just got worse and worse every week. All I can say is that I didn't finish last at Q School or any other tournament I played in, and I ain't giving up yet."

"Say, Harry," Charlie Collins called to me from the grill. "What did you tell those other guys out on the tour when they asked you where the Sag Harbor Golf Club is?"

"I told 'em it's right between Maidstone and Shinnecock."

My reply prompted an outburst of laughter that roiled the porch and echoed off the trees up and down the ninth fairway. It was as if I had just shared the funniest joke any of them had ever heard.

"Boy, that's a good one," Charlie allowed, almost choking on his own chuckles.

"You got that right, bub," said Jack the Rat, whose day job was cutting the grass and mowing the traps at Maidstone.

"I'm gonna tell everybody who asks the same thing from now on," said one of the younger guys out by the grill. "Wait'll the mucky-mucks at Shinnecock get a load of that."

Once the laughter quieted down, I noticed that Jimmy Schiavoni and Judge Bailey had a pile of legal documents on the table in front of them. When I asked if one of them was in danger of getting arrested along with me, they suddenly turned serious.

"While you were out trying to make the Tour, we've been trying to cover our asses so the State doesn't take over the golf course," Bailey informed me. "We just kicked out the old board of directors and elected a new one. Marshall's the new president. Jimmy's vice president and head of the greens committee. Kiselak and I are treasurer and secretary. Now the Department of Environmental Conservation is getting ready to do an audit. They want to see where all the money's been going."

"Unfortunately, the old board made such a fuckin' mess that we don't know ourselves," Jimmy interjected. "The books are a joke, the golf course is goin' to seed, and the guy they hired as the greenskeeper is missing in action. We want to make some major improvements around here, but first we gotta get by the goddamn audit."

I lifted my beer bottle and swallowed to the last sip.

"Sounds like it's time to rally the troops and crank up the old word processor like you guys did a couple of years ago."

Jimmy shrugged, frowning hard.

"We hope it don't get to that, but you never know. In the meantime, you might want to fill out a membership application so we can submit your name at the election meeting in December. We could use some more bodies around here if push ever does come to shove."

My face flushed bright red. I'd been thinking about applying to join the Sag Harbor Golf Club ever since Judge Bailey and Jack the Rat had arranged to list me on the handicap rolls following the member-guest tournament back in June, but I had first wanted to be sure that I was informally accepted as one of the guys lest my application be rejected out of hand. Although I was truly surprised and flattered to be offered such a direct invitation, I pretended to take it with a grain of salt.

"This is probably the only club on the East End of Long Island that would even consider having me as a member," I said.

"We're desperate," Jimmy replied with a deadpan stare. Then he winked at me and added, "Speaking of desperate, your buddy Toad is out on the course with his new girlfriend. You oughtta go check 'em out. What a fuckin' piece of work."

"Yeah, Harry, go check 'em out," Charlie chimed in. "I'd love to see the look on his face when you drive a ball over his head and land it on the green."

I shook my head from side to side.

"Sorry, Charlie, but you'll have to wait another week or two. My back's still too sore for me to hit a driver. I'm under doctor's orders not to swing anything longer than a five iron."

"Then go get your damn five iron," Whitey King insisted. "If you're gonna apply for membership, you gotta know about the traditions we got around here. One of 'em is the One Club Tournament we have every year where everybody plays the course with only one club. I was just gettin' ready to play a few holes with my four iron. You and I can give Toad a lesson he won't forget."

A few minutes later, I found myself standing on the outdoor-carpeted first tee clutching a five iron and a grass-smudged Maxfli. A wedge of ducks flew overhead followed by another gaggle of speckle-winged honkers. But except for the bird cries and the smack of Whitey's club face against his ball, the landscape was as quiet and still as an empty church.

I teed up the Maxfli and took the first practice swings I'd attempted in nearly a month. My back felt remarkably fine. So fine, in fact, that I proceeded to whallop my first five iron shot over 180 yards down the middle of the fairway. I turned to Whitey and grinned.

"You know, I really, really love this place."

"Yeah," Whitey said, nodding and grinning back at me. "There ain't nothin' like it."

Off in the distance, I spied the familiar froglike figure of my former member-guest partner, Toad, walking up number-two fairway. He was wearing a bright green sweater and a pair of faded jeans that failed to disguise his pouchy belly and widely splayed legs, and he was pulling a two-wheeled golf cart with one hand while making single-fingered gestures at Whitey and me with the other. An attractive middle-aged woman decked out in blue woolen slacks and a yellow cardigan was at his side. She had neatly coif-fured blond hair and a slightly embarrassed look on her soft-featured face.

"Hey, Dick," Toad shouted as we got within earshot. "Did you win your damn Tour card or what?"

I returned his single-fingered gesture, shaking my head.

"No, I busted out of Q School in Stage One. And it's all your fault."

"My fault?" Toad shouted back incredulously. "How do you figure that?"

Before I could answer, Whitey nudged me in the ribs and de-manded that I tell Toad what I had said to the other guys on the pro golf circuit when they asked about the location of the Sag Harbor Golf Club.

I duly repeated the line, which sent Whitey into another knee-slapping fit.

"That's exactly where we're at—just look at the damn map," Toad noted with a straight face. Then he turned to his companion, smiling as innocently as a choirboy. "By the way, guys, this is Sandy."

After Whitey and I had introduced ourselves to Sandy by name, Toad stared at me, furrowing his balding brow in puzzlement.

"So how come it's my fault you flunked out of Q School?"

" 'Cuz you bailed on me after the member-guest," I said. "You were supposed to be caddying for me all the way to the next U.S. Open."

"Sheet," Toad replied, rolling his eyes toward Sandy. "I told you I wouldn't carry your bag if you paid me a million dollars. Besides, I got a more important person to caddy for now."

Sandy grasped him by the hand, nuzzling his forearm with hers.

"You never said anything about a million dollars, Tom," she purred. "I would've let you do it for that kind of money."

"No friggin' way," Toad croaked, glaring at me again. "So whad-dya gonna do now, Dick—quit golf for another twenty-five years or start gettin' ready for the Senior Tour?"

"Nope, we're going back to square one and try again. Soon as my back heals up a little more, I'm starting a physical training program down at the gym so I can keep up with all those flatbellied kids I was playing against in Q School. I gotta get myself stronger and longer off the tee."

"Sheet," Toad returned as Whitey and I started down the fairway to find our balls. "You got plenty of length already, Dick. The thing you gotta work on is your head."

"Look who's talking," Sandy interjected.

"I was referring to golf, honey," Toad said, blushing.

"What do you think I was referring to, hon?"

Whitey started laughing so hard he nearly tripped on his four iron.

"Nice to meet you, Sandy," I called over my shoulder. "Just lemme know when you change Toad's mind about the million dollars. If you can stand to keep kissing his ugly mug long enough, maybe he'll turn into a prince after all."

the next morning, I celebrated my forty-fourth birthday by hiring a personal trainer at the American Fitness Factory in Sag Harbor. His given name was Giuseppe Antonio Ciafolo, but he went by the handle "Joe C." Although he was fifty-three years old and stood only 5'9", he was not the kind of dude you wanted to mess with. He weighed 190 pounds, not an ounce of which was fat, and he could bench-press 400 pounds. With his tatooed biceps, black toupee, and gaunt cheekbones, he could sometimes seem a little vampirish, an image that was permanently reinforced as we tackled the first station on the Cybex machines.

"These full moons really get to me," he confided, massaging his left elbow. "I've had five broken ribs and two broken legs, and my joints feel like shit."

In fact, Joe C. turned out to be a very likable fellow, but he was definitely not a country clubber. He had grown up in South Ozone Park, one of the tougher predominantly Italian neighborhoods in Queens, where, as he put it, "we used to have fights all the time." The son of a local barber, he played baseball and boxed in between street rumbles. He had started bodybuilding during his hitch in the army in 1963, and decided to make a career out of physcial fitness. He specialized in training weight lifters, football players, baseball players, boxers, and swimsuit models. But after I showed him a few sequence photographs of the swings of Greg

Norman and Nick Faldo, he intuitively grasped the kind of conditioning most appropriate for a golfer.

"What we're after is flexibility, suppleness, and stamina," he declared. "We want to strengthen your legs, your forearms, and your back and shoulders. But the key is to do plenty of stretching every day so you never get tight."

Joe C. outlined two basic types of golf conditioning programs for me, one for the "off season" and another to take on the road during tournament season. The "off season" program began with a warm-up session on the exercise bicycle followed by weight-bearing leg squats and calf curls, and non-weight-bearing calf springs for my legs. For my upper body, he recommended bench presses, military presses, rowing machine pulls, and two-handed "barrel squeezer" pulls using the cables attached to the Cybex machines. He later added some curls and chest extensions with free weights and some forearm rolls with a specially designed rubber-handled bar to which stacks of two-pound plates were attached on a nylon cord.

Joe C. made sure that I finished each workout with at least ten to fifteen minutes of stetching. Most of the stretches he prescribed were fairly conventional floor exercises targeted at my hamstrings, calves, back, and shoulders. But Joe C. and I also co-invented a golf-specific stretching and strengthening exercise on one of the Cybex machines. This simple to do but hard to describe regimen was basically a weight-bearing cable pull that conformed to the pattern of my backswing. I would grasp a pulley handle with both hands as if I were gripping a golf club, then turn perpendicular to the machine, sling the cable over my shoulder, stretch to a position equivalent to or slightly beyond the top of my backswing, and hold it. As our workouts continued, I would add more weight and try to stretch farther back, thereby increasing the extension of my backswing arc and toning the muscles involved.

The "on season" program Joe C. created for me was intentionally less strenuous but no less rigorous. Where our "off season" exercises focused on building up greater strength, the exercises designed for use on the road were mainly for maintaining suppleness and flexibility. Along with including the requisite leg and torso stretches, the daily regimen consisted of thirty minutes of jogging, jumping rope, or pedaling an exercise bicycle, a hundred push-ups, a hundred sit-ups, and an almost uncountable number of crunches, which Joe C. promised would simultaneously condition my belly and my back. I would never forget the way he introduced me to the crunches with a set of fifty repetitions.

"I want you to do a lot of these every day," he said when we were done.

"Please define what you mean by 'a lot.' "

Joe C. looked over at me on the mat, grinning.

"Oh, I'd say about a thousand."

I groaned, and asked if he wanted me to drop to the floor and rip off a set of one hundred crunches every hour on the hour throughout the day.

"No," he replied matter-of-factly, "you should try to do at least five hundred at a time. But once you get into it, you'll find that you want to do all your crunches at once to get them over with."

As usual, Joe C. was right. I started off doing five hundred crunches per day in sets of one hundred as an adjunct to our "off season" workout program. It took me about a week to build up to one thousand per day, but after that, the crunches no longer seemed so daunting. I discovered that I could complete the nonaerobic portion of my "on season" exercise program, including the crunches, in about forty minutes. Best of all, the routine was conveniently portable. The only piece of equipment I would need to take with me on the road was a jump rope for the aerobic portion of the program, and I could even do without that if I packed a pair of jogging shoes.

A week or so into our training, Joe C. suggested that I might make greater and faster progress by adding something to my daily diet—a packet of pills marketed under the trade name Biolean. At first I was more than a little wary; I'd heard too many horror stories about steroids and the like to be interested in taking a hand-to-mouth shortcut. But with the help of my wife, Alison, I consulted a couple of our family doctors, who pronounced Biolean "harmless" for anyone who was not suffering from a heart, kidney, or liver condition.

Given that the Biolean supplements cost about $90 a month, the question then became whether or not they were a useless waste of money. According to the label, the product was composed of "100% pure Chinese herbs and crystalline pure pharmaceutical grade free form amino acids." Each packet contained a white capsule consisting of 400 mg. of L-Phenylalanine, L-Tyrosine, and L-Carnitine, and three brown tablets consisting of Ma Huang, Green

Tea, and various roots, seeds, and berries with names like Angeli-
cae Sinsensis, Jujube, and Schizandrae.

"The Biolean will increase the rate at which your body burns
fat and give you a lot more energy," Joe C. assured me, adding,
"I've been taking it for months, and I plan to keep on taking it for
the rest of my life."

Once again, he seemed to be on the mark. The Biolean started
delivering exactly the kind of wonder pill results Joe C. claimed it
would in just a few short days. I found myself losing body fat at a
comfortably steady rate without losing much of my natural appe-
tite, if any. At the same time, I felt much perkier in the morning,
which was typically the down time of my biorhythmic cycle. Although I had no plans to keep taking the stuff until my dying
breath, I figured that it had to be better for me than the Schimmelpennick cigars I had been puffing, so I wrote out a check for a
three-month supply.

In the meantime, I began to complement my two-hour-a-day "off
season" training sessions with a freelance study of golf instruction
books from the Harry Vardon era through the present. This literary
inquiry was one of the keys to playing *Golf My Way*, which happened to be the title of the Jack Nicklaus book on my reading list.
My purpose was not merely to investigate the differences between
the great men of golf and their methods. In a quest that Dick Harmon surely would have characterized as the at-home version of
"The Search for the Perfect Swing," I wanted to identify the subtle
and not-so-subtle points of convergence, the common features each
world-class player and/or teacher believed to be essential to proper
ball striking.

I realized that it would take many months just to collect, never
mind complete, every golfing manual published in the twentieth
century. But with the use of some informed selectivity, I got a fair
sampling of the major swing theories by focusing on ten well-
known tomes. In addition to *Golf My Way* (1974) and Vardon's *The
Complete Golfer* (1905), my syllabus included *Bobby Jones on Golf*
(1966), Percy Boomer's *On Learning Golf* (1946), Tommy Armour's
Classic Golf Tips (published posthumously in 1995 but based on
methods of the 1930s and 1940s), *Power Golf* (1948) and *Five Les-
sons:The Modern Fundamentals of Golf* (1957) by Ben Hogan, Sam

Snead's *The Education of a Golfer* (1962), Harvey Penick's *Little Red Book* (1992), and *The Golf Swing* (1990) by David Leadbetter.

Surprisingly, I found that the so-called old-fashioned swings of Vardon, Jones, and Boomer, the teaching pro's teaching pro, were far more like the so-called modern swing outlined by Leadbetter than most contemporary students of the game might imagine. There were, to be sure, certain obvious differences in style. Jones, for example, was much looser at the top of his backswing than such Leadbetter pupils as Nick Faldo and Nick Price. But many of these differences were related to personal idiosyncracies or the exigencies of bending hickory shafts and early-model metal shafts.

The two most notable oddballs in the bunch were Jack Nicklaus and Ben Hogan. Because he had a physique distinguished by very large thighs and calves and very small hands, Nicklaus emphasized the importance of driving the legs through the ball. According to modern "big muscle" methodologies, which called for turning the hips and shoulders around a solid axis formed by the left side, the Nicklaus move would have been disparaged as a "slide." Hogan, who was shorter than Nicklaus but had stronger hands, recommended a pronating of the wrists through impact in his second book, *Five Lessons.* That prescription (which, interestingly enough, was not included in Hogan's first book, *Power Golf*) would have been pronounced "too handsy" by advocates of the modern "big muscle" method.

And yet, a majority of the great men on my reading list, which frequently included Nicklaus and Hogan, was in fundamental accord more often than not. From takeaway through impact, the masters of the modern era of stainless steel and graphite shafts made the same basic moves and focused on the same key concepts of proper form as their illustrious predecessors. I attempted to summarize their views on the main phases of the golf swing as follows:

The Setup/Ball Position: The ideal ball position was one of the few points of almost universal agreement. "I play every standard shot with the ball in the same position relative to my feet," Nicklaus declared in *Golf My Way.* "That position is opposite my left heel." His opinion on the subject was endorsed by the likes of Jones, Hogan, Snead, and Leadbetter, all of whom claimed to play and/ or advised their pupils to play the ball off the left heel on standard shots.

Ironically, this was also the one point with which I quibbled most, as did my personal swing coach, Eden Foster. The dispute ultimately boiled down to the definition of a "standard shot." We agreed that it made sense to play the ball off the left heel on the longer clubs such as the driver, the fairway woods, and the one through four irons. But when it came to hitting the five through nine irons and wedges, playing the ball off the left heel seemed to promote an unwanted draw. By moving the ball to the middle of the stance on middle irons and slightly farther back on the shorter irons, my own shots seemed to fly straighter.

I was much more comfortable in accepting a second concept concerning the setup—the idea of forming a solid triangular base with the legs and knees at address, while digging in with the inside soles of the feet. This notion was shared by "old-fashioned" and modern ball strikers alike. Boomer referred to it as "bracing," while Leadbetter protégé Nick Faldo likened it to "squeezing a beach ball" between his knees. But both proclaimed it essential to maintaining proper balance throughout the golf swing. Snead considered it the key to powerful shotmaking. "When I set myself to swing," he recalled in *The Education of a Golfer*, "I dug in with my cleats on the inside edge—not just the toe—of the right foot. . . . Upon contacting the ball, that inside sole pushed against the resistance of the left foot and gave me an added kick, which added up to power and 300-yard drives."

The Takeaway/Forward Press: This was the other point of almost universal agreement, and to my mind, the most important. Jones, Boomer, Hogan, Snead, Nicklaus, and Leadbetter unanimously emphasized the importance of initiating the golf swing with some form of forward press. This forward press could be the hip twist employed by Jones, the head swivel preferred by Snead, the knee kick advocated by Leadbetter, the club and body press favored by Nicklaus, or one of many variations that included an increase in grip pressure or a forward push of the hands. But as Nicklaus observed, "Every golfer needs something to 'trigger' his swing."

The action of the forward press was sometimes compared to the age-old motion employed in swinging a bucket full of water. Rather than merely jerking the water bucket backward, successive generations of mankind discovered that an almost effortless momentum could be created by first nudging the bucket forward and then swinging it backward. Hogan was the most articulate in explaining the practicalities and purpose of the forward press in the golf swing.

"One of the questions I am most often asked is how the club is started back on the backswing," Hogan noted in the opening pages of *Power Golf*. "But most of the golfers who ask me that question don't even wait for my answer. Instead, they quickly offer the suggestion that maybe it is started back by the left hand, the right hand, left arm or right arm. . . . Actually the club is not started back in any of the ways they suggest. It starts back on the recoil from the forward press.

"The forward press is nothing more than the movement forward of the hands, arms, and body just before the backswing," Hogan continued. "What it amounts to is that you address the ball with some movement, or waggle as the tournament professionals call it, and then go smoothly from the waggle into the backswing via the recoil from the forward press."

The Backswing/Pivot: Here again, I identified a commonality of views among such ostensibly diverse swingers as Jones, Boomer, Hogan, Snead, Nicklaus, and Leadbetter. All of them believed that a full turn or pivot was critical to making a powerful swing, and—here was the important thing—that this motion was properly controlled from the ground up by the feet, legs, and torso, not by the hands and arms. Leadbetter made the case from the perspective of the modern "big muscle" method by reference to the concept of centrifugal force.

"So how do we harness this important [centrifugal] force found in the swings of all good ball strikers?" Leadbetter asked rhetorically in *The Golf Swing*. "Simply, it is the efficient coiling and uncoiling of your torso in a rotary or circular motion which maximizes centrifugal force. . . . Just like a discus thrower who builds up power through the coiling motion of his or her body, you use your hands and arms merely as conductors of your torso-created power."

Snead said essentially the same thing in his own homespun way, though he placed more emphasis on using the feet as the anchors of torso rotation. "Watching the best players, I decided that footwork is the basis of hand action—rather than the other way around—and that the pivot called the shot all the way," he wrote. "It was the key to everything I did on the tee. Experts talked about swinging the club head, but they put the cart before the horse.

Although a good pivot includes hip, leg, and shoulder movement, it must start and finish with the feet."

The Downswing: There were at least two key points concerning the initiation and execution of the downswing on which I found widespread concurrence. The first was that the downswing was best begun with a change of direction triggered by the shifting of weight back to the left side. This subtle motion was what the late Harvey Penick aptly called "the magic move." As he reminded in his *Little Red Book*, "You've heard it from me many times, but I will say it again—to start your downswing, let your weight shift to your left foot while bringing your right elbow down to your body."

In contrast to Penick, some writers stressed the role of the lower body in starting the downswing, deliberately omitting any mention of the right elbow or the arms. Jones and Leadbetter, for example, advised turning the left knee back toward the ball. But the idea of shifting the weight to the left side, however accomplished, was considered to be of primary importance.

A second point of concurrence was the concept of "gradual acceleration" throughout the downswing, starting with the leftward weight shift at the top. As Jones observed in *On Golf*, "The one quality a golf swing must have is smoothness. The acceleration from the top must be gradual, and the motion must be unhurried and free from any sudden or jerky movement." Hogan echoed those sentiments. "The application of speed and power to the golf swing is not a hurry-up process," he noted in *Power Golf*. "Speed and power are gradually applied during the golf swing and increased until they reach their climax right on the ball."

Impact: I had read and heard thousands of times that the single thing all great ball strikers had in common was their position at impact. They might have gotten to that position via very different backswing and downswing motions, but according to conventional wisdom, a stop-action photograph would show that Jones, Hogan, Snead, Nicklaus et al. looked virtually identical at the instant the club head met the ball.

In fact, as I discovered upon close examination of the drawings and photographs in my library of golf books, that was not precisely true. While there were indeed remarkable similarities between the impact positions of the great ball strikers, they were not one-on-one matches. To cite just one comparative example, Hogan's body and weight appeared to be extremely well centered and his left leg fairly straight at impact, while Nicklaus appeared to have much more bend in both legs and almost seemed to be falling back from the ball. Hogan tended to hit low, driving shots; Nicklaus was known for his high, soft fades.

The one thing I did find in common among the great ball strikers, however, was the almost universal notion that impact was not the climax of the swing. To the contrary, they all seemed to agree on the importance of continuing to swing the club head beyond the point of impact without any regard to the presence of the ball itself. As Boomer put it way back in 1946, "You must swing past [the ball] as if it were not there." Nearly half a century later, Leadbetter advised his pupils that impact involved "no conscious hit at the ball, merely a swing through it" as if the ball was simply "in the way" of the club head.

Visualization/Feel: Last but by no means least, I learned that almost all the great ball strikers agreed on the one thing not to do when swinging a golf club—think. Instead, they emphasized the importance of visualizing the intended flight and direction of the ball during the preshot routine, then feeling rather than thinking their way through the swing itself.

In *Golf My Way*, Nicklaus offered a brief but informative section on his use of visualization in planning his shots and "seeing himself" execute them. During the tumultuous Vietnam War era of the early 1970s, such visualization exercises were still considered a little wacky by large segments of the general public in the United States, who associated them with the mysterious rituals of pot-smoking hippies and allegedly evil-minded athletes from the Communist bloc. Nicklaus made the concept of visualization easy for the average American golfer to grasp by referring to it as "Going to the Movies."

Boomer had outlined a similar method three decades earlier when he urged his pupils to draw on visualization and a "feel cabinet" in their shotmaking routines. "You never have to 'think out' a shot," he insisted. "You see the lie [of the ball] and the flight required, and this produces an automatic response, the right feel from the cabinet and so the right shot from the club."

As if to confirm his unique genius, Jones believed that the true secret to playing championship golf ultimately lay in integrating the visual, tactile, and conceptual functions of the brain. "It is not easy to teach golf either by personal instruction or by writing," he noted in *On Golf*. "In order to play well, the player must have the feel of the proper stroke." At the same time, however, he declared that, "A golfer who depends on finding the feel more or less accidentally can never hope to play consistently well, day in and day out, for this very reason. He must know how to hit the ball . . ."

I still wasn't sure that I *knew* how to hit the ball, even after digesting the dictums of the great ball strikers on my reading list. But I decided it might be worthwhile to put the books aside and fly back down to Houston to get some personal instruction from Dick Harmon's older brother Claude "Butch" Harmon Jr., the sibling who had been draped with their daddy's 1948 Masters champion green jacket at the tender age of four. As the director of golf at the all-male Lochinvar Golf Club, Butch was rapidly emerging as the true heir to his fabled father's legacy and the most sought-after teaching pro in Texas since the death of Harvey Penick the week before the 1995 Masters.

Butch had first won national recognition back in 1990 by rebuilding the game of Davis Love III, himself the son of a domineering teaching pro. In 1992, his reputation had begun to spread around the globe as he had guided then-slumping Greg Norman through a top-to-bottom mid-career swing change that eventually helped catapult Norman from fifty-third on the PGA money list to number one. He had later worked similar magic with Tiger Woods by showing him how to gear down his power game to win the 1994 and 1995 U.S. Amateurs.

Butch was about to share his golf-teaching secrets in a forthcoming book titled *The Four Cornerstones of Winning Golf*, cowritten by *Golf Magazine* senior editor John Andrisani with a foreword by Norman. I had arranged to get an advance copy of the book from Simon & Schuster, and had given it a quick perusal. At a retail price of $25 per copy, the book represented a major discount on the $200-per-hour Butch charged for nonmember lessons at Lochinvar and the tens of thousands of dollars a year he reportedly charged in his consulting contracts with Tour pros. But I knew that in golf, as in life, you got what you paid for, and that nothing beat the real thing. The experience of getting firsthand instruction from Butch Harmon was simply not available in book form, and I suspected that it might prove to be a bargain at twice the price.

The moment I laid eyes on Butch Harmon, I realized that he was nothing like his younger brother Dick. He ambled out to meet me on the Bermuda grass practice tee at Lochinvar with his collar turned up against his neck and a golf cap pulled down over his forehead, looking more like a working-class private detective than a country club teaching pro. Where Dick fairly bubbled with warmth and cordiality, Butch exuded an air of mysterious reserve. Though he appeared to be about the same height, he carried a little more weight around his middle, and he had a much bigger chip off the old block on his shoulders.

"Be sure to tell Dick that you didn't have to hit off plastic mats like they have at River Oaks," Butch said with a sly smirk after we shook hands. Then he gestured at the pile of shiny white Titleists at my feet, adding, "And ask him if he's ever gonna get rid of those ugly yellow range balls they've been using over there."

I'd already read enough of the autobiographical sections in *Four Cornerstones* to realize that the comments were classic Butch and should be taken in stride. One passage in the book particularly stuck in my mind. After recording some outstanding performances as a junior golfer in the New York area, Butch had won a scholarship to the University of Houston in 1962, only to find that he couldn't cut it at the golfing powerhouse that was on the verge of winning more than twenty NCAA championships. "I didn't like the school or the state," he had written, "something I find particularly amusing since I live in Texas today." Unsure about whether or not he wanted to turn pro, he claimed that he had "enlisted in the army . . . [and] spent two years in Alaska, during which I won several all-military tournaments and the Alaskan State Amateur."

Having heard the true story of Butch's departure from U of H, I knew that was a greater accomplishment than the uninformed reader might have suspected. Dick had told me his older brother's college golf days had actually come to a temperamental end after he duck-hooked a ball into a lake at a local country club. Incensed at his foozle, he tossed his entire golf bag, which included a set of irons their father had used on the pro tour, into the same lake and stomped off the course. Only then had he enlisted in the army. When he had called Claude Sr. to tell him what he had done, the old man had replied, "Well, at least you could've joined the navy so you could get my clubs back."

I quickly discovered, however, that Butch Harmon, like his father before him, had what teaching pros called "the eye," the instinctive talent to spot and diagnose swing flaws with only a few quick glances. He also had an unusually clear and complete overall concept of what playing golf was all about. In contrast to the overly mechanical tenets of a David Leadbetter or the Band-Aid solutions offered by so many less-talented golf instructors, his new book dealt with all the major elements essential to shooting low scores, assigning equal emphasis to ball striking, the short game, the mental side/course management, and physical conditioning. Butch took about half a minute to identify one of my basic faults and suggest a bona fide fix.

"Have the pros you've been working with said anything about your grip?" he asked after watching me push three drives straight right into the woods.

I shook my head. "Nope."

"Well, it's much too weak. The only way you can square the club face with that grip is to roll your wrists over at impact or come over the top with your right shoulder."

Butch advised me to strengthen my grip by rotating my left hand to the right so that at least two or three knuckles were visible to me as I looked down at it. I knew from all my reading that this change represented a significant departure from the classic Harry Vardon grip, in which the hands were "wed" more or less equally in parallel or "neutral" positions relative to the shaft. But in light of my instructor's reputation, I was willing to give it a try.

Butch then directed me to assume an extrawide stance with the insides of my heels planted on two imaginary lines running down from the outside edges of my shoulders.

"Now I want you to delay cocking your wrists as long as possible when you take the club back," he continued. "That's gonna help widen your arc and shorten your backswing by preventing you from letting the club drop past parallel at the top."

After a couple of clumsy mishits, I was amazed to find myself crushing drives with newfound power and control, drawing or fading the ball almost at will. As I later learned upon reading more of Butch's new book, he had prescribed precisely the same subtle changes—stronger grip, wider stance, delayed wrist cock—to Norman, Love, and Woods.

A few minutes later, Butch led me over to the putting green, where we went to work on the second of his four cornerstones, the short game. I told him that my sessions with Tom Jenkins had vastly improved my chipping, but complained that my putting, once the best part of my game, was now the worst.

Butch showed me a drill outlined in his book, enhancing it with a personal touch that could not be transmitted via the printed page. First, he marked a spot eight feet from one of the cups and placed a ball on it. Next, he sunk a pair of golf tees into the grass about six inches short of the cup so that they formed "goal posts" approximately the width of my putter head. Then he told me to put my putter behind the ball and then take my stance, rather than doing it the other way around as had been my custom. Finally, he took off his golf cap and held it against the left side of my face so that I could not possibly steal a glimpse of the cup out of the corner of my eye.

"Now stroke the ball," he said.

Although I felt half blind, I tried to follow his orders to the letter. I saw the ball leave my putter face, but kept my eyes focused straight down on the eight-foot spot. A split second later, I heard the sweetest sound in golf—the plop of the ball falling into the bottom of the cup.

"That's the sensation you should feel when you're out on the course," Butch informed me as he removed his cap from my face. "You should never see the ball go into the hole. Just keep your head still and listen for the sound. When you're practicing, you can use the goal posts to find out if you're pushing your putts or pulling them."

The clock ran out on my $200-an-hour lesson before Butch and I could discuss the last of his four cornerstones, the mental side/ course management and physical conditioning. In retrospect, that was probably just as well. When I subsequently turned to those sections in his book, I was sadly disappointed. His treatment of the mental side/course management lacked the psychological depth and attention to detail that Doc Rotella had provided, and the exercise program he recommended fell far short of the regimen I was already following with Joe C.

Even so, I flew back to Sag Harbor more optimistic than ever about my plans to make another run at the PGA Tour. I had rested enough to heal my battered back and repair my bruised psyche.

The reading I'd done had enhanced my understanding of the history and evolution of the golf swing. Thanks to Joe C., I was getting much more physically fit. Thanks to Butch Harmon, it looked like I was going to get longer off the tee and more proficient with my putter. And thanks to playing rounds of one-club golf at Barcelona Neck, a drill my friend Ben Crenshaw would later describe as "one of the best things you can possibly do with your practice time," I was beginning to acquire the elusive "feel" Bobby Jones had proclaimed to be essential to playing championship golf.

In fact, my latest encounter with Toad and the boys at the Sag Harbor Golf Club had reminded me of one of my favorite inspirational passages in Shakespeare. It was the speech Prince Hal, the then-prodigal future king of England, makes early in *Henry IV*, Part I, after he decides to quit horsing around with Sir John Falstaff and the fellows at the Eastcheap Tavern and get his life back on track.

> *I know you all, and will awhile uphold*
> *The unyoked humor of your idleness.*
> *Yet herein, will I imitate the sun,*
> *Who doth permit base contagious clouds*
> *To smother up his beauty from the world,*
> *That, when he please again to be himself,*
> *Being wanted, he may be more wond'red at*
> *By breaking through the foul and ugly mists*
> *Of vapors that did seem to strangle him.*
> *If all the year were playing holidays,*
> *To sport would be as tedious as to work.*
> *But when they seldom come, they wished-for come,*
> *And nothing pleaseth but rare accidents.*

Hal then goes on to observe that the great things he aims to do in the future will only seem more astonishing in light of the "loose behavior" he has indulged in for the past several months.

> *And, like bright metal on a sullen ground,*
> *My reformation, glitt'ring o'er my faults,*
> *Shall show more goodly and attract more eyes*
> *Than that which hath no foil to set it off.*
> *I'll so offend to make offense a skill,*
> *Redeeming time when men think least I will.*

Like Hal, I was prepared to redeem the time I had spent since my disaster at Q School by wielding my own bright metal golf clubs on the not-so-sullen grounds of a championship course. In less poetic words, I needed to test what I had been learning under real tournament conditions. And thanks to the rare accident of noticing a tiny advertisement in *Golfweek*, I stumbled across the perfect venue—the 40+ Tour of Florida.

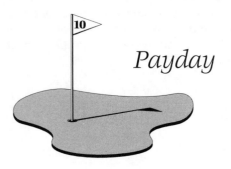

Payday

"**C**ongratulations—you've finally found a place where you can compete."

Jim Barfield flashed a toothy grin, pawing me on the back. It was late on the afternoon of Thursday, November 30, 1995, and we were posing for a photograph in front of the 40+ Tour of Florida scoreboard at the Grenelefe Golf and Tennis Resort in Haines City, some thirty-five miles south of Orlando.

"Make sure you take a couple of backup shots," Barfield told the photographer. "This is an historical moment, the first of many more to come."

Without further ado, Barfield then handed over the first check I had ever won in a professional golf tournament. The payment line was made out for $92, the amount I was due for taking a skin by making the only birdie of the day on the 380-yard, par-four fifteenth hole on Grenelefe's West Course.

"Thank you, Jimmy," I said, quickly adding, "I hope to hell you're right about the many more—and so do my wife and my creditors."

Barfield let loose a deep-throated laugh, pawing me on the back again.

"Shit, you've got a bright future ahead of you on the 40+ Tour. Out here, you're still a flatbelly."

Barfield himself was a roundbelly, a fifty-two-year-old broad-shouldered, brown-haired teddy bear of a fellow sporting a white Ashworth shirt emblazoned with the 40+ Tour of Florida's orange golf ball logo and a pair of blue Sansabelt slacks that barely encompassed his meat eater's girth.

By his own admission, Barfield was also a quixotic dreamer and schemer, an All American boy who would never grow up, which was one of many reasons I had taken a liking to him right off the bat. He had spent six years in the Los Angeles Dodgers organization as a would-be sub for Steve Garvey and close to thirty years in the life insurance business. A scratch amateur golfer for most of his adult life, he had quit his day jobs to turn pro at the age of forty-nine, only to get his butt whipped by the younger men he competed against for Monday qualifying spots in PGA Tour events.

In the fall of 1994, Barfield had organized the 40+ Tour of Florida in cahoots with his girlfriend, Loretta Sturgill. A similarly sweet-natured, Rubenesque brunette divorcee, Loretta came from a family that had built up one of the largest Tupperware franchises in America; she also boasted an entrepreneurial background in marketing. Loretta had provided most of the working capital to start the 40+ Tour, but Barfield had provided the inspiration and guiding vision.

"I had the same dream everybody else out here has," he confided after our photo session in front of the scoreboard. "We all get it by looking at the TV and seeing those guys on the PGA Tour and the Senior Tour playing for all that money. You sit there in your living room watching one of the pros screw up an easy shot, and you say to yourself, 'God, I could hit that shot.' But whether you could or not, you don't know until you get the chance. We started the 40+ Tour because there wasn't any place for guys in this age bracket who weren't already on the PGA Tour or the Senior Tour to chase the dream."

In the fourteen months since its inception, the 40+ Tour had staged some ninety-five golf tournaments during a season that ran from September to June. The majority were two-day and one-day events played on courses within a seventy-mile radius of the Barfield-Sturgill town house overlooking the fairways of Heathrow Country Club in Lake Mary, a suburb north of Orlando. As of the fall of 1995, the 40+ Tour claimed 275 active members, each of whom had paid a $100 annual membership fee. Pros paid $275 entry fees for each thirty-six-hole event and $150 for eighteen-hole events; amateurs anted up $150 and $100 entry fees.

The prize money offered by the 40+ Tour varied according to the number of players competing in a particular event. In most two-day tournaments, there were cash payouts for the nine low scorers, with the winner's share going as high as $1,250 in cash plus a free entry fee for a subsequent event. There were also separate pots for skins, which were up for grabs on every hole every day, and for second-day money in the thirty-six-holers. Even so, the 40+ Tour had quite a way to go before its purses rivaled the PGA Tour or the Senior Tour. The "lifetime" leader on the 40+ Tour money list had so far amassed only $24,552; Barfield ranked number eleven with $4,756.

As Barfield repeatedly reminded all concerned, the potential growth in 40+ Tour prize money and player participation was directly dependent on attracting commercial sponsors. The tour's main sponsor to date had been Central Florida Investments (CFI), which touted itself as the nation's leading developer and operator of time-share vacation villas. But the head honcho of CFI had never played a round of golf in his life, and for all its generous support, CFI was not in the same league as PGA Tour corporate sponsors such as Buick and AT&T.

In order to establish real credibility, the 40+ Tour needed to find a backer in the golf business, a major equipment manufacturer or ball maker with a well-known brand name. Barfield claimed to be holding talks with representatives of Cobra Golf and Snake Eyes. But so far, he and Loretta were still keeping the tour alive with money from their own bank accounts, a circumstance to which they had reluctantly become accustomed. As Barfield put it, "If you don't chase the dream yourself, nobody's gonna chase it for you."

When I retreated to my rented condo near Grenelefe's East Course that evening with my 40+ Tour paycheck in hand, I kept musing over Barfield's words and those of the late great Bobby Jones. "Golf is a game that must always be uncertain," Jones had observed in his book *On Golf.* "I don't believe that anyone will ever master it to the extent that several have mastered billiards and chess. If someone should do so, I think he would give it up—but that is a danger most of us would be willing to risk."

My perfomance in round one at Grenelefe West proved that I

was hardly on the verge of achieving mastery at this stage of my comeback. If anything, it made the $92 I received from Barfield for taking a skin more than a little ironic. I had always dreamed that my first check as a professional golfer would come as a result of outstanding overall play over the course of at least eighteen or thirty-six holes. Instead, it had come purely as the result of a lucky putt on one of the precious few holes where I had put my drive in the fairway and hit the green in regulation.

But then again, if Bobby Jones had been attemping a comeback on the 40+ Tour, he probably would have pointed out that such rubs of the green were just another part of chasing the dream. As I lay down on the bed to rest up for round two, I started thinking about the "historical" day that had just passed, the rather hysterical round I had played, and all the men I had recently met who were pursuing the same quixotic quest, mounting motorized steeds with bag racks on the back and tilting at windmills with graphite shafts.

during its relatively short life span, the 40+ Tour had attracted some exceptionally talented players, including a score of PGA Tour veterans. The best known was probably Gary Koch, the forty-three-year-old ESPN golf commentator. Koch had won six times in his fifteen-year career on the PGA Tour before he had semiretired to the broadcast booth. He had also won the first 40+ Tour event he entered, in December 1994, and had accumulated total winnings of $6,227, which put him at number six on the money list.

"I would love to see some of the guys from the 40+ Tour go on and qualify for the Senior Tour," Koch had confided in a recent chat, thinking perhaps of himself as well. Then he had leveled his eyes at me, adding, "I'd love to see you start playing better and shooting some low scores again, too. It would be great if you could win one of these things."

Almost equally well known in golfing circles was Koch's fellow Temple Terrace, Florida, high school alum, Eddie Pearce, a former U.S. Junior Amateur champion and a veteran of eight years on the PGA Tour. "E.P.," as he was called by our many mutual friends, had been the Tiger Woods of my generation, a prodigy once touted as the next Jack Nicklaus. At age forty-three, he was making a comeback after a long absence from competitive golf by tuning up on the 40+ Tour, the Hooters Tour, and the Tommy Armour Tour.

Prior to arriving in Orlando, I'd telephoned E.P. to congratulate him on making it through Stage Two of the 1995 PGA Tour Qualifying School. He was presently competing in the Final Stage down in West Palm Beach, where I planned to meet him later in the week.

The 40+ Tour had also become one of several happy hunting grounds for the unofficial king of the Florida minis, Jim Chancey. With his lean, pink-skinned physique and wizened blue eyes, Chancey looked much older than his forty-three years, but he had grown up competing against E.P. and Koch on the Florida high school and junior golf circuits. After turning pro at age nineteen, he had struggled for six years until he won his PGA Tour card. He had then labored for five more years on the major-league circuit, with his best showing a third-place finish in the 1978 Hawaiian Open.

In 1990, following a ten-year stint as a teaching pro, Chancey had attempted to make a comeback on the Hogan Tour, only to discover that he could not make a satisfactory living without re-qualifying for the PGA Tour, which he failed to do at that year's Q School. He had then returned to the Florida mini-tours, where he had enjoyed a competitive renaissance, sometimes playing two tournament rounds in separate events on the same day. In 1995, he had already risen to the top of the money list on the Tommy Armour Tour, which was open to all age brackets, with total winnings of roughly $70,000. Having nabbed $4,175 on the 40+ Tour and thousands more in other pro events, he expected to gross over $100,000 for the third year in a row.

Chancey was the first to admit that he was the exception to the rule among mini-tour players. "It's a great life, but it's really tough to make a living unless you can really play," he told me in an interview between tournaments. "Ninety percent of the guys who are not on the PGA Tour lose money every year. I'm divorced and don't have any kids to support, and I live within driving distance of most of the tournaments I compete in, so my only major expenses are entry fees."

Jim Hays already had his money in the bag before he teed it up on the 40+ Tour. A newly turned fifty-year-old pro from Tulsa with silver hair and robin's-egg eyes, he was a former college baseball player who had taken up golf in his twenties when he joined the Houston office of a major recreational property developer that owned and built over two hundred golf courses across the country. Following the oil price crash of the early 1980s, he had moved back to Oklahoma and purchased an embattled regional pipeline, which he rode to riches as oil prices gradually recovered. Hays had since sold his pipeline company "for more money than I can spend for the rest of my life," and started chasing his dreams full-time.

"A lot of these guys have no idea what it really takes to be a golf pro at this age," he told me, echoing Chancey's words. "I figured it's a three-legged stool: you've got to have financial backing, you've got to be in shape, and you've got to be able to compete. At least I've got two legs of the stool. I've taken care of myself financially, and I work out five days a week."

Hays conceded that he was still in the process of honing the third leg of the stool, his competitive prowess. Over the past year, he had won over $25,000 in various pro tournaments, including $900 on the 40+ Tour, which put him at number twenty-three on the money list. But he had also spent about $50,000 on travel and entry fees, which left him with a net loss for the twelve-month period. His ultimate goal was to make the Senior Tour, but he had admittedly "choked" in a recent Monday qualifying round. "I was pissed at myself," he recalled. "But I jogged harder and worked harder on the golf course the next day."

In fact, Hays possessed the indispensable "fourth leg" of his proverbial stool—a devotion to playing golf at all costs. He told me a story when we first met that illustrated the kind of unashamed obsession he shared with scores of other men on the 40+ Tour. The day after his wedding, he said, he had left his bride to play in a golf tournament that lasted nearly a week. He had returned on a Friday night and announced that he was heading straight for the golf course on Saturday morning.

"As I was leaving the house, my wife asked, 'Are you gonna play golf again today?' " Hays recalled. "I told her, 'Yes, and I'm gonna play at least three times a week for the foreseeable future.' Then she looked at me and said, 'If you had to make a choice between golf and me, what would it be?' I told her, 'Don't ever ask me to make that choice because you're not gonna like my answer.' She never asked that question again, and we've stayed married for the past twenty years."

Though I surely would have picked Alison over golf, I privately hoped that my own wife would never ask me to make such a choice. I certainly would never ask her to choose between her restaurant business, which was often at least as time-consuming as golf, and me. In my brief experience on the pro golf circuit, it had already become clear that the support of wife and family were the dowel rods that held together the legs of the stool. Although Alison had probably hit a golf ball less than a dozen times in her entire life, she had an actress's gift for mimicry, and she occasionally served as a kind of human instant replay camera for me when I hit balls on the practice range. More important, she was always there when I needed her after a bad round, putting up with my mood swings and comforting me with love and sympathy.

Several 40+ Tour players in the older age brackets had enlisted their wives as both caddies and coaches. Mike Long, a forty-nine-year-old former amateur standout whose bag bore the pink bunny logo of his sponsor, Energizer Batteries, had recently moved down to the Orlando area from Missouri with his wife, Vicki. An easygoing if sometimes long-suffering blonde, Vicki read the break and the grain on all of her husband's putts, wiped the mud off his clubs, and raked the sand traps after his bunker shots. Ron Widner, a fifty-one-year-old from Sanford, Florida, who was sponsored by a local Harley-Davidson dealership, received the same kind of help from his wife, Nancy.

Many of the younger guys on the 40+ Tour were club pros with seasonal jobs up north who lived the lonesome bachelor's life on the road. Some still dreamed of making the PGA Tour; others were getting a head start on preparing themselves for the Senior circuit. But almost all of them could play far better than the average assistant selling socks and sweaters back at the shop. Delroy Cambridge, a forty-four-year-old Jamaican-born punch shot artist, had made a name for himself in New York metropolitan area tournaments. Barry Hamilton, a forty-four-year-old former stockbroker from Arkansas, had been a national-class amateur before becoming a club pro.

Mike Thompson, who operated a driving range outside Philadelphia during the summer, was one of the most talented teaching pros on the 40+ Tour or anywhere else, and one of the more consistent players. At age forty-six, he had an impish grin and a shock of brushed-back light brown hair that made him look like the twin brother of rocker/golf nut Huey Lewis. "Swinging a golf club is like making love to your wife," he liked to say. "There's nothing fast about it. She wants you to take your time and make love nice and slow."

The amateurs generally lacked the overall golfing proficiency of the pros, but they shared the same basic ambitions even if many of them were admittedly sampling life on the 40+ Tour as a lark.

They also boasted an even greater diversity of career backgrounds. Hoyst Whitman, for example, was a fifty-two-year-old former Olympic skier from Kitzbühel, Austria, who had raced on the dream team with Franz Klammer. Dale Moore was a basketball coach from Kentucky. Perry Wergin had been a computer programmer at Texas Instruments for over twenty years; he now operated a mail-order business that marketed specially contoured car pillows with fanciful animal covers. Bruce Kulesza was a former Coca-Cola executive who had retired at the age of forty-seven. His modest goal was to "become a good amateur player or maybe even get good enough to make expenses on the Senior Tour."

Although some of the big names like Koch, Pearce, and Chancey had not signed up for the two-day event at Grenelefe, the thirty-nine-man field was still quite strong without them. Among the proven 40+ Tour winners were reigning World Woods champion Ron Terry, a forty-six-year-old African-American based in Tampa who had played three years on the PGA Tour and two years on the Nike Tour, and Dan Wood, a Stetson-hatted forty-nine-year-old from Winter Springs who had captured the Falcon's Fire Open earlier in the month.

There were also several tournament-hardened journeymen who seemed to be due for their first wins on the 40+ Tour. John Snyder, a lanky, laconic banana-munching forty-year-old from Brooklyn Park, Minnesota, had played in thirty-five PGA Tour events and three U.S. Opens. Buddy Hamilton, age forty-eight, was a born-again pro and former landscaper from Broken Arrow, Oklahoma, who had played on the University of Texas team led by Tom Kite and Ben Crenshaw. Denny Lyons, the fifty-year-old head pro at Niagara Falls Country Club, the home of the Porter Cup, was a short, neatly dressed straight hitter in the Deane Beman mold who boasted four decades of competitive experience.

Besides the prize money, one of the main draws for all the professional contestants on the 40+ Tour was the unusually high-quality rota of courses, and Grenelefe's West Course was arguably the most outstanding of all. Far too many Florida courses were nothing more than reclaimed swamps or retrenched orange groves, with fairways flatter than the parking lots at Disney World and Mickey Mouse greens composed of subsoil dug up to make the Daffy Duck ponds that guarded them in lieu of natural water hazards. Grenelefe West, on the other hand, was a par-72 Robert Trent Jones–designed masterpiece that featured rolling, tree-lined fairways and slick, elevated Bermuda greens protected by a plethora of well-positioned bunkers. One of the sites perennially chosen for the early stages of PGA Tour Qualifying School, it was the same course where my coach Eden Foster had suffered the baptism of wind and subpar firing competition that convinced him to become a teaching pro rather than a touring pro.

Grenelefe West measured an interminable 7,325 yards from the tips and had several par fours that ranged from 430 yards to over 450 yards. But few people other than would-be PGA Tour pros practicing for Q School and visiting sadomasochists ever played the tips by choice. In an effort to emphasize shotmaking skills instead of raw power, 40+ Tour events always had two pairs of tees. Pros age forty-seven and under played from the back tees. The amateurs and pros age forty-eight and over played from front tees planted ten to twelve yards up on each hole. Tournament officials had set up the tees at Grenelefe West so that the course measured about 6,800 yards from the back and 6,600 yards from the front, or roughly the length of the average Senior Tour course.

Like their counterparts on the Senior Tour, most 40+ Tour players elected to ride in golf carts rather than walk in order to keep their legs from tiring on long tracks such as Grenelefe West. I generally preferred to walk a golf course because I believed that covering each yard by foot gave me a better feel for distances from tee to green and enhanced the accuracy of my club selections. But at Grenelefe, I decided to join the cart riders to save caddy expenses and to get to know my fellow competitors a little better.

In round one, I had been paired in a transplanted Yankee foursome with Snyder, Lyons, and Ron Clark, a slightly pudgy, soft-spoken fifty-year-old amateur from Marshall, Michigan. All three of them turned in respectable if unspectacular rounds. Lyons fired a five-over-par 77, with most of his bogeys caused by bad bounces and unlucky lies rather than poor shotmaking or mental errors. Snyder seemed intent on overpowering the course and nearly did until a series of unwisely aggressive shots on the back nine inflated his tally to a one-over 73. Although Clark was by far the shortest knocker in our group, he was the steadiest scorer, capitalizing on almost flawless chipping and a couple of timely birdie putts to shoot an even-par 72.

By contrast, my own round had developed into an agonizing exercise in inconsistency whose otherwise unpredictable twists and turns seemed to have been forecast in the unusually prescient hole-

by-hole notations printed in the official yardage book. The first hole
at Grenelefe West, for example, was a tree-and-bunker-lined par
four that was playing somewhere around 430 yards from the forty-
seven-and-under tees. In words that reminded me of the horo-
scopes in the morning newspaper, the yardage book described
number one as, "A very tough opening hole, which requires an
accurate drive. The fairway bunker on the right catches a lot of
errant tee shots. Birdies will be hard to come by on this hole."

While I would have gratefully settled for a routine par on number one, such good fortune was apparently not in my stars. I tried
to draw my tee shot using the strong grip and delayed wrist cock
prescribed by Butch Harmon, but I wound up hitting a slider into
the fairway bunker on the right and had to struggle to salvage a
bogey. The yardage book declared that number two, a 408-yard par
four, offered "a realistic chance for a birdie" provided one's tee shot
carried the fairway bunker on the left. I sliced my drive underneath
a palmetto tree in the right rough and made a double-bogey 6.

That inauspicious beginning sent my Scorpio birth sign into a
fit of frustrated gyrations that continued for the remainder of the
front nine. The only high points were making a tricky par save on
the long par-three fourth hole and sinking a twenty-five-footer for
birdie on the 564-yard, par-five fifth. I somehow transformed the
551-yard, par-five eighth hole from what the yardage book called
"the best birdie opportunity on the front nine" into my second
double-bogey. The yardage book noted that a par four on the "long,
difficult" 458-yard ninth hole would "pick up some shots on the
field." I only picked up where I had started the day, with yet another bogey. As a result, my scorecard showed that I had shot my
age, a numerological coincidence that left me trailing most of the
field, since I was forty-four years old and the par was 36.

Mysteriously enough, the forces of the zodiac seemed to turn
in my favor when our foursome made the turn onto the back nine.
But after a series of solid pars, my briefly rising stars plummeted
to earth with a terrible thud on number fourteen. The yardage book
accurately characterized the dogleg-left par four, which we were
playing at 450 yards, as "the most difficult hole on the golf course,"
adding that "par is excellent here, but you should not be discouraged with a bogey." I had cause to be discouraged beyond all re-
deeming hope after hacking my way in and out of three sand traps
and soaring to a big fat 6, my third double of the day.

I didn't need Joyce Jilson to divine that I would have to birdie all four finishing holes just to break 80. Number fifteen, a 380-yard dogleg right, was duly described in the yardage book as "a relatively easy par four." It afforded "a definite birdie opportunity" so long as one's tee shot found the narrow strip of grass between the fairway bunker and the thicket of trees on opposite sides of the landing area.

I plastered my longest and straightest drive in many a moon, then reached the fifteenth green with a three-quarter eight iron approach that stopped twenty-five feet from the pin. Having misread almost every putt so far, I decided to go straight at the hole, and mindful of Butch Harmon's instructions, vowed to keep my head down no matter what. At the end of the seemingly eternal time period that followed the completion of my putting stroke, I heard but did not see my ball plopping into the bottom of the cup. Although my birdie was better than a flagstick in the eye or another bumbling double-bogey, no one in our foursome, most especially me, expected that it might be the only birdie of the day on this "relatively easy par four." I proceeded to par the last three holes without further incident, winding up with a two-over-par 38 on the pack nine.

My half-decent finish did not mitigate the despair I felt over shooting 82 for the day. Nor did it put me back in contention to win even a ninth-place paycheck unless I literally shot zero in the second round of the tournament. Ron Terry had carded a remarkable five-under-par 67, leaving me a full fifteen strokes out of the lead. Buddy Hamilton and another pro I did not know were tied with Ron Clark for second place at even par. John Snyder joined a threesome at one over. Twenty-four other players, or roughly 60 percent of the field, had also turned in lower scores than mine, including Barfield, who had managed a 78.

I found little joy in the fact that I had tied or beaten only six of my fellow contestants in the course of winning my first prize money as a professional golfer. As I drifted off to sleep that night, I began to wonder whether I was chasing the dream or it was chasing me. I closed my eyes muttering the same Bobby Jones line that had haunted me in the opening holes of the Nike Tour qualifier: "One always feels that he is running from something without knowing exactly what nor where it is."

*   *   *

When I awoke the following morning, I suddenly began to realize that November 30, 1995, had indeed been a "historical" day, just as Jim Barfield had proclaimed. The fact that I had finally won some money, however paltry the sum, confirmed me a real pro, at least in the unblinking eyes of the USGA, if not by my own personal standards. I had a paycheck to put in the bank, albeit by virtue of taking a skin, and that was certainly preferable to being shut out forever. Mine happened to have been one of only four skins claimed that day, and the $92 I had received was a better-than-average payout for a skin on the 40+ Tour.

When I looked at my first payday in historical perspective, it didn't seem so embarrassing, after all. I had read in an authoritative biography of Ben Hogan that the former caddy from Fort Worth who would go on to win three U.S. Open championships in a row had won his first check as a pro in Phoenix; the amount was $50. Jack Nicklaus's first check at the 1962 Los Angeles Open was only $33.33. I had bested both of them in absolute dollar amounts, and even accounting for the rate of inflation since the 1930s and the early 1960s, I figured that the three of us were about equal, give or take a few bucks.

While I wasn't going to get my name in the newspaper for winning $92, I reminded myself that it was a greater accomplishment than most jaded sportswriters suspected. Anytime and anywhere there was money at stake, you could be sure of competing against hard-bitten pros who would fight tooth and nail to beat you out of it. That was just as true on the 40+ Tour as it was on the Hooters Tour, the Nike Tour, or the PGA Tour. To paraphrase Barfield, you might think you were capable of matching the money winning scores you read about in the newspaper, but the only way you could prove it was to do it. I had done it—at least on one hole.

More important, I had found a place where I could prepare to take the next step in my ongoing quest to make the big time. You couldn't make a decent living solely by playing on the 40+ Tour; even mini-tour king Jim Chancey bagged most of his loot on other professional circuits. But the 40+ Tour definitely offered a chance to gain experience playing under pressure against some pretty stiff competition in a relatively short amount of time. According to the schedule Barfield had distributed, he and Loretta planned to host an average of two events per week for the next six months, punctuated only by a brief hiatus during the Christmas holidays.

The 40+ Tour calendar happened to coincide with the timing

of my second run at the PGA Tour. The major-league circuit had already gone on hiatus following the Tour Championship in late October. I would not have a chance to enter my first Monday qualifier for a PGA Tour tournament until the 1996 season. In early January, the Tour would commence its annual swing through the West Coast, the Arizona desert, and Hawaii. At the end of February, however, the action would shift back to Florida for a three-week series that started with the Doral Ryder Open in Miami and the Honda Classic in Fort Lauderdale, just half a day's drive south of the 40+ Tour headquarters in Orlando.

On the posthistorical afternoon of December 1, 1995, I teed off in the second round of the 40+ Tour tournament at Grenelefe West with a new game plan for the future in mind. I was also determined to put some of my hard-learned lessons to use in the present. After double-bogeying the treacherous opening hole, I tried to emulate Hogan's performance after he doubled the first hole at the Colonial Invitational years ago. Unlike the Hawk, I did not rally for a sensational 69, but I did play the next seventeen holes in four over par, carding a face-saving 78.

I realized that my score could very well have been an 87 if I had succumbed to the same demons that had waylaid me at the Nike Tour qualifier and other tournaments. But rather than panicking or dwelling on my initial misfortunes, I demonstrated a new mental toughness by sinking a twenty-foot putt to save par on number two, and a fifteen-foot putt for birdie on number three. I also began to strike the ball better and manage my game more wisely, as evidenced by my solid par on number fourteen, which I had doubled the day before, and my eight iron shot to two feet, setting up a birdie, on number seventeen.

My second-round score was not low enough to earn me another paycheck. I did not take another skin, nor did I claim a share of the pot reserved for second-day money. And like every other player in the field, I was unable to overtake first-day leader Ron Terry, who shot his second straight 67 and won the tournament with an incredible ten-under-par total of 134. But I did tie Jim Barfield's second-round score, and leapfrogged several other players to finish just below the middle of the pack rather than dead last. I also came away from the round knowing that I had forged invaluable new friendships with fellow dreamers like Barfield and Loretta Sturgill, Jim Hays, Mike Thompson, and Barry Hamilton.

Shortly before the sun set on Grenelefe West, I signed up to play in a series of 40+ Tour events during the first three weeks of February 1996 to get some more tournament experience before entering the Monday qualifiers for Doral and Honda. Then I hopped into my rental car and drove straight to West Palm Beach, where my pal E.P. was chasing his own dreams and a really big payday was in store for one of my former Q School classmates.

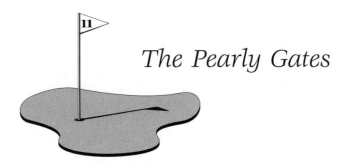

The Pearly Gates

"**b**irdies Fly, Eagles Soar."

The cute epigram displayed on the marquee at the Comfort Inn on Palm Beach Lakes Boulevard scarcely hinted at the high level of tension in the air just around the corner. A far better indicator was provided by the predatory birds hovering in the cloudless Saturday morning sky above Bear Lakes Country Club. Local residents had various euphemistic names for the black-winged creatures. Some called them palmetto parrots. Others referred to them as beach buzzards. But as far as I could tell, they looked exactly like sci-fi movie vultures.

Appropriately, the vultures had the only unobstructed overview of the 190 men fighting for their professional lives on day four of the Final Stage of PGA Tour Qualifying School. Day four was the seventy-two-hole cut day. At the end of the afternoon, only 100 players would remain in contention for the 1996 PGA Tour cards, which would be awarded to the low 40 scorers and ties after the completion of two more rounds on Sunday and Monday.

If the vultures did not devour their carcasses first, the other 90 also-rans would be sent packing with the questionable consolation of having earned conditional status on the 1996 Nike Tour, which, as I would soon learn, often turned out to be worth less than my $92 check for taking a skin on the 40+ Tour.

From the moment the valet parkers acknowledged one of my many expired press passes at the entrance gate, I could see that Bear Lakes was as existentially eerie in its West Palm Beachy little way as my Stage One site back at The Ranch in McKinney, Texas. The clubhouse had pink stucco walls and an orange tiled roof reminiscent of The Breakers in Palm Beach proper, but the place had all the charm of a fast-food franchise converted into a sanitorium. The members mingling with the general public in the gallery seemed to be a politically incorrect, somewhat inebriated contingent of WASP wanna-bes in chartreuse slacks and silk-banded planter's hats, and nouveau riche rednecks with fuzzy beards and TV test pattern shirts.

There were two golf courses, the Lakes and the Links, connected by a concrete tunnel burrowed underneath the entrance road. Both courses had been designed by Jack Nicklaus (hence the name Bear Lakes), and both were par 72s that measured 7,062 yards and 6,962 yards, respectively. But unlike Grenelefe West, they were tediously flat Florida wind fields dimpled with manmade lakes and pimpled with Bermuda grass bumps intended to substitute for naturally rolling terrain. The Links, which was generally regarded as the lesser of the two tracks, with a slope rating of 129 compared to a slope of 135 at the Lakes, was also scarred by several sprawling waste areas splotched with fuzzy clumps of marsh grass that resembled the hirsute chins of some of the members.

Despite all this weirdness, the Final Stage of Q School seemed a bit like a high school homecoming for me. I had competed in tournaments with at least two dozen of the players in the 190-man field during the past few months, and I was anxious to find out how they were making out. The giant scoreboard in front of the clubhouse revealed that my buddies from the Hooters Tour and Stage One of Q School were having experiences that, like the local weather forecasts, ran the gamut from sunny and fair to partly cloudy to dowright nasty.

Brett Quigley, the winner of the BB&T/Granddaddy Classic in Myrtle Beach, was tied for seventy-ninth place with a fifty-four-hole score of three under par. That meant that he was in danger of missing the cut if he played poorly on day four. Javier Sanchez, the Mexican immigrant with the miraculous success story, was at eight over par, just four strokes out of last place. Sadly, Javier was now certain to miss the cut even if he shot a course record score on day four.

Mike Swartz, the stone-faced University of Arkansas alum nicknamed Lurch, was sitting pretty in a tie for ninth place at eleven under, only three strokes behind the third-round leader. His traveling mate, Jack O'Keefe, had bittersweet reason for envy. O'Keefe had recently beaten Swartz out of the Naturally Fresh Foods Bonus Points championship on the Hooters Tour, netting over $180,000 for the year, but O'Keefe's fifty-four-hole total in the Final Stage of Q School was one over par, which put him in a tie for 140th place. Deane Pappas, another Hooters Tour veteran, who had won medalist honors in Stage One at The Ranch, was also tied for 140th place, and was therefore likely to miss the day four cut along with O'Keefe.

I was pleasantly surprised to learn that two of my best buddies from tournaments gone by—Eric Epperson and Shane Bertsch—appeared to have odds-on chances of actually winning 1996 PGA Tour cards. Eric had fired opening rounds of 69-70-67, which put him in a tie for fifteenth at ten under par. Shane had shot 71-68-68, and was tied for twenty-first at nine under. Even so, both Eric and Shane had to keep up the pace by continuing to shoot under-par scores on days four through six or they could easily be overtaken by the thirty-one players who were just two shots behind the low forty finishers at the end of day three.

Ironically, Shane's impressive performance so far had been overshadowed by the highly publicized bumbling of Marco Gortano, his fellow Texas A&M alum and traveling mate. Gortano had been disqualified on day one for missing his tee time because he had misread the pairing sheets. Believing that he was supposed to start at 10:03 A.M. instead of 9:03 A.M., he had been sitting in the clubhouse eating breakfast when his group was called to the tee. The *Sun Sentinel* had recounted the episode in embarrassing detail, noting, "No wonder Aggie jokes are a cottage industry in Texas."

The predicament of my friend and former junior golf idol Eddie Pearce, however, was no laughing matter. E.P. had fired opening rounds of 73-75-67, which put him in a tie for 114th place at one under. Like Quigley, O'Keefe, and Pappas, he was precariously close to the projected cut line. I decided to hurry over to the back nine of the Links course, where he was scheduled to start his fourth round, and offer some moral support before it was too late.

Traversing the concrete tunnel connecting the clubhouse and the Lakes course with the Links course turned out to be as dangerous as trying to walk across Interstate 95 during rush hour. Frustrated contestants and their caddies were careening their golf carts into and out of the tunnel with reckless abandon and without any regard for other human lives. One particularly distraught player with sun-blistered lips and a scowling face actually flipped his middle finger at me when I plastered myself against the tunnel wall to avoid his oncoming cart.

"Eat shit and die, motherfucker," he shouted, pounding for the center of his steering wheel as if to honk an automobile horn.

I eventually caught up with E.P. as he was coming off the tenth green, where he had made a routine par. He was wearing a pair of shiny white Footjoys, khaki slacks, a white shirt with yellow side-stripes, and a white cap bearing the Titleist logo. He still had the long-legged six-foot frame, sloping shoulders, and charismatic smile that I'd seen in so many photographs documenting his exploits as a junior and amateur star. But now there were crow's-feet on the corners of his eyes, crosshatched wrinkles across his neck, and wisps of gray around his blond-haired temples.

E.P. was quickly surrounded by a loyal if somewhat subdued support crew led by his third wife Linette, a petite brunette dressed in extradark sunglasses, black shorts, and a black visor.

"Hey, everybody, let this guy through," E.P. blurted when he saw me approach. "He's a real pyscho."

"Look who's talking, hon," Linette quipped.

She shook my hand, then introduced me to her husband's sports psychologist, Wayne Burroughs, and thirteen-year-old Eddie Jr., the only child of E.P.'s second marriage. Short, pudgy, and pale-complexioned, Eddie Jr. lived with his mother up in Buffalo, New York, most of the time, and he bubbled with a baby-faced innocence that both his father and I had lost in the crucible of junior golf competition at a much earlier age.

"My dad says he's got to shoot a 68 today," Eddie Jr. whispered to me while E.P. prepared to hit his drive off number-eleven tee, "or maybe even a 67."

"Your dad's a good guy," I whispered back.

"Yeah, he is."

As Eddie Jr. and I started down the eleventh fairway, I mused over the long and often tortuous road his father had traveled since he was a child prodigy playing out of Temple Terrace Country Club in suburban Tampa. The godson of legendary athletes George and Mildred "Babe" Didrikson Zaharias, E.P. had grown up with the double-edged blessing of great expectations, and had done a rather remarkable job of fulfilling them during his teenage years. In addition to winning virtually every major junior golf title in our age brackets, he had played with fellow future touring pro Gary Koch on a nearly invincible high school championship team.

At age sixteen, E.P. had won the 1968 U.S. Junior Amateur Championship at The Country Club in Brookline, besting a field that included Koch, Ben Crenshaw, Bruce Lietzke, and my hometown buddy John "Fat Cat" Walzel. Two years later, he had entered Wake Forest University on an Arnold Palmer scholarship, following in the footsteps of then-budding PGA Tour star Lanny Wadkins. He had been named to the All American team as both a freshman and a sophomore, and was in position to win the 1972 U.S. Amateur Championship until his opponent in the finals holed out a nine iron shot to beat him one down. In 1973, he had dropped out of college to turn pro, and had won his card on his first attempt at Q School, coming in second overall behind Crenshaw.

"Everybody said I was a lock to make it big on the PGA Tour, and I believed them," E.P. had recalled in one of our conversations prior to this year's Final Stage. "I put a whole lot of pressure on myself to win a major championship right away. Looking back on it, I guess it was just too much pressure, too many expectations."

Although he finished second five times, E.P. never won a tournament outright in his eight years on the PGA Tour. He started smoking and drinking and, as he put it, "doing everything else you can imagine." He got married and divorced. Then he got married again, had a son, and got divorced again. In 1981, he decided he'd had enough. He gave away everything he owned that had anything to do with golf—his clubs, his bags, his shoes, and, much to his later regret, four Sportsman Wizard putters that were now worth $3,000 apiece.

After quitting the Tour, he did not play an even half-serious round of golf for almost nine years. Instead, he went back home to Tampa and got into the used-car business. He was later recruited by a used-car dealer in Corpus Christi, Texas, to help with a turnaround project that was supposed to take ninety days to complete. He had wound up staying in Corpus for three years. His boss convinced him to join one of the local country clubs, but he actually played there less than half a dozen times. He kept smoking and drinking, and allowed his weight to balloon to over 250 pounds. When I had asked what inspired him to return to golf, E.P. had given full credit to Linette. He had told me that they met in 1986 at an automobile dealership up in Abilene, Texas, where he was working at the time. Linette, herself a divorcee who had spent an itinerant childhood as an army brat, had just left her former life in Anchorage, Alaska. As I stood next to her beside the eleventh green at the Links watching E.P. finish off his second routine par of the morning, I asked for her version of their first encounter.

"I went looking for a new car, and I found him," she replied, adding, "Eddie thought he was being smart. He convinced me to sign a back-end lease with a sixty-month term. Then he asked me out on a date. As it turned out, I only made the first four payments, and he ended up making the rest."

Linette went on to confess that she had no idea about the true nature of her husband's golfing prowess until shortly after they got engaged. ("Everybody used to tell me what a great player Eddie was when he was younger, but you can't believe people in the car business.") The kicker came when she agreed to fly to Tampa to meet his parents. E.P.'s mother, Doris, proudly showed off cases and cases full of trophies he had won in days gone by. Linette had drawn an audible breath, astonished by the array of silver and gold before her eyes. In the spring of 1991, she finally issued a challenge to the former golf star who had become an increasingly restive couch potato.

"One afternoon, I walked into the den and saw Eddie watching another PGA tournament on televsion," she recalled as we headed for number twelve, a dogleg-right par four. "I looked him in the eye and said, 'I know what you're thinking, and you've got to make a decision right now. I don't want to spend the rest of our lives hearing about how you coulda-woulda-shoulda played on the Tour.' Eddie thought about it for a while and realized that I was right."

That summer, less than twelve weeks before the start of the 1991 Qualifying School, E.P. had committed to a four-year plan for making a comeback. Having already recorded lifetime earnings of $300,000 on the PGA Tour, he was given an exemption into Stage Two. He made the Final Stage, but just as he did, his father went into the hospital with a terminal illness. E.P. spent all day on the golf course and every evening at his father's bedside. Not surprisingly, he missed the cut in Q School that year, and though he earned conditional status on the Nike Tour, he was not able to join the circuit until after his father's death in March 1992. He played in only the last ten tournaments on the Nike western swing, winning less than $10,000, hardly enough to cover travel and living expenses.

In the event, E.P. did succeed in getting his weight down to 225 pounds, and getting his competitive spirits up. At the next Q School in the fall of 1992, he regained his PGA Tour card by a one-stroke margin, finishing thirty-sixth overall to the chagrin of skeptics in the golf media. If the breakthrough was admittedly something of a fluke, the 1993 season brought E.P.'s expectations back down to earth. He played in twenty-two tournaments but made only five cuts and won less than $19,000, far too little to earn an automatic exemption for the following season.

After failing to regain his PGA Tour card at the 1994 Q School, E.P. had decided not to risk another frustrating season on the Nike Tour. Having earned only a conditional Nike exemption, he would have needed to make cross-country road trips with no guarantee of getting into any tournaments until the second half of the season. Instead, he elected to retool on mini-tours within driving distance of Tampa, and continued to lose weight.

"Eddie says his swing's changed because he's dropped so much weight recently," Linette reported when E.P. pushed his drive on number twelve against a Bermuda-grass-covered bump in the right rough. "He's down to a hundred and seventy pounds, and he looks great. But he's probably lost a good forty pounds since January, and that's a lot in a short amount of time. He says that he keeps turning his hips through much faster than he used to."

A few moments later, E.P. stumbled to his first bogey of the day as a result of some uncharacteristically poor play around the green. I noticed for the first time that he had resorted to using one of the long-shafted putters favored by many Senior Tour players afflicted with the yips.

"Eddie hates this Links course," Linette whispered when we reached number-thirteen tee. "I don't like to think negatively, but I just knew he wasn't going to play well today. It's all mental."

"There's still plenty of holes left," I assured. "If he can pick up a quick birdie or two, he might be able to make a charge on the second nine."

Unfortunately, E.P. had a tough time just getting up and down for pars on two of the next three holes, and blew his only good birdie opportunity by missing a ten-foot putt on the 412-yard, par-four fourteenth hole. On number sixteen, a 189-yard par three, his hopes of making the day four cut effectively vanished along with his ball as he duck-hooked his three iron tee shot into a lake in front of the green. The errant three iron led to a double-bogey that put him at three over par on the day.

On the par-five seventeenth hole, E.P. crushed a drive well over 300 yards down the left center of the fairway. But I could tell from his narrowed eyes and downturned mouth that he was silently flagellating himself for screwing up the sixteenth, realizing that he would now have to birdie at least seven of the remaining eleven holes to shoot a 68, an almost impossible task. He showed how he felt about his prospects by foregoing his customary preshot routine and halfheartedly swiping a three wood shot that died well short of the green.

"Dad's just given up," Eddie Jr. observed. "He went up to that last shot and just whacked at it."

I tried to sympathize, allowing that E.P.'s errant tee shot on the sixteenth had been the killer.

"Yeah, I know," Eddie Jr. replied. "It's always one hole."

After watching her husband fail in his transparently lackadaisical attempt to make a twelve-foot birdie putt on the seventeenth, Linette pulled E.P. aside and read him the riot act.

"If you're gonna give up, let's just walk in."

"I ain't giving up," E.P. insisted. "I'm trying as hard as I can."

"Doesn't look like it to me."

"Fuck you. Get away from me."

E.P. proceeded to smash his longest drive of the day down the middle of the eighteenth fairway, then stormed off without her.

"I just pissed him off big time," Linette told me a few moments later. "He's gonna beat the shit out of every shot from here on. Now I'm the ball."

It quickly became apparent, however, that the symbolic role reversal was not going to save the day. Despite evincing some renewed determination, E.P. made bogeys on two of the next four holes to go five over on the day and four over for the tournament. At that point, even his wife conceded that all was lost.

"Eddie was so positive coming into Q School, and he worked so hard." Linette sighed as we wandered down the fifth fairway. "There's nothing I can do to console him except tell him that I love him and that I'm proud of him."

I asked her if they had made contingency plans for playing somewhere besides the PGA Tour in 1996.

"We haven't thought about it," she admitted. "We haven't wanted to think about it."

I reminded her that E.P. would earn conditional status on the Nike Tour by virtue of making the Final Stage, and that he might still be able to launch another assault on the PGA Tour from there.

Linette shook her head, rolling her teary eyes.

"No, this time we're gonna have to take a bite of reality. With a conditional exemption, Eddie won't be able to get into any tournaments until the end of the year, and we've gotta live."

Then she paused to take a deep breath, and added, "We've heard that Jack Nicklaus may be starting a new tour here in Florida sometime next spring. Maybe if we can get someone to give us fifteen thousand dollars . . ."

Linette's voice trailed off as E.P. three-putted for another bogey on number five.

I soon felt my own eyes welling with tears. Here was the man whose youthful exploits had won him acclaim as the best and the brightest of my golfing contemporaries, the guy who was supposedly destined to shoot it out with Watson and Crenshaw and Kite in historic battles for all the major championships. He had once carried the hopes and dreams of all us less-talented PGA Tour wanna-bes, and now he was hacking his way back into obscurity, becoming just another Q School sob story not even worthy of mention in the next morning's newspaper. He deserved better than that, by God, and I prayed that he would be blessed with success if he got a chance to try Q School again in 1996.

In the meantime, the pain of witnessing E.P. go on to bogey number six, then gamely regroup to finish with three straight pars for an inglorious 79, was almost too much to bear. I waited beside the ninth green while Linette smothered him with kisses. When she was done, I walked over and embraced him with both arms, choking on my own words.

"Just want you to know that I'm really, really proud of you."

"Thanks, pal, I appreciate that," E.P. replied, patting me on the shoulder. "Let's stay in touch."

Then he took Linette and Eddie Jr. by the hand and disappeared into the tunnel underneath the entrance road.

*   *   *

by the morning of day six, even the vultures circling above Bear
Lakes Country Club looked worn out, and no wonder. There had
been sufficient carnage on day four to satisfy the most bloodthirsty
of the flock. E.P. had gone down along with Javier Sanchez, Deane
Pappas, Jack O'Keefe, and eighty-six otherwise able-bodied men. If
the difference between them and the hundred men who survived
to day five was tantamount to life and death, the survivors were
still struggling for their respective places in a PGA Tour hierarchy
roughly equivalent to Heaven, Hell, and Purgatory.

Heaven was reserved for the low forty finishers and ties who
would enter what I had begun to call the P. G. of A.—the Pearly
Gates of Affluence—by winning their 1996 Tour cards. Hell was
almost an understatement for the self-immolation that might con-
sume those who were in contention for one of the card-winning
spots coming into the last day of Q School but lost their souls by
shooting a high score in the final round. Purgatory was the effective
fate of those who had barely made the day four cut and were destined to spend the 1996 season on the Nike Tour no matter how
well they played on the final day.

At the end of day four, the cut line demarcating the P. G. of A.
had been drawn at the remarkably low seventy-two-hole score of
nine under par, but it had dropped even lower by the start of the
sixth and final round of the Final Stage. Brett Quigley had made
the day four cut by firing a two under 70, which put him in a tie
for seventy-sixth place at five under for the tournament and four
strokes back of the magic forty. On day five, he had turned in a
71, only to lose ground against the low forty as the cut line fell to
minus eleven.

I had gone to bed on Sunday evening elated by the fact that
two of my best buddies in the field seemed assured of entering the
Pearly Gates the following afternoon. On day five, Eric Epperson
had shot a 70, his fifth straight subpar round, and was tied for tenth
at seventeen under. Shane Bertsch had carded a 69, which put him
in a tie for sixteenth place at fifteen under along with Mike Swartz.

I felt the first of many day six jolts shortly after arriving at the
clubhouse overlooking the Lakes course, which was now the site
of all the action. Starting on the weekend, the Golf Channel had
been broadcasting coverage of the Final Stage, which made it pos-

sible to monitor hole-by-hole changes on the leaderboard via the television sets in the grill room. Had I made it to the Final Stage, the presence of the TV crews would only have further unnerved me, and it seemed to be having a similarly disturbing effect on some of my friends.

Just as I sat down in front of one of the screens, I saw Shane duck-hook his tee shot off the par-four first hole directly toward the out of bounds markers on the left side. Then, as if guided by some invisible hand from above, the ball caromed off a tree and bounced back into the light rough safely within bounds.

I exhaled a sigh of relief when Shane started striding down the fairway. He was dressed in the same Swoosh-marked white cap and mottled blue shirt he had worn back in Stage One at The Ranch, and I could almost hear him chortling with relief as he flipped his Oakleys up and down.

Several minutes later, I saw another chilling picture appear on the clubhouse TV sets. Eric Epperson had just hit his approach shot on number four, a 382-yard par four. The ball seemed to be heading straight for the flag, and it actually landed on the fringe of the green. But instead of bounding toward the pin, it spun back into the green-side bunker. I could tell even from the remote camera angle that Eric's ball had tumbled into an awkward lie just below the lip of the bunker. I held my breath as he blasted out short and right of the pin, then missed his par-saving putt.

The real-time leaderboard at the bottom of the screen showed that Eric's bogey on number four had dropped him back to fifteen under for the tournament. That meant he must have also bogeyed another one of his opening holes. Although he was still a comfortable four strokes below the morning's P. G. of A. cut line, this was not a good sign. I had planned on trudging out to the course to join his gallery so that I could cheer him into the clubhouse, but given his shaky start, I figured it was better to keep my distance until he turned things around.

Eric's predicament quickly went from not so bad to extremely tenuous. He pushed his drive against the upslope of a Bermuda-grass-covered mound on the long par-four fifth hole, and stumbled to his third bogey of the day. He had a good opportunity to get himself back to fifteen under on the 554-yard, par-five sixth, but his ten-footer for birdie hit the edge of the cup and refused to fall. On the seventh, he three-putted for yet another bogey. After a safely executed par on the lake-guarded ninth hole, he finished the front nine four over on the day, and only thirteen under for the tournament. For the past two days, the P. G. of A. cut line had been falling by two strokes per round. Assuming that it dropped at the same rate on day six, Eric was right on the edge. Another bogey would knock him out of the low forty and ties.

Unable to sit still any longer, I bolted out of the clubhouse and jogged down to number ten, a 394-yard par four lined by the same lake that fronted the ninth and eighteenth greens. Then I huddled next to a tree and watched Eric negotiate his way around the water for a two-putt par. On the eleventh, a 170-yard par three that required carrying a smaller lake, he smacked a sweet-sounding five iron shot that plopped down about twenty-five feet short of the flag. A few minutes later, I saw him three-putt for his fifth bogey of the day.

Acutely aware that the last thing Eric needed at this point was another distraction, I ran in the exact opposite direction to check in on Shane Bertsch, worrying with every fleeting step that he was in the midst of an identical catastrophe. I reached the grassy slope behind the fourteenth green just as Shane's threesome, which also included Mike Swartz, arrived on the tee. There was a Q School official with a walkie-talkie standing nearby, and I asked him for an update. His responded with the kind of report I had been hoping for.

"We've got Swartz at fourteen under," he informed me. "And we're showing Bertsch at nineteen."

Unfortunately, my friends still had to get past a 213-yard par three with yet another very large lake in front of the green and a waste area on the left. Shane hit one of his patented punch fades safely into the light rough right of the green, but Swartz chunked his tee shot into the water. After taking a penalty stroke and a drop, Swartz hit a rather mediocre approach shot that eventually led to a two-putt double-bogey. I felt my pulse start to throb once again when Shane charged his pitch about eight feet past the hole, but he then proceeded to ram his par putt in the back of the cup. He walked over to me and held out his hand for a congratulatory slap.

"Hey, Harry," he said, as coolly as if he were in the middle of another routine practice round. "Whatcha doing—just hangin' out?"

I nodded. "Thought I might walk you in for old time's sake, if that's okay."

"Sure," Shane replied, chortling. "Come on."

The well-deserved good fortune that befell my former Q School classmate during and after the next four holes at the Lakes course was a beautiful thing to behold, the exact opposite of what had happened to Eddie Pearce two days before and what was in the process of happening to Eric Epperson that very same day. I would have given my King Cobra Tour Model irons, all my Maxflis, and my firstborn child to have been walking in Shane's shoes. He was living the dream I had been chasing since my comeback quest began. But since my hopes of qualifying for the PGA Tour had to be postponed until another day, I was happy to settle for the rare privilege of witnessing my friend's heroics in the role of his alter ego.

When I had caught up with Shane on number fourteen, he was already four under on the day. The bounce off the tree on number one had undoubtedly prevented the round from becoming a nightmare at the outset. Following that lucky break, however, he had put on a short game display that had awed even his caddie, Jaimie Adam, a veteran PGA Tour looper in Day-Glo green pants and a wide-brimmed straw hat, who thought he had seen everything.

"We've already had four up and downs today, big ones," Jaimie reported as I stood beside their golf cart on the fifteenth tee. "I told him, 'The best part of your game is your putting. If you keep it up, we might just win this whole thing.'"

Shane immediately let us know that he aimed to do exactly that. He laid up with a perfect three wood on the water-guarded fifteenth, lofted a seven iron to twenty feet, and drained his birdie putt, pumping his fist in the air as the ball disappeared into the cup. On the sixteenth, a couple of discourteous gallery wandered across the fairway just as he was starting his downswing, and he pushed his tee shot into a fairway trap. Shane simply shook his head in disbelief, blasted his second shot to within five yards of the green, and got up and down for the fifth time that day.

On the 501-yard, par-five seventeenth hole, Shane reached the front of the green with a boldly faded seven wood approach shot and two-putted for another birdie. His perfomance simultaneously seemed to energize the stone-faced Swartz, who recovered from his double on the fourteenth by matching Shane's birdies on fifteen and seventeen.

On number eighteen, a 437-yard par four that marked the 108th hole of the Final Stage and the 252nd hole of the 1995 PGA Tour Qualifying School, Shane pounded a resounding drive that rolled so far I feared he might have made it all the way to the pond, some

320 yards off the tee. Happily, we found his ball lying in a tuft of light rough just short of the water and only 140 yards from the green. From there, he hit a nine iron, slightly pulled, that deposited his ball about thirty feet from the pin. Two putts later, he was in the hole with a 66 for the day that put him at an incredible twenty-one under par for the tournament. Swartz then two-putted for a final round 73 that put him at minus fourteen.

the moment Shane stepped off the eighteenth green, his life changed more quickly and dramatically than either of us could have ever imagined. It was already clear to the teeming throng of agents, managers, equipment company reps, commercial sponsors, and endorsement hounds hanging around the scoreboard that he was assured of finishing among the lowest of the low forty scorers. Before we could even walk the two dozen yards to the clubhouse, he was deluged with flyers, pamphlets, manila envelopes, and offers shouted at him from all sides.

"Oh, man, let's get out of here," Shane said, chortling again. "I need to get something to eat."

As we climbed the clubhouse steps leading to the grill room, a familar figure from out of our Nike Tour past pulled us aside. It was Glenn Karp, the management executive I had met at the Sonoma Open. Karp congratulated Shane on his round, then he congratulated me on my recently published *Sports Illustrated* article about Stage One of Q School. He no longer seemed worried about the distracting effect my poor play might have had on the other guys I was paired with in Stage One; he could tell from having watched me walk down the eighteenth fairway with Shane that at least one of my former playing partners and I had gotten along just fine. Now the only thing on his mind was convincing Shane to listen to his solicitation spiel.

"I'd like to talk after you've had a chance to get out of your nails," he told Shane, using the pseudo-hip term for golf spikes. "Why don't you and Harry meet me upstairs, and I'll buy you guys a beer."

A few minutes later, Shane and I found ourselves sitting at a table in a quiet corner of the grill sipping Michelob Lights and listening to Karp. I glanced up at one of the TV sets just in time to see the final scores flash across the screen. Shane's six-day total of

411 turned out to be good enough to tie him for fourth behind medalist Carl Paulson, who finished with a twenty-three-under-par total of 409. A total of forty-two players won their 1996 Tour cards with scores of thirteen under or better. Swartz made it by two strokes, while Eric Epperson carded a final-round 78 and missed entering the Pearly Gates of Affluence by two strokes.

The financial implications of those two strokes were staggering. As the fourth-place finisher, Shane would collect a check for $4,200. Less than half of the $15,000 Carlson would collect for finishing in first place, that amount would not even cover his $3,000 Q School entry fee and the travel expenses he had incurred while playing in the three stages of the tournament. But the Q School check was only a token of the paydays that were due in the months ahead.

Simply by qualifying for the PGA Tour, Shane had won the opportunity to play for a share of purses that would average $1.5 million a week in 1996. He had also set himself up for an income stream that would grow for the next year even if he did not win a tournament or make a cut. He could look forward to receiving $400 to $500 a week from Callaway Golf in return for using a Big Bertha driver and fairway woods. He could anticipate similarly sized weekly checks from Karsten Manufacturing for playing Ping irons, and from Nike for wearing their Swoosh-marked clothes and shoes.

If Shane did make some cuts on the PGA Tour and win a fair amount of official prize money, he could also claim proportionately greater shares of his equipment sponsors' year-end bonus pools. He had already told me about how the bonus pool had affected one friend, who had earned $190,000 on the Tour the previous year; though his official winnings only ranked him in the bottom tier of the top 125 money winners, he had received a $90,000 bonus check, which boosted his actual income to over $280,000. If Shane actually won a tournament outright, endorsement contracts and bonus checks would rain down on him.

Eric Epperson, on the other hand, would leave Q School without a dime of PGA Tour prize money for his nearly three-month-long efforts. By virtue of at least earning exempt status on the 1996 Nike Tour, he could look forward to getting some weekly checks from the makers of his clubs and balls. But as Shane could testify from personal experience, the amounts would be less than half of what was offered to PGA Tour players. Likewise, the purses offered in Nike Tour tournaments were less than one-fifth of those on the PGA Tour.

"At Triangle Management, we preach integrity," Karp declared after staring up at the TV screen, then looking back at Shane. "What you did out there today by shooting a 66 to finish fourth was huge. But the next few weeks are going to be overwhelming. You're going to get lots of different offers from all kinds of people, and there are gonna be lots of management companies coming up to you."

"They already have," Shane interjected. "The second day here, I shot 68, and this guy came up to me and said he wanted to take me to a ballgame. I said, 'I don't want to do any of that stuff now. It's only the second day.' "

Karp nodded sympathetically.

"That's the kind of thing I'm talking about. Like I was saying, there's lots of management companies out there, and some of them are a lot bigger than we are. IMG, for example, is obviously one of the biggest ones. And in the past, they have represented a lot of the biggest names like Palmer, Price, and Norman. But don't make the same mistake a lot of guys who are new on the Tour make. Don't go by who are the big companies. You can look at their lists of clients and see where you'll be. Shane Bertsch won't be at the top.

"At Triangle Management, we're not really just a management company, we're your advisers," Karp continued. "We put together a promotional package for you. We write letters to various people for you, sponsors and so forth, to make them aware of Shane Bertsch. That can be very important in getting you into tournaments next year. As you know, you're only going to get into the first three or four events on the basis of finishing fourth at Q School. After that, there's going to be a reshuffle based on how much money you win in those first few tournaments. But at each event, there are usually at least eight sponsor's exemptions, four restricted and four unrestricted. We can be a big help in getting unrestricted exemptions."

Karp paused to take a sip of his beer and leaned closer to Shane.

"You've got to remember that as a professional golfer, you're basically an entertainer," he said. "That doesn't mean you have to be funny or witty or clown around out on the golf course. Just be yourself. But remember that you are in the entertainment business. That's the reason you'll be playing for over a million dollars in purses every week. If all those volunteers had to be paid for the time they put in helping out with PGA tournaments, you'd be surprised at how quickly that million dollars would shrink to half a million or less. So there's a lot of courtesy things you should keep in mind. One of the things we do, for example, is send letters to the people you play with in pro-am events, thanking them. I'd like to see you play in three to five of those events next year to help you get the kind of exposure you need to have."

Karp took another sip of his beer.

"Now, by the same token, you don't want to spread yourself too thin each week," he cautioned. "Mondays and Tuesdays are very important days because those are the only days when you'll have a chance to play your practice rounds on the courses you've never seen before. Wednesdays are basically your laundry days because the courses will be closed for the pro-am events. Remember, the golf course is your office and so is the practice range. People will be showing you stuff all the time. There's thousands of things coming on the market all the time, new shafts, balls, grips, gloves. It's okay to look, but you've got to be careful not to let yourself get too distracted. The point of being out there is to prepare yourself to win a PGA Tour tournament."

"Yeah, I know," Shane said, obviously becoming a little impatient with Karp's lecture. "It was like that this year on the Nike Tour. So tell me, what kind of contract deal do you guys want to have with me?"

Karp cleared his throat and smiled.

"You're the chairman of the board," he said, "and I'm the president. I handle the day-to-day stuff, but I do what you tell me to do. We insist on signing our clients to a two-year contract because we don't make any money the first year, it's just the setup. And we don't take any percentage of the things that you've already got going; those deals are your business. We take 20 percent of the things we do for you, and we take 10 percent of the things that come independently but only if you ask us to check them out for you. Some of the big companies take 25 percent of everthing, including 25 percent of the deals you've already got with Nike and Ping."

Shane nodded, muttering under his breath.

"That's a pretty big chunk."

"Yes, it is," Karp agreed. "That's why I'd like you to take plenty of time to think about what we've been discussing. You don't have to give me an answer right now. Call some of our clients and hear what they have to say about us. You probably know Jerry Foltz from the Nike Tour. Call Jerry and ask him. Call Lennie Clements, he's another one of our clients who's on the PGA Tour. Ask Lennie what he thinks. All I ask is that you get in touch before the end of the month and let me know what you want to do. Then I can get you started off right away after the first of the year."

Shane said he'd do that and pushed away from the table, thanking Karp for the beer. I got up with him.

"Go have yourself a good time tonight," Karp called out as we headed for the door. "But don't set your hair on fire."

Shane chortled again, elbowing me in the ribs and rolling his eyes.

"Don't worry, Glenn," he called back over his shoulder. "I won't."

A twosome of PGA Tour officials stopped Shane in the middle of the hallway and ushered him inside one of the clubhouse offices, where three more officials were making travel arrangements for the forty-two men who had won their cards that afternoon. Like the others, Shane would be flying to PGA Tour headquarters in Ponte Vedra, Florida, the following morning to attend a mandatory three-day seminar for rookie players. We slapped hands, wished each other luck, and said good-bye.

I waited until Tuesday morning to track down Eric Epperson, hoping that would give him enough time to get over what must have been one of the most traumatic rounds of his life. To my surprise, he was in remarkably high spirits when he answered my phone call.

"It didn't exactly go the way I wanted it to," Eric admitted, "but I haven't been planning to commit suicide or anything like that. I think the mistake I made yesterday was that I tried to go out and just shoot for pars on every hole instead of trying to make birdies. I wasn't just going through the motions, but I wasn't being nearly aggressive enough. When I went three over after the first five holes, I told myself, 'Okay, start over. It's no big deal. If you can just stay three over, you're fine.' But before I knew it, I got to four over, and then I started trying to force my shots."

Eric added that his sponsor, the owner of a Dallas-area cable television firm, had also gotten over the initial shock of his day six disaster. "My sponsor told me he's pleased with what I've accomplished in such a short amount of time, and to be honest, so am I. I didn't play golf in college, and I've only been playing for two years as a pro. This was the lowest Q School cut in PGA history. I average 69.9 for the six days even with the 78 on the last day, and I still don't get my card. That just shows you how tough it really is."

Before we signed off, Eric told me that he planned to take full advantage of the fact that he had played well enough to earn fully exempt status on the 1996 Nike Tour. "I want to get better at everything before Q School comes around next year," he said. "The strongest part of my game is tee to green. The weakest part is putting. But one of the things I've found out is that you can't really have a weak point. I know even the best players have some parts of their games that are weaker than others, but they also have stronger parts to make up for it."

I hung up the phone, marveling at the bravely optimistic words I had just heard. Eric Epperson had been through the Hell of the PGA Tour Qualifying School's Final Stage. He had—there was no other word for it—choked. But he was already rebounding from his misfortunes, learning from them, and preparing himself to move on to better things. I was reminded of a passage in *Golf Is Not a Game of Perfect*, the bestselling book by my own ad hoc consulting sports pyschologist, Bob Rotella.

"Choking is not synonymous with having a flawed character," Rotella had pointed out. "Some nasty, miserable people have triumphed under pressure. And some of the finest, most admirable human beings in the world have choked in tight situations. If you play golf long enough, you are bound to encounter some pressure situations in which you will perform at less than your best. They will help you learn how to cope with pressure, which is a skill that must be learned, and once learned, constantly maintained."

When I flew back to New York the evening after the Q School finals, I started revising my comeback strategy in midair. It was not enough to have won a check for $92 or to have avoided finishing in last place in the pro tournaments I had entered so far. It was not acceptable to shoot scores in the high 70s and low 80s every time I teed it up for money. Like Eric Epperson, I wanted to—and needed to—get better at everything.

If I couldn't achieve the breakthrough accomplished by Shane Bertsch, I desperately wanted to avoid the kind of relapse suffered by Eddie Pearce. Since the next Q School would not come around again until the fall of 1996, my immediate goal was to get into at least one PGA Tour tournament in the spring of 1996 via a Monday qualifier. Given the low percentages involved in "four spotting," I also set a secondary goal. I felt that I needed to match or beat the 72 I'd shot in the first round of the U.S. Amateur qualifier under the heat of professional competition. Otherwise, I would consider my comeback attempt to be for naught.

After I talked it over with Alison, she reminded me that, as usual, I was putting an awful lot of pressure on myself. I said, so be it. I had to discover once and for all how I would perform when the chips were down. Would I wind up being just another choker? Or would I prove myself to be a real pro at long last? There was only one way to find out. And as we sat down that Christmas Eve to say grace over the sumptuous dinner she had prepared, I bowed my head and prayed that the golf gods would guide my every swing along that way.

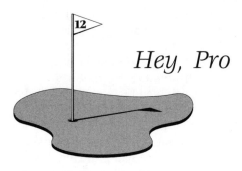

Hey, Pro

Palisades Golf Club perched atop a bleak and barren weather-blistered hillside about a forty-five-minutes' drive northwest of Orlando. The property's steeply undulating slopes had formerly cradled a fruit farm, but with the groves long since felled and furrowed over, the place now appeared best suited to be a goat ranch or the set for a horror film based on Dante Alighieri's *Inferno*. The fairways and greens were chewed down to a grassless pulp. The clubhouse was nothing more than a rickety little blue-gray mobile home. And the entire golf course reverberated with relentless winds that seemed to block out the sun.

"I came to a place where every light is muted, which bellows like the sea beneath a tempest," Dante reported in Canto V. "The hellish hurricane, which never rests, drives on the spirits with its violence: wheeling and pounding, it harasses them. When they come up against the ruined slope, there are cries and wailing and lament, and there they curse the forces of the divine."

I had cause to curse the forces of the divine for abandoning me in the second round of the 40+ Tour tournament at Palisades on the afternoon of February 20, 1996. This windblown midwinter Tuesday was my late father's birthday. Had he been alive, he would have been ninety-seven years old. Along with lamenting his passing, I was bemoaning the fact that my pitiful performance on the front nine had raised the very real possibility that I might shoot my old man's age. That specter was further eroding my all-but-depleted self-confidence.

"I am going through Hell," I had written in my golfing journal the night before. "I feel embarrassed, humiliated, pissed off, stupid, incompetent, and chickenshit. My hands shake over every putt. My head goes dead on me every other hole. I make one wrong decision after another. And it just gets worse and worse every day."

The two-day event at Palisades was the fourth 40+ Tour tournament I had played in during the past two weeks, and in the seven rounds I had completed so far, I had broken 80 only twice. The official tour record books listed only one sub-80 round beside my name, however, since I had compounded my misery and my score on the second day of my first 40+ Tour tournament of the month by signing an incorrect card. I was getting into the kind of rut John Daly dug for himself on the all-too-frequent occasions when he got off to a bad start and then quit trying—except that I *was* trying, at least most of the time.

To make matters worse, the Monday qualifier for the Doral Ryder Open was now just six short days away, and the qualifier for the Honda Classic was scheduled for the week after that. Unless I miraculously turned my game around right away, I would only descend deeper into the flaming inferno.

But I arrived on the tenth tee at Palisades seething with the kind of anger and self-hatred that did not bode well for any attempt at redemption. For the second day in a row, I had double-bogeyed number nine, an uphill par four that was playing about 430 yards long from the back markers. What had killed me each time was "the hellish hurricane," which always seemed to be quartering against my second shot from left to right. Twice I had tried to reach the green with a four iron, and twice my ball had ballooned haplessly off to the starboard side.

My short game had been even more damning. Twice I had tried to spin my third shot on number nine close enough to the pin to save par, and twice I had scooped it into the green-side trap. On day one, I had left my first bunker shot in the sand. On day two, I had done it again. Both times, I had wound up having to sink a ten-foot putt just to salvage a 6. The only difference between the implications of the two doubles was that I had carded a 41 on my most recent front nine, two strokes lower than my 43 the day before but two strokes higher than the pace required to break 80.

Number ten was a 520-yard par five that might normally have yielded the birdie I needed to turn my day around. But here again, our threesome was playing into a mini-gale quartering from left to right. Having long since forfeited the honor to the two amateurs in my group, I impatiently waited my turn in the back corner of the tee box, then whipped my driver back and through with a wide-eyed rage. The ball barreled off the club face in a wind-cheating slide that traveled a good 270 yards down the right side of the fairway.

For the first time that afternoon, I actually welcomed the angle and intensity of the wind as it influenced the flight of my second shot on number ten. I had no choice but to hit my hook-prone three wood in order to get anywhere close to the green. The big blow quartering against me from left to right perfectly offset my hook, holding the ball on line until it rolled to a stop about 100 yards short of the green.

It was my third shot that presented the same dilemma that had bedeviled me for the last few weeks. If I lofted a pitching wedge to the green, there was a good chance that the ball would be grabbed by the wind and thrown right back in my face. The situation called for a knockdown nine iron that would come in low to the ground with a controlled draw. Over the weekend, the always obliging 40+ Tour's founder, Jim Barfield, had agreed to tutor me in the fine art of hitting knockdowns, a shot that was indispensable to scoring on Florida golf courses but heretofore untried by me in tournament competition.

Barfield happened to be playing in the threesome ahead, and they were taking their sweet time lining up their putts on number-ten green. Realizing that it was now or never, I yanked out my nine iron and started to review the pointers he had given me about hitting knockdown shots. While I waited for Barfield's group to clear out, I also began to think about all the words of advice and encouragement he and so many other pros on the 40+ Tour had been offering me. And the more I reflected on the support I had received from my newfound friends, the more I felt gusts of self-doubt and insecurity bellow over me.

*   *   *

exactly one week prior to the event at Palisades, I had played in another 40+ Tour tournament at Grenelefe West. The computerized pairing system had put me in a threesome with Eddie Pearce, who had fired a solid 69 to demonstrate that he was well on his way to recovering from his Q School debacle. I had desperately wanted to shoot a decent round to impress E.P. with my own progress. But instead of making a step forward, I had regressed several yards in the opposite direction. My driving and iron play were erratic, my short game abysmal, my putting pathetic. Each time I hit my ball into trouble, I followed with a shot that got me deeper into jail. I ended up carding a humiliating 86.

Following the round, my embarrassment grew by quantum leaps when I retreated to the practice range to diagnose my ailments. E.P. came out to offer his help. So did Mike Thompson, the Pennsylvania-based teaching pro who looked like Huey Lewis, and Barry Hamilton, the former amateur star from Arkansas. Before long, Barfield and Gary Koch joined my postround consulting team. I was deeply touched by their attention, but I knew that they all had better things to do. I felt like they were wasting their collective time, and told them so even as I thanked them for their advice.

"You're too hard on yourself," Mike Thompson scolded afterward, echoing similar comments I'd gotten from E.P., Barry, and Barfield. "You're someone who wants to learn, and that's the best kind of person we could have. You've got so much talent in that body of yours. You've just got to let it out. Eddie and I both said we wished we had a magic wand that we could touch you with, but we don't."

I returned to my $36-a-night room in the TraveLodge in Kissimmee and made a list of the swing points Mike had emphasized. They sounded awfully familiar. I thumbed through my golfing journal to some entries I'd made way back in June 1995 after my first lessons with Eden Foster. He had told me the same things virtually word for word that I'd just heard on the practice range at Grenelefe. "We've got to slow your tempo down to a blur. . . . You need to take the club back straighter, it's too inside. . . . You've got way too much tension in your hands and arms and shoulders, try to relax more." The only variation on this litany was Mike's favorite dictum, "Swinging the golf club is like making love to your wife. . . . She wants you to take your time and make love nice and slow."

Although my wife, Alison, arrived the next day to work her wonders on my notoriously quick tempo, the wands in my golf bag continued to dig up plenty of dust, almost none of it magical. I shot 81 in the second round at Grenelefe West. That came on the heels of the previous week's 40+ Tour tournament at Ridgewood Lakes, where I had shot 82-80, signing off on an incorrectly calculated second-day card that should have been a 79. When Alison and I sat down inside a cozy restaurant in Winter Park for a Valentine's Day dinner, I informed her that I didn't care how long it took or how much it cost, I was going to keep entering these damn pro golf tournaments until I shot 72 or better.

"Okay, then, that's what you'll do," Alison replied. "And I'll keep coming down to see you on your days off."

Then she added, apropos of the holiday we were celebrating, "Just remember, sweetest, you have to love every hole just like all the other holes, or the other holes will get jealous."

I bussed her on both cheeks, laughing.

"I love you for sure, honey one. But that's just a cute little way of restating one of the oldest clichés in golf. It's the same as saying you've got to take it one hole at a time."

"No, it is not," Alison insisted. "I know from being an actress that telling you to take one hole at a time is poor direction. It's too passive. You have to have active directions. You can't just 'take' a hole—you have to *love* the hole."

Two days after the Grenelefe event, the 40+ Tour moved on to Bay Tree, a Gary Player–designed course in Melbourne, just down the beach from the Cape Kennedy launch pads. My score in the first round at Bay Tree rocketed like a Saturn V missile to an 84. In the second round, I tried to combine Alison's "love every hole" direction with Mike Thompson's "making love" swing thought. The blend worked almost like an aphrodisiac. I didn't shoot lights out, but I did fire a respectable 77 under windy conditions to tie Mike himself for third place in the second-day money race. Barfield wrote me a check for $75, the second check I had won as a pro golfer and the first for a performance on a full eighteen-hole round.

When we got to Palisades, however, even my wife had to admit that she did not love any part of the layout, much less every hole. Alison rode with me on a Sunday afternoon practice round, making wisecracks about the golf course and the cookie cutter condos springing up on the periphery that had my playing partners in stitches. When one of them informed her that the property was about to be purchased by a group of Korean investors, she rejoined,

"I read in the newspaper that they're working on an atomic bomb. I bet you they're buying this place just so they'll have somewhere to test it."

The next morning, Alison had to return to her restaurant business in New York, and I must have wanted to reach out and touch her with the help of AT&T, because my scores on the first seven holes of the front nine at Palisades sounded like the digits of a telephone number. I started out 4-2-9-8-6-5-5. Although I parred the eighth hole, my double on number nine put me at ten over on the day. I made another double-bogey on the eleventh after plunking my approach shot into a water hazard, then went on to bogey the last three holes of the back nine for an 87, my worst score in any tournament round so far.

Unlike Eric Epperson after his choke in the Final Stage of Q School, I was furious at myself and the world around me. I tried to hide out on the far end of the practice range, as much to contemplate suicide as to work on my game. Barry Hamilton came over offering to critique my swing, but I told him in so many words to buzz off. I didn't want to see anybody, talk to anybody, or listen to one more goddamn piece of advice.

"Oh, honey, I'm so sorry about what happened today," Loretta Sturgill sighed when I called in from the TraveLodge later that evening to get my tee time for round two. "I wish I was there to give you a hug."

I told Loretta that I wished she could give me a brain transplant. The most maddening thing about my 87 was that, with a few notable exceptions, I had hit most of my shots pretty well. Alison's pithy remarks during the Sunday practice round had helped me relax, which, in turn, had helped slow down my tempo. My only swing thought during warm-up on the practice range was to pretend to be Freddy Couples and emulate his "lazy" motion. I had almost birdied the opening hole of the day, and had come within inches of a hole-in-one en route to my birdie on number two.

My downfall had resulted from a total disconnect of what Butch Harmon called "the mental side/course management." I had tried to cut off too much of the lake-lined dogleg on number three, a par five that was not reachable in two shots anyway. On number four, I had neglected to account for a crosswind that pushed my not-so-badly-struck tee shot out of bounds by less than a foot. At that point, I felt that my round and my entire life were in ashes. John

Daly came in to the game to replace Couples, and I proceeded to play out a self-fulfilling prophecy of doom.

Upon commencing round two, I had sworn to concentrate on my course management skills even if I started ringing up phone numbers again. The challenge had become that much greater when I three-putted number one from the fringe for a careless bogey. But I succeeded in parring the next five holes in a row, and had almost salvaged a par on the 185-yard seventh hole after a sudden gust of wind knocked my tee shot back into the front bunker. If I had not three-putted the eighth hole and had merely bogeyed the ninth, I would have turned in 39, my first sub-40 nine since Bay Tree.

When Barfield's threesome finally replaced the flagstick on number ten and walked off the green, my state of mind underwent a subtle but important change. The interlude of reflection during the long wait had spawned a new devil-may-care attitude. My anger had subsided and my hands had stopped shaking. I was no longer thinking, "This is hell." Instead, I was telling myself, "Hey, what the hell—let's go for it."

I stood over the ball so that it was positioned off my back foot, choked down on my nine iron, and hooded the face ever so slightly. Then I brought the club back low and punched into the shot with a slight roll of my wrists and an abbreviated follow-through. The ball bored low into the wind, curved leftward toward the flagstick— and disappeared.

"Oh, Lordy," I groaned. "The little bastard's run all the way over the green."

One of my amateur playing partners started waving his hands excitedly, shouting above the wind.

"No, no, no," he cried out. "I think you just knocked it in the hole. Go up and take a look."

Moments later, I stepped onto the putting surface, walked right past the flagstick, and peered at the embankment that sloped down to a water hazard on the far side of the green. My ball was not there. I groaned again. Then I turned around and headed back toward my golf bag to get another ball and check the rules sheet for the designated drop area. On my way past the pin, I decided to glance down into the cup just in case.

"Holy shit," I cried, blinking my eyes in disbelief at the white object below the lip. "The little bastard did go in the hole."

My amateur playing partners came over to offer their congratulations.

"I told you so," one of them reminded me, grinning. "Nice eagle."

When we got to the eleventh tee, Barfield and his group were still waiting on the threesome ahead of them. I told him what had just happened. Then I flipped my Bolles up and down and gave him a bear hug, chortling like Shane Bertsch.

"Guess even a blind pig finds an acorn every once in a while."

"You weren't no blind pig on that one," insisted the amateur who had called the ball in the hole. "That was a real nice shot."

"Owe it all to Jimmy here," I allowed. "He's the one who showed me how to hit a knockdown. Thanks again, big fella."

Barfield flashed one of his toothy grins, pawing me on the back.

"You're welcome, young man," he said.

In the venerable history of the game of golf, there have been a number of mighty and decisive blows that have turned around major championships—and in some cases, entire careers. Among them was the 175-yard iron Bobby Jones hit from a fairway bunker on the seventeenth hole at Royal Lytham and St. Annes to set up his victory in the 1926 British Open. Another was the 250-yard four wood that Gene Sarazen hit in the 1935 Masters to hole out for a double-eagle on the par-five fifteenth. Both shots have been acclaimed in golfing annals as "The Shot" of their respective years and duly memorialized with plaques beside their respective sites.

The knockdown nine iron I holed on the tenth at Palisades was neither as long nor as historically important as the Jones and Sarazen shots, but its impact on me was almost as monumental. That single and singular blow not only turned around my day, it reversed the terrible slide I had been undergoing in tournament after tournament. Like Sarazen's double-eagle, it marked the beginning, not the end, of a series of triumphant shots. For just as Sarazen had to survive a playoff against Craig Wood the following day to win the 1935 Masters, I had to survive the last eight holes at Palisades to insure that my golfing fortunes were once again on the ascent.

I ended up feeling even more proud of my performance on those last eight holes than of my eagle on number ten. Nicely struck or not, my knockdown nine iron shot had been a classic lucky break; the best I could have reasonably expected to make without a dash of serendipity was an easy birdie. My play on holes eleven through eighteen, however, was the result of all the new knowledge, experience, and instruction I had gleaned over many months.

Instead of chunking my approach shot into the water hazard on eleven for the second day in a row, I armed myself with plenty of club and went for the middle of the green. On twelve, a terrifying 450-yard par four, I exploded from a downhill lie in the left greenside bunker to within a foot of the pin. I made an almost equally satisfying par save on the sixteenth, where I got down in two putts from a mound of green above the hole that was so hardpacked and steeply sloping my spikes could scarcely keep me from falling off it. On number eighteen, where I had had to come in with a five iron the day before, I drove the ball far enough to go with a pitching wedge on my second shot, and hit it stiff.

Despite jacking a five-footer for birdie on eighteen (one of my amateur playing partners later claimed my ball bounced off a spike mark), I now had cause to quit cursing the divine and thank the golf gods for smiling down upon me. I carded a two-under-par 34 on the back side, the lowest nine-hole score in round two of the tournament. My eighteen-hole total of 75 was one stroke too high to claim a share of second-day money, but I did take a skin worth $26.50 for my eagle on the tenth.

That night, I celebrated my miraculous turnaround by treating Barry Hamilton to a four-course dinner at a fancy Italian joint across the street from Church Street Station in Orlando. After apologizing for my rude behavior on the practice range the previous afternoon, I popped open a bottle of champagne and toasted him for being a friend in need and deed. Then I telephoned Mike Thompson and Jim Barfield and Loretta Sturgill, and thanked them all for believing in me when I had lost faith in myself.

The next morning, I stopped by one of the local Edwin Watts golf shops on my way out of town. Everyone had been telling me that I was too hard on myself; I decided it was time to treat myself to a present. Combined with my skin at Grenelefe and my second-day money check from Bay Tree, my skin at Palisades had increased my total winnings to only $193.50. All I could afford was a little present, but I found an appropriately meaningful one: a $19.95 copper bracelet.

The pamphlet that came with my purchase claimed the copper bracelet would prevent and/or alleviate the symptoms of otherwise incurable arthritis and rheumatism. Since I had been plagued with just about every other golf-related physical affliction, I figured it made sense to avoid those two if possible. But my real reasons for buying the bracelet were symbolic and cosmetic. This was the one piece of jewelry many of the players on the big-league tours wore. It was a mark of being a pro. Feeling like Prince Hal on his way to fulfilling his destiny in *Henry V*, I slipped the copper strip around my wrist, climbed into my rental car, and watched the bright metal glitter in the sun beaming through the windshield as I drove south to the site of the Doral qualifier.

"**H**ey, pro—how's it going?"

Dan Wilkins strode through the predawn darkness enveloping The Club at Emerald Hills in Hollywood, Florida, like a man on a mission. It was not quite 6:30 A.M. on Monday, February 26, and the full moon in the making was shrouded by a foggy mist. Only moderately tall but supple in the forearms, torso, and legs, Wilkins was dressed in tan slacks and a windbreaker with the collar of a pastel golf shirt poking out the top. He had a pair of wraparound Bolles identical to mine propped on top of his brown-haired head, and a businesslike look on his flat, lightly freckled face.

As the club's head professional, Wilkins had come to assist officials from the local PGA section in organizing the eighteen-hole qualifying round for the Doral Ryder Open. He had also come to play in the qualifier against the other 179 men competing at Emerald Hills for three of the four available spots. The fourth qualifying spot would simultaneously be contested by 56 men at Inverrary in nearby Lauderdale Hills.

"Up early today, huh, pro," Wilkins muttered on his way past the putting green. "Thought I'd be the first one here."

I stared blankly at him for three or four seconds until I realized that he was talking to me. No one had ever addressed me as "pro" before. The experience sent a warm tingle up my spine and across the back of my neck.

"Got paired in the first group off number one tee at seven-thirty," I moaned, shaking my groggy head. "Who the hell did I piss off?"

Wilkins answered my complaint with a knowing smile.

"That's good for you," he said. "The wind usually doesn't pick

up around here until after 9 A.M. You can make some birdies on
the front nine, get yourself two or three under par, and have a
good chance of qualifying if you can make it around the back side
without any bogeys."

Wilkins informed me that in past years the players who shot
69 or better on the par-72 Emerald Hills course had invariably qualified for Doral. Then he added, "If you shoot 70, you'll probably be
in a playoff."

I nodded solemnly, trying my best to look like the seasoned
pro Wilkins had mistaken me for being, and started toward the
practice tee to warm up.

"Play good, pro," I called over my shoulder.

"You, too, pro," Wilkins returned.

Less than a week before, the idea of my shooting a 69 or a 70
to qualify for a PGA Tour tournament would have been more pre-
posterous than the notion that I might replace Troy Aikman and
quarterback the Dallas Cowboys to the next Super Bowl. But in the
past few days, I had begun to feel more like a real pro and actually
play like one, too.

On Thursday afternoon, Bart Richardson, a former Texas junior
golf buddy turned Florida real estate developer, had arranged for
us to get on the par-72 Dunes Course at Palm Beach Polo and Country Club. I had shot two under par from the tips, which were set
up at over 7,000 yards long. Combined with my 34 on the inward
nine in the second round of the 40+ Tour tournament at Palisades,
that put me at four under for my last forty-five holes of no-
mulligan, play-them-as-they-lie golf.

My practice rounds at Emerald Hills had been somewhat spotty
due to the disorienting nature of the locale. The whole scene had
a sepia-tinted, time warp quality, like a clip from *Good-bye, Colum-
bus* or an old Robert Wagner film. The early-1960s-vintage cube-
shaped clubhouse was trimmed with glass bricks and surrounded
by dead or dying palmetto clumps. The porte corchere was constantly bustling with bleached blondes in Corvettes and ragtop Jag-
uars, and there was a burbling interior waterfall where blue-haired
old ladies whined about the perpetual tardiness of their luncheon
companions.

The golf course, however, seemed to suit me from tee to Bermuda grass green. It was a narrow guage track crisscrossed by tree-
shaded lanes variously lined with post–World War II vacation
bungalows and modernesque red-tile-roofed condos. From the

markers selected for the Doral qualifier, it measured about 6,800 yards, or roughly the same length as the 40+ Tour courses I had been tuning up on. There were water hazards fronting or flanking the relatively tiny, double-tiered putting surfaces on three of the par-five holes, which neutralized the easy birdie opportunities for long hitters. And the longest par fours were all within four iron approach range for short knockers like me.

Shortly before seven A.M., the first rays of sun streaked over the horizon, and some of my fellow competitors began to join me on the Emerald Hills practice range. According to the pairings sheet, the field promised to include several players who had been on and off the PGA Tour in recent years. Adam Armogast, a smug thirty-two-year-old former All American at the University of Florida, was short in stature and short off the tee, but he also boasted one of the best short games of any pro on the minor-league circuits. Chris DiMarco, age twenty-six, another former All American at Florida, had finished eighty-fifth on the PGA Tour money list in 1994 but had lost his card in 1995 and failed to regain it at Q School back in December. Bart Bryant was an up-and-coming Orlando-based pro and the younger brother of Tour veteran Brad Bryant, a.k.a. "Dr. Dirt."

The would-be Doral qualifier closest to me in experience and playing ability, however, was thirty-six-year-old Ivan Lendl from Czechoslovakia, the former number-one-ranked tennis player in the world. I had met Ivan following a warm-up tournament at Emerald Hills on Sunday afternoon, and bonded with him almost immediately. In sharp contrast to his Ice Man image on the tennis court, he couldn't have been friendlier or more good-humored about his so-far-mediocre two-year-long record as a professional golfer. "I have no business being pro," Ivan had admitted during lunch in the clubhouse. "But I feel I have to play as a pro because I had a contract with Ram from tennis which included a set of golf clubs."

Ivan told me he had started playing golf back in the early 1980s as a way to relax between matches. After a back injury forced his retirement from tennis, he had started taking golf lessons at a course near his home in Connecticut. In 1995, he had gone to David Leadbetter for more advanced instruction. Renowned for his power game in tennis, he was not exceptionally long off the tee, but he had a gifted touch around the greens. And oddly enough, he played golf from "the wrong side" of the ball as a southpaw. "I can't explain why I decided to play left-handed," Ivan had confided, "I don't think it is because my right hand is stronger. But my mother is a left-hander and so is one of my daughters."

Despite his relative lack of big-league golfing experience, Ivan approached the game with the same highly competitive determination he had displayed in his tennis career. He told me he practiced a minimum of three hours per day, spending the vast majority of that tme on his short game. ("I am always having to grind for pars, but I don't mind—that's the way you get better.") In the summer, he played on the North Atlantic Tour in New York and the New England states. In the winter, he played on the South Florida PGA Tour against veterans like Armogast.

"I love this game as much as I love tennis," Ivan had declared. "The thing that is similar is the role of will. You have to will the ball close to the hole, and you have to make yourself hit good shots. The difference is that there is not so much margin for errors. In tennis, I can whiff thirty forehands and still win 6-2, 6-2. You hit two bad shots in golf and you're done. For me, golf is also more mentally challenging. My second tournament as a pro was a qualifier for the U.S. Open, and I have never been more nervous in any sporting event in my life. I couldn't even see the ball on the first tee."

Like most touring pros, Ivan had complained about the loneliness of being on the road without his family. He had noted that situation was only that much worse due to the fact that, like me, he had mostly been carding scores in the high 70s and low 80s in pro tournaments. "I would like to be with my wife and kids all the time, but it's hard for them to travel because the oldest is only six years old," he had said, adding, "I feel bad when I shoot a high number. I don't like to call home and say that I shot 82 today. It makes me feel guilty."

Unlike me, Ivan had drawn a postnoon starting time for the Doral qualifier, which meant that I would be finished with my round before he even teed off. Although my foursome would have an open course ahead of us unblemished by spike marks, both my body and my brain would have preferred to trade groups with Ivan. I had spent Sunday night in a motel less than ten minutes' drive from the golf course, but I still had to set the alarm for 5:30 A.M.

in order to complete my daily regimen of stretches and one thousand stomach crunches.

These minor personal hardships, however, paled in comparison to the guilt I felt when I saw my erstwhile coach, mentor, and friend Eden Foster approach the Emerald Hills practice range rubbing sleep from the corners of his eyes. Several months back, just before closing down The Maidstone Club for the off-season, Eden had offered to caddy for me in the Doral qualifier. He and his wife, Laurie, were spending the winter in Naples, on the opposite coast of the Florida peninsula, which meant that he, too, had had to rise at 5:30 A.M. to get there in time to loop for me.

"Mornin'," Eden mumbled, tugging at the hand towel hanging from the belt loop of his khaki shorts. "Wha's happening?"

I started chortling like Shane Bertsch.

"Oh, just hanging out in the dew. Thought we might take a little stroll in a few minutes—if you're up for it."

Eden answered me with a game face stare.

"I'm ready, man," he said.

I stopped clowning and looked him in the eye.

"Good. I'm ready, too."

"Okay, then. Let's go qualify for Doral."

at the stroke of 7:30 A.M., I stepped onto the first tee at Emerald Hills with driver in hand and my own game face focused on a hurricane fence that was just beginning to become visible through the rising mist. The opening hole was a 558-yard par five that angled in a sharp dogleg left about 250 yards off the tee. A stand of hanging oaks guarded the inside corner. A rectangular pond lined the left side of the chute that led to the green, and there was out of bounds marked by the fenceline along the right side of the chute.

My battle plan called for a deliberately conservative three-shot approach to the green. It was tempting to try to cut off a chunk of the dogleg by drawing your drive around the hanging oaks on the corner. A truly mighty blow might allow you to get very near the green on your second shot. But if your draw off the tee turned into a duck hook, your ball could get caught up in the branches, and you'd be looking at a costly bogey or maybe even a double. I wanted to get a nice solid par under my belt before shifting into an attack mode.

I took dead aim at one of the middle fence posts well to the right of the corner, a target line that allowed plenty of margin for error left. It was a wise choice. Most of my early-morning tee shots tended to slide to the right until I woke up enough to turn all the way through the ball at impact. But on this particular morning, my adrenaline was evidently flowing full bore. I not only got through the shot, I actually made it draw. My playing partners grunted approvingly as they watched my ball curve underneath the hanging oak to the left edge of the fairway.

"Good swing."

"Ball."

"Play."

I could tell from their jargon that all three men were pros. As I'd learned on the 40+ Tour, amateurs tended to praise their playing partners with overly enthusiastic phrases like "Great drive" or "Beautiful shot." Pros tended to be more restrained and succinct. They seldom even said "Good shot." They merely complimented your "good swing," or expressed appreciation for your shot trajectory or your strategy with shorthand terms for "good ball" and "smart play."

I had not bothered to find out any personal details about the men in my foursome prior to teeing off, and I was not interested in expanding my knowledge after we started down number-one fairway. I hadn't come to Emerald Hills to socialize; I was out there to qualify for the Doral Ryder Open.

I knew the tall guy with glasses and blondish hair was named Scott Spier and that he hailed from a town called Veirico, Florida. I learned that the skinny guy sharing my golf cart was Kevin Wood and that he had a club pro job somewhere up north during the summers where he had met Eden Foster. The third member of our group was a short, muscular, swarthy guy named Mike Malizia who hit one irons off the tee; I soon surmised on the basis of a frustrated and rather annoying remark Malizia would repeat time and again in the holes ahead that he had played on the PGA Tour in years past.

After making two more good swings with a three wood and a fifty-two-degree gap wedge, I got down in two putts from the back fringe of the first green for the solid par I'd wanted. Spier also parred, and Wood sunk a nice little twelve-footer for a bird. Malizia, however, stubbed a slightly shorter birdie putt and had to settle for a five. He then gave all of us an unsolicited hint as to why he was

having to sweat through another Monday qualifier instead of enjoying an exemption into the Doral Ryder Open.

"Look at that damn shit," he cursed, turning to his caddy and
shaking his head from side to side. "That's exactly why I lost my
card."

Eden winked at me and smiled, whispering that it was a good
thing for the PGA Tour that Malizia had lost his player's card. Then
he hopped on the bag rack of the golf cart I was sharing with Wood
to ride across the street to the next tee.

Number two fanned away from the cart path in another dogleg
left that was playing about 425 yards from our markers. A kidney-
shaped fairway bunker defied any attempt to cut the inside corner,
but the landing area to the right offered a spacious bailout area.
The real trouble awaited at the green. The putting surface slanted
precipitously from right to left, and it was protected by a centrally
positioned pot bunker about four feet deep. The pin setters had
planted the flagstick directly behind the pot, so I hit a hard five
iron second shot safely to the back middle about twenty feet above
the cup.

Wood happened to fly his second to a similar position just a
few inches outside my ball. I watched closely as his first putt slid
down the slope and curled in front of the cup, leaving him a three-
foot tap-in for par. Having gotten a good read off Wood's ball, I
chose to play mine a little more on the high side. It started out on
what appeared to be precisely the right line and for a full three
seconds I thought it was sure to fall in the hole. But at the last
instant, it picked up a burst of speed and missed the edge of the
cup by less than a millimeter.

"Oh, man, nice roll," Malizia blurted as my ball tumbled eight
more feet past. "Thought you had that one."

Moments later, I got a painful reminder that the difference between a great round and a mediocre one often boils down to just
a couple of lucky or unlucky breaks. I saw a little leftward slope
in my eight-foot uphiller to save par. Eden read it as straight in,
and advised me to hit the putt firmly. I nodded, and told myself to
keep my head down. Although I stroked the ball firmly, I never
heard the sweet plopping sound I was waiting for. When I finally
looked up, my ball was resting outside the left edge of the cup. A
momentum-building birdie had suddenly become a bogey.

I reckoned that I had to make at least a par on the 160-yard
third hole to stay in the qualifying hunt. Here again, Eden and I

had a difference of opinion. The pin was cut back right. I wanted to go straight at it with a six iron; he counseled me to hit a seven iron and keep it left. Though I was technically the boss, my caddie was also my teacher. My seven iron shot landed thirty feet below the hole, a one-club margin. A tentative first putt left me with another knee-knocker of roughly the same length as my uphiller on number two. Remembering my conversation with Ivan Lendl, I crouched over my second putt without bothering to get a read from Eden and simply willed the ball into the hole to save my three.

Now I was back on track, temporarily. The yardage book listed the fourth hole at 364 yards, which made it the shortest par four on the course. To my mind, it was also the trickiest and the most unfair hole on the course. The extremely tight landing area dipped into a crusty swale flanked by a bunker on the right. Set atop a pyramidal mound that rose a good fifty feet above fairway level, the green looked like the Egyptian pavillion at one of the amusement parks up in Orlando. Its steeply sloping perimeter could repel all but the most perfectly targeted invading balls.

I popped a kind of Corey Pavin drag bunt three wood off the tee, and given the towering elevation of the putting surface, elected to go with an easy seven iron approach from 135 yards out. The ball left the club face sounding a little thin, nicked the front fringe, then spun backward down the pyramidal embankment. Another half a foot of carry would have set up a makable birdie. Instead, I faced an uphill pitch-and-putt to save par. It was not a particularly demanding sequence of shots, but my short game failed me under the pressures of pro competition, and I wound up making my second bogey of the morning.

In past tournament rounds, this would have been the cue for John Daly to come into the game for Freddy Couples. I was two over after only four holes, and well aware that it would take at least two under or better to qualify for Doral. I felt the overheated glow of the I-don't-give-a-shit light starting to flicker inside my brain. But I refused to fold. While I might have already shot myself out of a chance to play in my first PGA Tour event, I vowed that my days of staggering home with ignominious scores in the 80s were over.

"Come on, let's regroup," I said to Eden on the next tee. "We can still get it back with a couple of quick birds."

"Yep," he replied. "Just keep it smooth."

My renewed resolve produced a display of bold shotmaking

that led my playing partners to believe that I might still be in contention after all. The fifth hole was a 548-yard dogleg left with a watery moat around the green that made it unreachable in two shots. I got away with a solid two-putt par there, then smacked a six iron to ten feet on the par-three sixth. Malizia hit an equally impressive tee shot on number six, only to lip out his birdie putt and remind us once again why he had lost his PGA Tour card. I also missed my bird, but shrugged it off and headed for the next tee.

Number seven, a 390-yard par four, offered a birdie opportunity only for the brave at heart. The fairway was bisected by an L-shaped lake that fronted the desired landing area and hugged the left side of the hole all the way up to the green. A row of mounds covered with Bermuda grass rough dotted the bailout area on the right. All three of my partners chose to play it safe by hitting long irons off the tee. I cracked a driver 270 yards straight down the middle, then punched a three-quarter pitching wedge to five feet. My birdie seemed so assured that the other members of my foursome were already walking off the green as I bent over my putt. I missed it on the low side.

"Shit, that really pisses me off," Eden groaned. "Who do those assholes think they are, walking off like that when you haven't even finished?"

I shrugged again, dismissing their breach of etiquette as merely another hardball move to write down in the book.

"Welcome to the big leagues, Eden old pal."

I completed the front side with testy par saves on the 440-yard eighth and the 418-yard ninth, getting up and down from jail cell lies in the green-side rough on both holes. As it turned out, my score of 38 was the low number in our foursome; Malizia was one stroke back with a 39. But Eden and I both knew that I needed to shoot for the pins on the back side to have any hope of qualifying.

We gave the inward nine a gallant run. After barely missing birdies on ten and eleven, I came to the 554-yard, par-five twelfth feeling more pumped up than a fire hose. A well-placed drive followed by a half-topped, worm-burning three wood advanced my ball to about 110 yards short of the pin. I went with a sand wedge and nailed it, hammering my ball straight over the pin and over the green. A sloppy chip and a misread putt led to my third bogey of the day. Undaunted, I smashed a 300-yard drive off the thirteenth tee, stuck my pitching wedge approach twelve-feet above the hole, and canned the birdie putt, pumping my fist in triumph.

By now, Malizia had mounted a charge of his own, draining birdies on eleven and thirteen to get back to one over par. Having gotten myself back to plus two, I could overtake him again and possibly put myself in contention to qualify with birdies on four of the last five holes, which included two par threes and a par five. On the tee of the 152-yard fourteenth, however, we were greeted by a swirling wind that confounded club selection. Eden and I finally decided on a smooth six iron. We held our breaths as my tee shot zoomed straight at the pin. The ball actually hit the top of the flagstick, then ricocheted into the back trap. The ill-fated bounce resulted in a fried egg lie. Rather than facing a desperately needed birdie opportunity, I was hard-pressed just to salvage a bogey.

Although my chances of qualifying had become more remote than those of an alligator in the middle of the Everglades, I ordered Daly to stay on the bench and kept trying to play the last four holes like Couples. My otherwise admirable plan was quickly made problematic by the adrenaline that kept rushing through my veins. Although I swung smoothly, I started to fly my iron shots almost as far as Freddy's. Every time Eden suggested a club, I took one less club, and still smacked the ball beyond my targets. But thanks to his calm and accurate readings of the greens, I made scrambling par saves on fifteen and sixteen, bounced a birdie pitch off the pin on seventeen, and negotiated a precarious two-putt par on eighteen.

I walked into the scorer's tent with a respectable three over par 75. That was low enough for the tournament officials to write my name on the leaderboard two slots behind Malizia, whose subpar second nine gave him a 73 for the day.

My second-place standing did not hold up for long. Adam Armogast, who had teed off in one of the other early-morning foursomes, fired a sizzling 65 to win medalist honors. Then Chris DiMarco came in with a 66 to take over second place. Before the day was done, three other players carded 67s to tie for the last qualifying spot. One of them was host pro Dan Wilkins, who made the turn in only one under, then birdied four of the last six holes on the inward nine. He eventually lost out to Bart Bryant in a marathon playoff that continued until dark and resumed the next morning.

*   *   *

despite failing to qualify, I left Emerald Hills with a sense of genuine accomplishment. It was one thing to shoot a 75 in a 40+ Tour tournament against a field of mostly older players, quite another to shoot the same score in a Monday qualifier for a PGA Tour event. I had finished in the upper third of a highly talented open field, and I had bested my latest alter ego, Ivan Lendl, who had carded a 77. As I bid good-bye to Eden under the porte cochere, the once-distracting sight of the club's resident bleached blondes zooming off in their vintage sports cars provided a perfect backdrop for our departure.

"We got some tough breaks." Eden sighed. "I don't know if you had a 67 in your bag, but with a little better luck we sure as shit could have shot a 69."

"Yeah, maybe," I replied, oggling a towhaired lass in a yellow Jag. "But we could have just as easily shot another 81 if we hadn't kept grinding after the bogeys on two and four. And you know what? If this had been last week, I probably would have."

That evening, I drove down to Miami, where the greatest golfers in the world were preparing for the start of the Doral Ryder Open. My hope was to learn something by watching the best in action even if my burning desire was still to battle them head-to-head out on the golf course one day. As I sped down Interstate 95, I flipped open my golfing journal, braced it against the steering wheel, and scribbled a line that reflected the new meaning of the bright metal copper bracelet glittering on my wrist.

"Today," I wrote, "I finally became a real pro."

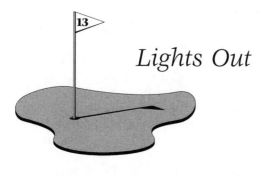

Lights Out

the Shark knew the best way to approach the Blue Monster, and it was not by land or by sea. The fastest and most direct route for Greg Norman was by air. It was also the most breathtaking. After climbing into his $4 million twin-engine Bell 230 helicopter and zooming down the Florida coastline from his home in Hobe Sound at 140 knots, he merely had to veer several degrees south by southwest to get a panoramic overview of the lush green Doral Golf Resort and Spa sprawling across the lakelands next to the Miami International Airport.

Norman needed only a few more quick flicks of the control stick to have the chopper hovering over Doral's signature hole, the water-lined, 425-yard, par-four eighteenth, which had been the scene of so many monumental triumphs and tragedies. From there, it was almost as easy as a pitch and a putt to set down across the street from the four-story pink-tile-roofed clubhouse and make his grand entrance to the cheers of 35,000 golf fans.

When I arrived in the media room on the Tuesday afternoon prior to the start of the 1996 Doral Ryder Open, Norman was sitting up on the stage next to Raymond Floyd. Although they had just competed in a skins game with John Daly and Fred Couples, most of the questions from the two dozen assembled reporters were about Norman's record the year before and his outlook on the year ahead. The tone of his answers was upbeat, but his animated, deeply dimpled face looked rather pale in the wake of a viral infection that had recently sidelined him for ten days.

"If you have a bad year, you forget about it," Norman was saying, brushing a lock of shiny blond hair from his forehead. "If you have a good year, same thing. You can feed off positives, but I like to have a fresh approach to the year. I'm not one to look back too much."

In 1995, Norman had walked away with Player of the Year honors thanks to performances most other golfers would have loved to look back on. Despite entering only sixteen events, he had finished number one on the 1995 PGA Tour money list with $1.6 million, and had overtaken Tom Kite as the number-one money winner of all time, with more than $9.5 million in official career earnings, a figure itself eclipsed by the tens of millions more he had earned in commercial endorsements and private investments. The Shark had also brought the Blue Monster to its knees in the not-too-distant past, shooting a course record 62 to take first place in 1990, then winning again in 1993.

In 1995, however, the Monster had bitten back. Norman had come into the eighteenth hole in the final round at Doral with a one-stroke lead. After driving into a snarl of heavy rough, he had yanked his approach shot into the water en route to a double-bogey that handed the championship to Nick Faldo. He had then gone on to suffer more disappointments in the four majors, tying for third at the Masters, blowing a final-round lead at the U. S. Open, and failing to contend for the lead at the British Open and the PGA.

At the age of forty-one, Greg Norman had a marketing name on a par with Arnold Palmer and Jack Nicklaus, and an international image that transcended the game of golf. Along with designing a score of courses around the globe, his corporate persona, Great White Shark Enterprises, would soon be debuting a line of sportswear intended to compete with Calvin Klein and Donna Karan. But even though he had topped the Sony World Rankings for a record 266 weeks, he rankled at having only two major championships to his credit, the 1986 and 1993 British Opens, compared to Nicklaus's eighteen major championships and Palmer's six.

"Before coming here, I've been working quietly on my game because of what we all know is coming up in a few weeks," Norman said, alluding to the 1996 Masters, which would start on April 11. "I'm excited about playing this year. I think I'm a very confident individual. I'm a believer in my ability and I have a strong passion for the game. I hope it gives me an edge."

According to a report in *Sports Illustrated*, Norman had recently "fired" Butch Harmon, his swing coach for the past four years. Butch had told me that he had just changed from being a full-time coach to a part-time consultant. Whatever the case, the Shark informed his audience in the Doral media room that he had been working out in his private gym six days a week and "pushing just a little bit harder" in his ball striking sessions on the practice range.

When the floor was opened to questions, I asked Norman about the current status of his relationship with Cobra Golf. Back in 1991, the Shark had given the then-struggling equipment maker a financial shot in the arm by purchasing a 12 percent interest for $1.9 million. In late 1995, Cobra Golf had been acquired by American Brands, the owner of Titleist and Footjoy, for a reported $700 million in cash.

"I am no more on the board of Cobra," Norman said, "but I still have my contract with Maxfli to play their balls, and I would rather stay with Cobra clubs until the day I stop playing golf."

One of the reporters in the back of the room shouted out a question pertaining to Norman's personal gain in the Cobra–American Brands deal.

"Hey, Greg, tell us, how does it feel to make twenty-six million?"

"Who said it was twenty-six?" Norman shot back.

"Well, how much was it?"

"I'd rather not say. Any good investigative reporter could find that out with a little digging."

"One way a good investigative reporter might try to find that out," I interjected, "is to ask an authoritative source such as yourself. Besides, it was all publicly traded stock anyway, wasn't it?"

"Yes, the stock was all public."

"Well, then, how much was it?"

Norman stared at me, his crystal-blue eyes glinting.

"I made just about forty million," he said. Then he added with a deep-dimpled grin, "Last year was the most exciting year of my life, flying out to the Cobra board of directors meetings in San Diego that were highly confidential because of what was happening with American Brands. You don't have the opportunity to do that very often. When you play business and hit a bad shot, you may not get to hit another one."

Norman went on to insist that the $40 million he had made on the Cobra sale was not such an enormous sum of money in the grand scheme of things. "It's a very expensive world out there. That little bit can go very quickly, and you're back to square zero. I still remember when I was making twenty-eight dollars a week and I was eight hundred down on the golf course. But I hate talking about money. I don't think it's anybody's business. It doesn't affect the way I play, and it doesn't affect the way I live my life. If it does, I'll have to reassess."

Twenty-four hours later, I had to reassess my view of Greg Norman, an exercise that I would repeat many times in the months ahead. It was common knowledge that the Shark was not the most popular player on the PGA Tour; in fact, his only close friend was his Florida neighbor Nick Price. I could easily see why he might evoke that basest of all emotions, male jealousy. He was handsome, talented, rich, famous. He was the kind of guy who seemed to be good at everything. And as I soon discovered, he was also hyper-sensitive.

We were standing eyeball-to-eyeball on the practice putting green at Doral. I had just introduced myself as one of the reporters who had been asking him about Cobra Golf at the press conference the day before. The morning editions of some of the local news-papers had made headlines out of Norman's "revelation" of netting $40 million on the sale to American Brands, and he was in the process of chewing my head off.

"The next time, I wish you'd just pull me aside instead of ask-ing me questions like that in front of forty people," he snarled. "There are a lot of kooks out there, and I've got to be protective of my wife and family."

Norman's reaction really threw me for a loop. He had arrived at Doral in a private helicoptered fanfare. He had often boasted of owning his own private jet, a second helicopter, and half a dozen Ferraris. He had been photographed flying fighter jets off the decks of aircraft carriers. And now he was suggesting that I had endan-gered his family's security by asking a few follow-up questions about a transaction that had already been widely reported in both the financial and golf press.

"I don't see why I always have to be defending myself to the media," Norman complained. "I'm really getting sick and tired of constantly correcting all the facts they get wrong about me."

Seeing Norman up close was also something of a shock, his diatribe notwithstanding. Prior to our run-in the day before, I had seen him only on television. He had always appeared to fill up the TV screen with his booming drives, his broad-brimmed akubra hat, and a build that seemed to resemble the physique of a middle-weight boxer. In person, the Shark looked downright minnowy, more like a ballet dancer. Although his shoulders were clearly quite muscular, their breadth was accentuated by his extraordinarily narrow hips and slim torso, and even with his trademark hat on, he was much shorter than my own measured height of 6'2".

"Look, man, you don't have to defend yourself to me," I said, holding up my palms in a sign of mock surrender. "I happen to think you handle yourself pretty damn well, especially considering the spotlight you're always under. One of the things I wanted to tell you is that I believe you deserve every penny you made off the sale of Cobra Golf. The second thing I wanted to say is that I'm glad you invested in them way back when because Cobra's been very supportive of me and this little project I'm in the middle of right now."

I started to give Norman a quick synopsis of my ongoing attempt to make a golfing comeback, and once again his reaction disarmed me. I expected the Shark to nod politely for a second or two, then blow me off. Instead, he listened attentively, grinning and chuckling as I recounted some of the recent highlights and lowlights of my quest. Sensing that the iciness between us might be melting, I informed the biggest moneymaker in golf, age forty-one, that he was looking at the smallest moneymaker, age forty-four.

"My total winnings to date are exactly $193.50," I said.

Norman leaned on his putter and roared with laughter.

"Well, at least it's a start," he allowed. "Keep me posted on how you do."

I shook Norman's outstretched hand, promising to send him a copy of the article I'd written for *Sports Illustrated* about my misadventures at Q School. Then I wished him luck in the tournament and retreated behind the ropes.

Over the next four days, the Shark threw me and just about everyone else in the golfing world for several more loops. He started the 1996 Doral Ryder Open on Thursday morning with a five-under-par 67, only to find himself in a tie for eleventh place, four strokes behind first-round leader Lee Janzen, who shot an even more incredible 63. On Friday, while Janzen was soaring to a 76, he fired a 69 that moved him into a tie for fourth with Vijay Singh. (I noted, by the way, that Monday qualifiers Adam Armogast and Bart Bryant missed the two-day cut of even par by a single stroke, while Chris DiMarco missed by three.)

On Saturday, the third round of the Doral Ryder Open was interrupted by a torrential thunderstorm as Norman's group stepped onto the fifteenth tee. Play was suspended for the rest of the day, forcing him to complete the last four holes of round three on Sunday morning. Both Norman and Singh carded scores of 67, which put them in a tie for the lead going into the fourth round later that same day.

By then, I'd spent several hours watching Norman out on the course, trying to identify all the factors that separated his scoring ability from mine. One of them was the unheralded strength of his short game. His high-arching 300-yard drives might awe the galleries and move TV commentators to gush with encomiums of praise. But I was more impressed with the way the Shark clenched his jaws and got down to business every time he missed a green in regulation. I saw him save pars from calf-high rough and downhill lies in the trap. I marveled at the way he turned a likely bogey into an unlikely birdie by blading a sand wedge from the fringe into the cup.

But for all his timely scrambling, I could also see that Norman was not happy about the way he had been striking the ball off the tee. As he walked out of the scorer's tent on Sunday morning after finishing off his rain-delayed third round, he spotted Butch Harmon up in one of the nearby broadcasting towers doing commentary for a News Corp. television unit. The Shark beckoned his allegedly fired former mentor to come down from the tower and follow him out to the practice range.

"Greg was complaining that he didn't have anything on his drives and that Vijay was outhitting him by sixty yards," Butch told me afterward. "As it turned out, Greg was aiming so far right, he had to come over the top with his right shoulder just to get the ball in the fairway. First, I helped Greg straighten out his alignment.

Then he called his wife back at home in Hobe Sound and told her to get four of the new King Cobra Titanium drivers from his work-bench and bring them down to Doral in their other helicopter. Greg hit seven shots on the practice range with one of the drivers and decided to go with it."

That afternoon, Norman played lights out. He made seven bird-ies in seventeen holes and, by his own account, "never missed a shot on the tee" with his new driver. Coming into the Blue Mon-ster's eighteenth hole, he held a three-stroke lead over Singh and twenty-nine-year-old Michael Bradley. Rather than risk a repeat of his 1995 disaster, he took a cautious three-shot route around the lake and onto the green, then two-putted for a bogey. His final-round 66 was good enough for a two-stroke victory.

On Sunday night, as Norman celebrated his third Doral Ryder Open win, he announced that he was already looking forward to the 1996 Masters. "I know April is five weeks away," he told re-porters inside the media room. "But time flies out here on the tour, especially when I'm playing three weeks in a row. And playing three weeks in a row, you don't have a whole lot of time to work on your game. So I know that I've got to start getting ready now, because it takes a good two or three weeks to get to where I'd like to get."

the morning after Norman reconquered Doral, I teed off in the Monday qualifier for the Honda Classic at Inverrary Country Club in Lauderdale Hills. The lair of the late Jackie Gleason had long since sacrificed its original "How sweet it is" charm to an onslaught of high-rise and low-rise condominiums. The surroundings now re-sembled a cross between a prison colony for senior citizens and a clash of competing franchise unit designs for the International House of Pancakes.

Like the Shark, I quickly realized that it was going to take me at least two or three more weeks—and possibly several more months—to get where I wanted to get. Even though my buddy Bart Richardson was housing me and looping for me, I also began to feel the mental and physical toll of being on the road for over four straight weeks. The weather bureau had issued day-long gale warn-ings, and caught between the ravages of nature and the similarly unruly behavior of one of the local residents, I kept losing my rhythm, my concentration, and my balls.

On our second hole of the day, a double-dogleg par five, I duck-hooked my tee shot toward the out of bounds stakes fronting a prison colony–style high rise on the left. Bart noticed an elderly man in a mix-and-match striped shirt and shorts wandering around in front of the building hunting for stray golf balls. I asked if he had picked up any balls in the last few moments. He looked at me with the innocent smile of the truly guilty, reached into the left pocket of his shorts, and pulled out a mud-splattered Top Flite.

"Is this it?"

"No, sir," I replied. "Have you picked up any other balls?"

The man reached back into the same pocket and pulled out a beat-up old Wilson Staff. That wasn't it, either. I asked him to try his other pocket. With the baleful frown of a burglar caught in the act, the man reached into his right side pocket and pulled out a shiny new white Maxfli stenciled with a blue *H.*

"Now, sir, we're playing in a tournament," I informed him. "It's very important that you tell me where you found that ball. Was it in bounds or out of bounds?"

"Oh, in bounds," the man assured me, pointing to a spot several yards farther up the left-side rough. "It was right over there next to that tree."

Remarkably enough, I almost made a birdie on the hole after dropping my ball on the spot the man had indicated, wondering all the while why he had picked up the damn thing if it had been in bounds all along. Two holes later, I hit another duck hook and started wishing that the old fellow would reappear to bless me with another lost-and-found drop. It was not to be. I foozled my way to the first of two straight double-bogeys and wound up staggering in with a weary, wind-battered 84.

The day after my implosion at Inverrary, I returned to Sag Harbor hoping to regroup amid the comforts of home. Although Alision welcomed my arrival with a feast of roast lamb, mint jelly, string beans, mashed potatoes, and espresso chocolate swirl ice cream, Mother Nature once again bared her teeth. The landscape was already soggy from a second straight winter of record snowfall, but there were still additional tons of white stuff on the way. It snowed intermittently throughout the month of March. It snowed on Easter Sunday, April 7. Then it snowed again two days later.

The intractable weather forced me to spend most of my time indoors rather than out on the golf course. My personal trainer, Joe C., made sure that it was time well spent. He studied the sequence photographs I had collected of Greg Norman and created a new series of medicine ball tosses and torso twists designed to sculpt my body into the streamlined shape of the Shark's. Although there was no chance that a stranger passing by in an airport might mistake me for Norman anytime in the near future, I started to gain much greater strength and flexibility.

When the snow temporarily melted off, I charged out to Barcelona Neck and played all nine holes with one club, my trusty King Cobra five iron. The Tour Model mashie became the next best thing to a magic wand. I used it to hit low rolling draws from 185 yards, high fading cut shots from 145, bump and runs from 125, and chip shots from the fringe. Even though I left my putter in the Jeep, I soon got proficient enough with the five iron to break 40 with ease.

I also played imaginary major championships of short game skill against Norman with my sand wedge. After blading several pressure-packed bunker shots, I telephoned Dick Harmon for advice. He told me to pretend that he was standing about three feet behind me propping a rake at a 60 degree angle to the sand; the idea was to break my wrists quickly so that my backswing was as steep as the rake handle. Once I got the hang of it, my bunker play became like child's play on the beach, and the Shark was dead meat.

Every so often, I ran into Toad and Sandy somewhere in town. The two of them invariably acted like lovebirds, holding hands and eyeing each other with desire, and Toad invariably chided me that my problems out on the pro golf tour were all in my head. But I sensed that there was trouble in paradise. When I pulled Toad aside to ask if things were all right, he insisted that he was doing just fine, then added in a tone that signaled his reluctance to elaborate further, "Sandy ain't feelin' so great lately, though."

On Sunday, April 14, I packed my bags and flew back down to Orlando, where I was scheduled to play in another series of 40+

Tour tournaments prior to entering the Monday qualifier for the Shell Houston Open. It so happened that Norman and Faldo were teeing off in the final round of the 1996 Masters just as I was piling into my rental car at the airport. The Shark had a six-stroke lead, and I had heard through my hometown grapevine that Butch Harmon was planning to join him in Butler Cabin when he put on the Masters champion's green jacket.

By the time I arrived at Heathrow Country Club, the situation down in Augusta was changing dramatically. Faldo had bogeyed the fifth hole, but his miscue had been offset by birds on two, six, and eight, and he was making the turn at two under par. Norman had bogeyed the opening hole, birdied the second, then faltered again with bogeys on number four and number nine. He was now two over on the day, and his lead had dwindled to two strokes.

The Shark's stunning reversal of fortune created an unanticipated dilemma for me. To watch or not to watch? Although I had never set foot on Heathrow Country Club before, I had heard there was water on fourteen holes. The only way I could hope to make a decent showing in the 40+ Tour tournament the following morning was to play a practice round so I could find my layup areas. I had originally planned to watch the highlights of Norman's presupposed victory march on the evening news. But if I went out on the course at this point, I might miss one of the most thrilling finishes in golf history.

After mulling it over for a few minutes, I decided to stick with Plan A. Something told me that the Shark was going to self-destruct on the back nine. The last thing I needed to see before teeing it up in my first pro tournament in over a month was the tragic spectacle of my sometimes adversarial idol choking away another major championship. If, on the other hand, Norman pulled himself together and held on, the finish would be merely anticlimactic. Should he and Faldo wind up tied after seventy-two holes, I could probably finish my practice round in time to watch the playoff.

In retrospect, my decision to proceed with my practice round at Heathrow was the wisest move I had ever made in golf. Jim Barfield and Loretta Sturgill came out to greet me on the back porch of their condo, overlooking the sixteenth hole, and filled me in on the gory details of the Shark's final-round 78 and Faldo's come-from-behind victory. By that time, I had become resigned to the fact that the severe penal style of the 6,800-yard Heathrow course made it unlikely that I would achieve my goal of shooting an even-par 72 in the morning. My revised goal was just to work on my game some more and try to shoot a 75.

"Y'all got more water out here than fairway grass," I teased Barfield. "When I get back to the hotel, I'm gonna have to give my golf balls the old Trevino toilet treatment."

"What's that?" he asked.

"I'm gonna dunk 'em all in the commode like Lee used to do so they won't get thirsty and decide to go in the drink tomorrow."

When I got back to my room in a nearby Ramada Inn later that evening, I decided that it made better sense just to rinse my sleeves of Maxflis in the bathroom sink. Then I cleaned my clubs and flopped down onto the bed to watch TV. Every time a clip from the Masters appeared on the screen, I immediately changed the channel. Shortly before 11 P.M., I turned out the lights, closed my eyes, and tried to visualize my tournament round hole by hole.

The early-morning haze wrapped Heathrow's well-scrubbed red-brick clubhouse in a soft, surrealistic halo. Although the forecast called for a warming trend, the air was still cool and moist, and beads of condensation glistened on the lampposts in the parking lot. The property was triangulated by a shopping center, a sprawling mid-rise office park, and a subdivision of private homes under construction, and I could hear nail guns hammering and radios blaring as the 40+ Tour starter, Patrick Staveley, called my foursome's 8:20 A.M. starting time.

My stomach felt slightly nauseous from a breakfast of bananas and decaffeinated instant coffee, and the excessive number of mulligans I'd hit during my practice round the previous afternoon had reaggravated an old shoulder injury. Upon arriving at the driving range, I had put on a lightweight blue sweater to help warm up and loosen my back muscles. But the sun was just now starting to burn through the haze, and my golf shirt was getting soaked with sweat. I decided to take off the sweater.

"Hey, man, turn around for a second," Patrick called out as I steered my golf cart to the first tee. "It looks like you spilled coffee all over your shoulder."

The 40+ Tour starter was a compact, clean-shaven fellow in his early thirties, neatly dressed with brushed-back brown hair. He stared at me with a bemused smile.

"Nah, not to worry, young man," I said, deciding at that very moment to put my sweater back on. "It's just a big glob of Tiger Balm us oldsters use."

Patrick nodded and winked at me, then introduced my assigned playing partners. The elder statesman of the three was Jay Moore, a short, white-haired fifty-one-year-old pro from Tampa who had twice finished second in the World Putting Championship back in 1981 and 1982. Moore was nattily attired in a silver shirt and slacks and custom made white shoes with gold plated toes. The junior member of our group was forty-one-year-old Rick Powers, a tall, blond, transplanted Pennsylvanian who bore a striking resemblance to the baseball pitcher Roger Clemens. My cart mate was Dr. Jon Buchman, a forty-nine-year-old with black hair, a black mustache, and a brooding demeanor. At first glance, I figured he had to be a shrink, but it turned out that he was a dentist.

Our foursome happened to be the last group to tee off, so we had the entire field in front of us. As usual, I wanted to get a nice routine par in the can to settle my nervous system, especially since this was just a one-day, eighteen-hole event. Number one afforded a fairly easy go at it if you didn't get greedy. It was a 397-yard dogleg-left par four with an upsloping bunker on the inside corner and an elevated green. On the practice range, most of my drives had been drifting right, so I aimed halfway between the right edge of the bunker and the middle of the fairway. Like a flashback to the Doral qualifier, my tee shot jumped to the left and rounded the corner, prompting a chorus of admiring grunts from my playing partners.

The opportunity to make a routine par quickly evaporated when I found my ball in a hanging lie formed by the upslope of a tiny furrow cutting across the width of the fairway. The hanging lie caused my eight iron to catch a fat wad of grass, and my approach shot stopped forty feet short of the pin, which was tucked in the back right corner of the green. My first putt barely covered three-quarters of the required distance, and I found myself facing exactly the kind of situation I had hoped to avoid, a tricky ten-footer to save par on the very first hole of the day. Miraculously, it went in.

"Thank you, Lord," I whispered, pretending to scratch my face while actually making a grateful Sign of the Cross.

The second hole was a 527-yard par five that curved to the right over a lake the size of the nearby shopping center parking lot. This time my drive did slide to the starboard side of the fairway, leaving me only 220 yards from the green. It was tempting to go for it in two, but the shot was almost all carry and the hour was awfully early. I decided instead to hit my trusty King Cobra five iron over the near left corner of the lake. Then I spun a sand wedge to six feet and made the birdie putt, silently complimenting myself for following what Butch Harmon would surely have endorsed as sound course management procedures.

On number three, I whalloped a drive that outdistanced the tee shots of my playing partners by a good twenty yards. The 453-yard par four was another dogleg right around a lake, and the fairway yardage marker showed me with 154 left to the pin. I knew from my practice round, however, that the hole played long, so I chose a smooth six iron for my approach and stuck it within seven feet of the flag. Before the work crews across the street could reload their nail guns, I was in the hole for another birdie.

Number four, a 165-yard par three, confronted me with my third major decision-making crisis of the morning. The wind was quartering against us from right to left, but it felt pretty light on my face, and I knew its direction would help promote a draw. My macho side argued for a hard six iron, while my smarter side insisted it was a smooth five. I elected to go with the club that had proved to be my magic wand back at Barcelona Neck, and watched with an almost mystical inner peace as my ball sailed right toward the flagstick and disappeared behind the hump of the front green-side bunker.

"Goddamn, you just hit the pin!" Jay Moore exclaimed. "I think it might have gone in."

I shrugged, having lost sight of the ball after it cleared the bunker.

"Just hope the sucker stopped somewhere on the putting surface."

Jay stared back at me, shaking his head from side to side.

"Sure wish you'd give me some of that shit you've got on your shoulder," he said. "Stuff must be pretty powerful."

When Dr. Jon Buchman pulled our golf cart to a stop beside the green a few moments later, I spied my three playing partners' balls lying between fifteen and twenty feet from the pin. It appeared that mine had run over the back. But just as I started to survey the rough, Jay raced onto the putting surface and peered into the cup.

"I was right," he announced, turning around to wave at me. "You knocked it in the hole. Wanna come get it out?"

I nodded, trying desperately to keep my emotions under control. Every part of my being wanted to jump and shout for joy. But a faint voice kept urging me to stay calm and collected like a true professional. As I strode across the green, I exhaled a long breath, then smiled and informed my playing partners that this was my first hole-in-one.

"You mean the first one in a tournament?" Rick asked.

"No," I replied. "The first one in my entire life, ever."

"Well, good for you. Congratulations."

After retrieving my ball from the cup, I shook hands all around, then walked off the back of the green and stood in the shade of an oak tree. It was impossible not to add up my score and marvel over what had just happened. I had started out par, birdie, birdie, hole-in-one. Four holes, four under par. That matched, and in a certain way even surpassed, Arnold Palmer's fabled start in the final round of the 1960 U.S. Open. Arnie had gotten to four under with a string of birdies. My run featured an ace.

I now faced a decision-making crisis that was uniquely different from any that had confronted me so far. Should I keep on playing? Or should I walk straight into the clubhouse? Although my revised aim had been merely to work on my game and try to keep my score down around 75, the stunning events on the first four holes had put me in a position to go after my original goal of shooting a 72 or better. But they had also insured that the holes ahead were certain to be less perfect than the four I had just completed.

"Go for it, you chickenshit," I whispered to myself at long last. "You wanted to feel the heat. Now you're in the kitchen. Let's see you cook."

"Okay, you got it, big guy," I heard myself whisper back. "Forget about the damn hole-in-one. It's just like you made a five or a six. It's over. Remember what Alison says, you gotta love all the holes just like all the other holes or they'll get jealous."

Despite such inspirational self-talk, my seminauseous stomach started to knot up with invisible golf balls. That, in turn, reminded me that I had yet another important decision to make. Should I stash my blessed Maxfli 1 in the bag for safekeeping? Or should I stick with the ball that had brought me so much luck so far? Although there were water hazards on twelve of the next fourteen

holes, I elected to keep playing the same ball, figuring that it preferred the dank of the cup to the chill of the drink. My cart mate
immediately made me second-guess my choice.

"Gee, you've been having a dream start," Dr. Jon noted, more
than a little gratuitously, while we drove across the access road to
the next tee. "Hope you remembered to put your hole-in-one ball
away."

"Sure did," I lied, squinting at him with an annoyed frown. "But
I'm still gonna be playing the same number."

When the foursome in front of us cleared out, I took two extra
practice swings and several deep breaths before I attempted to hit
my drive on number five, a 435-yard dogleg-left par four. The ritual
didn't help much. My archetypal hole-in-one hangover shot skidded
off the club face with a tinny clank and sliced all the way from the
left side of the fairway into the right rough. But the golf gods were
obviously smiling on me. I found my Maxfli sitting up just a few
yards short of a nasty tree root. My nerves started to settle down
after I drilled a two iron to the front apron. Then I chipped to five
feet and yanked my par putt off the left lip.

"Too bad," Dr. Jon muttered. "Your first bogey of the day."

Although I resented his remark, I realized that in a perverse
sort of way it was probably good to have made a bogey just to get
it out of my system. But enough was enough. Two bogeys in a row
would destroy all the momentum of my dream start. The par-three
sixth, a 185-yarder dead into the wind and over water, had the
potential to make or break the rest of the day.

After my three iron tee shot ballooned off to the far right corner
of the green about fifty feet from the back left pin, I found myself
facing the kind of teeth-rattler that had lockjawed the Shark at Augusta National on Sunday. I needed to rap my lag putt hard enough
to climb an undulating uphill slope that slanted sharply to the left
about twelve feet short of the cup, then pray that it didn't pick up
more speed and slip off the edge of the putting surface.

My stomach knotted up again when the Maxfli died a good five
feet below the cup, leaving me with a treacherous sidehiller to save
par. When I eased my par putt up the side of the hill and saw it
fall, I let loose the whoop that my playing partners had expected
to hear following my hole-in-one.

"Jesus H. Christ—I sure needed that one!"

"Nicely done." Rick Powers grinned. "Good recovery."

Compared to the first six holes, the rest of the front nine was almost like a massage for my overexcited soul. On the seventh, I threaded a three wood between the sand and water hazards and made my first routine par of the day. On the short par-five eighth, I reached the fringe of the green in two, chipped to three feet, and made the putt. On the ninth, I nearly birdied again from twenty-five feet.

Patrick Stavely was waiting beside the clubhouse with clipboard in hand to record our scores at the turn. When he asked how I stood, I told him that I was three under, forgetting that I had birdied number eight, because the hole seemed more like a par four.

"Hurt—three under," Patrick repeated. Then he looked up from his clipboard and grinned. "Congratulations, you're tied for the lead with Joe Gutterman."

"Hold on, that's not right," Jay Moore protested. "Hurt's not three under, he's four under. He had one bogey, three birdies, and a hole-in-one."

"No shit, a hole-in-one?" Patrick said, arching his eyebrows at me. "Well, let me congratulate you again on that, and congratulate you one more time. You're our new leader."

Given what had happened to Greg Norman the day before, I would have preferred to remain ignorant of my status in relation to the rest of the field. But Patrick's report did not send me into a tailspin. I did not expect to keep the lead, much less extend it. In fact, I really didn't think I had a chance of winning the tournament. All I wanted to do was shoot a good score, some kind of new personal best. And I knew the only way to do that was to keep loving all the holes ahead just like the holes behind me.

Even so, my heart started pounding louder and harder than all the nail guns in metroplitan Orlando when I stepped onto number-ten tee and almost hooked my three wood into the lake on the left. A passage from *On Golf* began racing through my mind. Paraphrasing J. H. Taylor, who had been one of the game's original Big Three along with Harry Vardon and Ted Ray, Bobby Jones had written that "the difference between the winner and the near-winner is the ability of the successful contestant to be ever on the lookout against himself. Never too certain of what the result may be, he plays not one shot carelessly or with overconfidence."

My definition of winning on this particular day was merely to hold it together long enough to par every hole on the back nine. Having just played my first and only really careless shot, I vowed to stay on the lookout against old you-know-who. Myself breathed an audible sigh of relief when I drained an eight-foot downhiller on the tenth green to save par. On the par-five eleventh, I chipped my third shot to within four feet to set up another bird. Then I jacked the putt, though not out of carelessness. I just misread the deceptively sharp break.

"Gee, too bad," Dr. Jon said when we got back in the golf cart. "That's the only short birdie putt you've missed today."

I simply shrugged, even though I felt like punching him in the mouth.

"Those things happen," I said with a forced smile.

The next three holes tested both my patience and my powers of concentration. After narrowly lipping out a pair of twenty-foot birdie putts on twelve and thirteen, I missed the green of the long par-four fourteenth with my three iron approach into the wind. My ball was sitting on the fringe a good forty feet above the flagstick, and it had to traverse another slick Augusta-style ridge protecting the cup. I gasped for air as my lag putt tumbled down the slope, then checked up on a spike mark five feet below the hole.

Seconds after I sunk my par saver, Patrick appeared on the cart path leading to the fifteenth tee. He had obviously come to update my score.

"For the moment, I'm still four under," I informed him, hastening to add, "But please don't tell me about anybody else. I don't want to know."

Patrick acquiesced to my request, but I could tell from the expression on his face that I was still the front-runner. Although I had never led a professional golf tournament, the position I was in now seemed like a reverse déjà vu of far less savory positions I'd been in before. I could par in and shoot a 68. But I felt almost exactly the same way as I had felt when I was on my way to shooting an 86. I just wanted the holes to go by and be over with as fast as possible, especially since my mind was chattering away nonstop.

"Shut up, mind," I whispered to myself. "Quit counting up your score."

"Can't shut up," my mind answered back. "There's nothing else for me to do but scheme and dream and calculate."

"Fine, be that way. But remember, if you think about just trying to par in, you're guaranteed not to do it."

I tried to silence my infernal inner dialogue by reviewing the short list of swing thoughts scribbled in my pocket notebook. On the par-three fifteenth, I reminded myself to "squeeze the beach ball" between my knees like Nick Faldo, and whacked a four iron to fifteen feet for an easy two-putt. On the sixteenth, I told myself to "watch the ground where the money is," another Alison-inspired admonition to keep my head down, and walked off with another par. The seventeenth was a 435-yarder with a landing area guarded by water on two sides. I focused on a "compact backswing" that helped me put my drive safely in the fairway and my approach shot in the middle of the green.

Now all that remained between me and the liquor cabinet in the clubhouse bar was the 434-yard eighteenth, but it could be a killer of a thirst quencher. My tee shot had to carry a lake that bordered the inside edge of the dogleg-left fairway; my approach had to avoid portions of the same lake on two sides of the green. I aimed well right and launched one of my best drives of the day, drawing the ball to the center of the short grass. After studying the pin sheet and pacing back from the nearest yardage marker, I figured that I had 179 to the flag. That was normally a smooth four iron for me, but the wind was swirling, so I decided to go with an easy three iron.

My beloved Maxfli rifled into the wind and bounded all the way over the green into the back bunker. When I saw the lie I'd caught, my heart started outhammering the nail guns again. The Maxfli was sitting on a downslope just inches in front of the rear lip of the bunker, and I could see the lake water shining ominously on the far side of the green behind the flagstick. I didn't dare think about what might happen if I bladed another sand wedge. Instead, I pretended that the rear lip was Dick Harmon holding a rake handle. Then I brought the club back with an extra sharp wrist break and hit down and through.

Watching my ball pop onto the eighteenth green was more thrilling than making the ace on number four. In addition to being able to follow the flight of the shot all the way, I knew that it resulted entirely from acquired skill rather than any lightning flash of good fortune. My incorrigible self was so intent on making certain that we broke 70 that I was almost persuaded to lag my ten-foot par putt and settle for a tap-in 69.

"Shut up, chickenshit," I whispered. "We're gonna try to make it for 68."

We did.

"Congratulations one more time," Patrick cheered when I reported to the scorer's table. "You won."

I had to stare at the scoreboard for a good sixty seconds just to confirm that it wasn't a dream. The total columns showed that Don McCart, a fifty-year-old European Senior Tour hopeful from Scotland, had taken second place with a two-under-par 70. Joe Gutterman, a curly-haired forty-one-year-old former college basketball player who had already won a handful of 40+ Tour tournaments, was tied for third at two over par. I could see that Joe had been two under coming into seventeen, where he had made an 8. I asked him what the hell had happened.

"I knew you were four under at the time, and I figured that I needed to birdie the last two holes to force a playoff," Joe reported. "I got too aggressive with my tee shot and dumped it into the hazard."

That was the first time any other pro golfer had ever felt threatened by a score I might shoot. But then, this was a day of incredible firsts for me. My first ever hole-in-one, my first sub-70 round in competition, and most important of all, my first pro tournament victory. I happily accepted two checks from Barfield. One was for the first-place prize of $600, an amount that happened to be exactly equal to what Sam Snead had won for his victory in the 1946 British Open. The second check was for taking a $60 skin with my ace on number four. But I would have been just as elated if Barfield had paid me a total of sixty cents. The money was secondary to the pride and joy of exceeding everyone's expectations, including my own. I was a winner, a bone fide champion.

When I got back to the Ramada Inn, I telephoned Alison to tell her what had happened and to thank her for the love-all-the-holes litany that had helped me win out. Then I called my brother Bill and just about everyone else who had encouraged me along the way—Eden Foster, Dick Harmon, Tom Jenkins, Eddie Pearce, Mike Thompson, Barry Hamilton, Jim Hays. That evening, I treated myself to a champagne dinner capped off by a shot of tequila for my birdies and my hole-in-one, and then two more shots for my saves.

Two days later, the 40+ Tour moved on to Deer Island, a course that had water hazards on seventeen holes, and I proved that my dream round at Heathrow wasn't just a fluke. I shot a four-over-par 76 the first day despite hitting three balls into the drink. In round two, I reached only eight greens in regulation, and still carded a hard-grinding 73 to finish fourth overall behind Jim Chancey, Joe Gutterman, and Mike Long. I also finished first in the contest for second-day money, and collected a check for $150 plus a $26.50 check for winning a skin. That boosted my total career earnings as a professional golfer to $1,030.

It seemed fair to assume that Greg Norman wasn't losing any sleep over the giant leaps I'd made at Heathrow and Deer Island following his collapse at the Masters. To the contrary, I'd read that he was enjoying an unprecedented outpouring of public sympathy and support as evidenced by some 45,000 faxes and letters he'd received from all over the globe. I'd also read that rather than undertaking the impossible task of answering each and every one, he was planning to say thank-you to all his newfound fans by buying full-page advertisements in various newspapers.

In the event, I was more than a little surprised when Alison called to tell me that a letter bearing the Shark's trademark red, blue, and green logo had just arrived in our Sag Harbor mailbox. I asked her to open it right away and read it to me over the phone. The letter was dated April 19, 1996, just five days after the final round of the Masters. The salutation was styled "Dear Harry," and the first line thanked me for sending along my *Sports Illustrated* article about Q School.

"If the book is in the same class," the Shark's letter continued, "I think you will do very well with it. Thank you for thinking of me. Yours sincerely, Greg Norman."

After Alison reread the letter one more time, she declared that the short and simple missive was proof positive that the Shark had a lot of love in his heart after all. She added that it also proved he was thoughtful and considerate, since he had taken the time to write me when he was being deluged with post-Masters fan mail. I told her that I agreed, and that I really, really loved her. Then I asked her to make sure to file the letter away in a secure place until my return.

As I packed my bags for an early-morning flight to Houston, I felt the same warm tingles that had overcome me the first time I had been addressed as "pro." My breakthrough pro tournament victory and the letter from Greg Norman were enough to make anyone consider my golfing comeback a success even if I had not qualified for the PGA Tour. But thanks to my brother, I was about to make my unfulfilled dream of playing head-to-head against some of the best golfers on the planet come true in a way that would have made our late father proud.

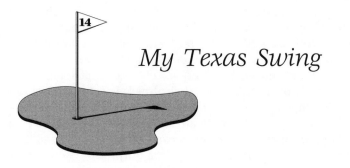

My Texas Swing

The old man's ghost blew into River Oaks Country Club on a breezy spring day so fresh and fine it had to have been heaven sent. Claude Harmon Sr.'s spirit was surely beaming like the Texas sun at the golfing royalty who had arrived to honor him in competition. There were princes and potentates from the PGA Tour and the Senior Tour such as Fred Couples, Davis Love III, Jay Haas, Mark Calcavecchia, Curtis Strange, Lanny Wadkins, Bobby Wadkins, Scott Verplank, Billy Ray Brown, Blaine McCallister, Brian Henninger, Tom Scherrer, John Schroeder, and on-and-off-course jester Peter Jacobsen.

Along with them had come the deans and deacons of the teaching profession, traveling from near and far. Jim McLean flew in from the Doral Golf Resort and Spa in Miami. Don Callahan made his pilgrimage from The Country Club in Brookline, Massachusetts. Paul Marchand represented the city's rival realm of hookers and slicers, Houston Country Club. And, of course, there were the old man's four almost equally famous sons, Butch of Lochinvar, Craig of Oak Hill, Billy of Newport, and host head pro Dick of ROCC.

There were also two newly beknighted first-time winners enlisted in the noble field. One was Tim Herron of Minnesota, a.k.a. "Lumpy," who had led wire-to-wire in capturing his first PGA Tour victory and $234,000 at the 1996 Honda Classic back in March. The other was Harry Hurt III of Houston and Sag Harbor, whose victory worth $600 at the 40+ Tour tournament at Heathrow Country Club had been reported to the golfing kingdom in the latest edition of *Golfweek*.

The grand banners, leather carry bags, and designer golf shirts emblazoned for the occasion bore the logo of the Claude Harmon Memorial Pro-Member-Guest. The tournament, held annually at River Oaks since 1990, was an eighteen-hole event with a shotgun start for the twenty-seven teams comprising the current field. The touring pros, who were all present or former students of the Harmons, ordinarily commanded five-figure daily appearance fees, but they had donated their time for free. Members paid entry fees of $1,500 per team, with proceeds going to the Harmon Foundation's junior golf program.

Normally closed on Monday, the practice range at ROCC fairly crackled with excitement as the visiting lords of the links went through their warm-up routines. The caddy corps was composed mostly of top-ranked area college players, while the gallery consisted of resident oil barons, industrialists, financiers, doctors, lawyers, and the like. They gathered in murmuring, goggle-eyed huddles beside the bag stands and behind the roped-off periphery to wonder at the way Couples wielded both driver and short irons with the same gracefully slow tempo, and to marvel at how Love lofted his long irons as easily as lob wedges.

As I warmed up beside my far more famous fellow pros, I asked myself the same question they were probably asking: Who the hell is that and what the hell is he doing here? The short answer was that I had been invited to play in the Claude Harmon Memorial by my younger brother, Bill, who was a full-fledged dues-paying member of River Oaks Country Club. His last-minute invitation had come on the heels of my victory at Heathrow, but he would've asked me to play with him win, lose, or draw, just because he was my brother and he was proud of me for attempting my middle-age crazy golfing comeback.

The real reason I was there, however, was the same reason my brother was a member of ROCC in the first place. We owed it all to Harry Hurt Jr. And although the elite tournament we were preparing to compete in officially memorialized the Harmon family patriarch, I intended to make my performance a tribute to our own father, whose ghost was everywhere as present as Claude Sr.'s.

Glancing back over my shoulder, I could see the putting green where the old man had taken me to try out my first set of cut-down clubs at age seven, and the tenth fairway where he had cheered me for hitting my drive beyond the cart path at age ten. Less fondly but no less vividly, I recalled the time he had accidentally clipped me above the eye with his sand wedge while attempting to show me how to hit a shot out of the left green-side bunker on number one. A small bucket of blood had gushed from my forehead as my father rushed me to the clubhouse to find Houston's most prominent heart surgeon, who diagnosed my seemingly mortal wound as a mere scratch.

I could still picture the smiling, somewhat awed expression on my father's face when he presented me with my first set of pro model woods to reward me for breaking 80 for the first time at the age of twelve. He had never beaten me in golf from that day forward, which is not to say that he didn't try. ("Damn it, Buzz, I've got to turn those hips," he would say, "so I can hit the long ball.") And while he desperately wanted me to become an oilman rather than a golf pro, he would get up before sunrise to chauffeur me to the sites of my junior golf tournaments. "This is just like logging a well," he would remind me. "It's dark, it's cold. And you never know if it's going to be a dry hole."

Fittingly, the team my brother had formed for the Claude Harmon Memorial was uniquely different from all the rest. The format called for each fivesome in the tournament to consist of one club pro, one touring pro, a member, and two amateur guests. Bill Hurt, who claimed a fifteen handicap, had recruited Jim Crane, an air freight entrepreneur with a two handicap at Lochinvar, as his amateur guest. He had also drawn a particularly appropriate club pro/ tour pro combination at the Calcutta on Sunday night. We were paired with Billy Harmon and 1995 Ryder Cup team member Jay Haas.

Both our team's pros were warming up in the slot next to mine on the practice tee, and I could already tell that playing with the two of them was going to be an invaluable learning experience. Six feet tall with moist brown eyes and a straightbacked casual gait, Jay Haas was forty-two years old, just twenty-five months younger than me, but he was still one of the most consistent ball strikers on the Tour. In fact, he had just capped off an impressive string of making over twenty consecutive PGA Tour tournament cuts in 1995 and 1996. Billy was the youngest, blondest, and most easy-going of the Harmon brothers. He was also unanimously acclaimed to be the best player of the four.

What set the Hurt-Harmon-Haas-Crane team apart, besides the two Bills and the three *H* names, however, was my special playing status. Although I was entered as my brother's guest, I was the only invitee who was going to be competing as a pro from the back tees. That necessarily meant our team would be disadvantaged in the low-net category since we'd be getting fewer total handicap strokes than the other twenty-six teams. But as my brother pointed out, it also meant that our old man's spirit could sit right beside Claude Sr.'s and elbow him with paternal pride as they gazed down on the proceedings from their clubhouse in the sky.

"You ready, Buzz?" Bill called to me shortly before eleven A.M. "We're going off number-one tee as soon as Dick and Lanny's group gets out of our way."

I nodded, chuckling at the way he had referred to the fivesome led by Dick Harmon and Lanny Wadkins as if they were just another bunch of duffers.

"We gotta take it nice and slow, bro," I said. "Remember, it's get set in the saddle like a rodeo cowboy, then uh-one-and-uh-two like Lawrence Welk."

Those were brotherly code words for the key elements in what I had dubbed my new and improved Texas swing. Exactly one week earlier, I had played in the Monday qualifier for the Shell Houston Open, the first leg on the PGA Tour's annual three-part "Texas swing," which also included the Byron Nelson Classic in Dallas and the Mastercard Colonial Invitational in Fort Worth. My hopes of qualifying for the Shell Houston Open had been dashed before I finished the front nine due to a series of inexplicable duck hooks with a recently purchased Great Big Bertha driver. Bobby Dylan once said, "There's no success like failure, and failure's no success at all." But my failure to qualify had led to some very successful readjustments, of which Bobby Jones would have approved.

Upon returning to the bag room at ROCC, I had discovered that the Great Big Bertha's swing weight was only C8, a heft more appropriate to a lady pro's golf clubs. Resident repairman Earvin "Magic" Wilson had immediately upweighted my new driver to D2 by attaching a few strips of lead tape to the back of the club head.

The reduction in my tempo and the concomitant increase in my distance off the tee were nothing short of amazing. On the 40+ Tour, I had rarely hit a drive more than 260 yards. All of a sudden, I started busting the ball an average of 285 yards, and often over 300 yards downwind.

While I was anxious to test my Texas swing under tournament pressure, I was somewhat more concerned about how Bill might hold up. With his curly hair and sharp facial features, my no-longer-so-little brother looked like a heavily muscled, slightly paunchy John McEnroe, but he acted like a Wayne Gretsky. At the age of forty-one, he still played hockey twice a week in a local club league whose teams featured several NHL veterans. I was forever urging him to make his golf swing emulate the smooth tempo of a tennis serve. But much like the comedy film character Happy Gilmore, he insisted on manhandling his clubs as if he had to nail a game-winning slap shot from the blue line before the buzzer sounded.

"Let's play good, guys," Billy Harmon said as he shook hands with Bill, Jay Haas, Jim Crane, and me beside the back markers on the first tee. "And let's have some fun even if we are going to be playing behind my brother all day."

The fun started as soon as we saw Dick Harmon and Lanny Wadkins waiting on the back slope of number-one green, and it was all at our expense. The opening hole at River Oaks happened to be a 364-yard dogleg-left par four. A forest of pines and oaks dripping with thick sashes of Spanish moss lined both flanks, and there were fairway bunkers on either side of the corner. Jay, Billy, and I hit three woods off the tee, and our balls came to rest in a neat little row just short of the sand pits.

After pacing back from a nearby sprinkler head, I figured on having about 129 to the pin. The wind seemed to be swirling, primarily in an unfavorable direction, so I tried to hit a smooth nine iron. I wound up dumping it in the front right green-side bunker, directly opposite the trap where my father had drawn blood from my forehead with his sand wedge over thirty years before. Billy, who was a couple of yards closer, tried to hit the same kind of shot and suffered the same result, plopping his ball next to mine in the front right bunker. Dick and Lanny howled with glee.

"What happened, little brother?" Dick shouted. "Somebody must have given you the wrong number."

Then he nudged Lanny in the ribs and gestured toward me. "Looks like both of them got the wrong number."

Thankfully, Jay and Jim Crane landed their balls on the green. I had a fried egg lie in the trap, and had to settle for a two-putt bogey. Billy Harmon had to accept a similar fate, while Bill Hurt chipped back and forth across the putting surface, wasting his handicap stroke on a double-bogey. Jay and Jim put nice rolls on their birdie putts, but when both of them lipped out another chorus of catcalls resounded from number-two tee.

"You guys might think about keeping it down to a dull roar," Billy Harmon suggested as his brother's fivesome started down the second fairway. "I understand there's a golf tournament out here today."

"Yeah, and if you're not careful," my brother interjected, "a hockey game might break out."

Dick choked down on his driver shaft, spread-eagled his legs, and began blaring out an imaginary play-by-play analysis like a TV sportscaster.

"We've got Bill Hurt on the breakaway. He's across the blue line. He shoots—he scores!"

Unfortunately, the hockey references seemed to inspire my brother to take a forechecking approach to the second hole, a 398-yard dogleg-right par four that was so tight that we almost had to walk it single file to stay clear of the tree branches. About 275 yards off the tee, there was a gape-mouthed bunker in the bailout area on the left and a stand of hundred-foot-tall pine trees blocking the shortcut on the inside corner. At that point, the fairway plunged abruptly downward toward a green protected by another battery of bunkers. The oval-shaped putting surface was pasted on a flattened ridge whose far sides sloped precariously toward Buffalo Bayou, and the pin was tucked back left.

Number two challenged all of us to adjust to the unusual complexities of the Claude Harmon Memorial's team format. According to the rules sheet, the team score on each hole was a combination of the best ball of the touring pro/club pro pair and the best ball of the other three members of the fivesome. There was both a low gross best ball category and a low net best ball category that allowed the amateurs on each team to utilize their handicaps. In effect, Billy and Jay merely had to look out for themselves and each other when it came to deciding who should play for a safe par and who should shoot for the pin to set up a birdie attempt. I had to look out for my brother, Jim, and myself.

After Jay and Billy laid up short of the left fairway bunker with three woods, I asked Bill and Jim if they felt confident about laying up to the same spot. They both said yes, so I whipped out my Great Big Bertha and cranked a drive down the left side that curved past the bunker and tumbled on down the hill. My Texas swing appeared to be holding up just fine. When we finally got to the ball, it measured 310 yards off the tee.

I was unable to shoot for the back left pin, however, because of what happened to my brother and Jim. Both hit near-perfect layups as promised. But rather than aiming their approach shots toward the middle of the green, according to proper team play protocol, Bill and Jim went for the pin. Both of their balls bounded over the green toward the bayou. Unnerved by their miscues, I tried to guide a wedge to the center of the putting surface and ended up thirty-five feet short of the hole.

Our old man's ghost must have been observing this unfolding predicament and decided to intervene with an unseen hand. That was about the only way to explain the fact that my brother's ball miraculously stopped on the slope behind the green just a few yards short of the jungle. Instead of being stymied, Bill had an unobstructed swing. He chipped to within fifteen feet, then two-putted for a bogey. Thanks to his handicap stroke, his gross score of 5 went down on our team card as a par four in the low net column.

Now it was my turn to falter. Since I was playing scratch, our best chance to win any money was by posting a good score in the low gross category. Like my brother, Jim had made a 5 on the hole, so it was up to me to keep the low gross column on our scorecard bogey-free by salvaging a par or a birdie. But our dad must have wearied after assisting Bill, figuring that his elder son could go it alone. I hit my thirty-five-foot approach putt less than two-thirds of the distance to the cup and missed the par saver.

"Sorry, bro," I muttered as we trudged off the green. "That was the stupidest fucking three-putt of my life."

My brother tried to console me, patting me on the shoulder.

"It's okay, Buzz. Remember, we're just supposed to be having fun out here."

Some fun, I thought to myself. So far, I had hit two fairways just like Jay Haas. But I had made two sloppy bogeys, and Jay had made two routine pars. I was two over after two holes. Jay was even. If I was learning any lessons from my PGA Tour partner, the content of the tutorial was nothing new. I was continuing to make the same kind of ridiculous and easily avoidable mistakes that had dissembled me in pro tournaments past.

I guess the old man's ghost decided to bequeath another timely break when we arrived on the tee of the par-three third hole. There was a two-group stackup in front of us. Dick and Lanny had not yet teed off; the fivesome ahead of them was still puttering about on the green. When our fivesome sat down on the teeside benches to cool off, Jay Haas, Billy Harmon, and I started talking about the subjects most pros talk about when they're killing time—other pros and themselves.

"The thing you've got to understand is that I'm the exact opposite of Butch," Billy was saying. "So is Craig, and so is Dick."

I shook my head, grinning.

"No way, Billy, old boy. It's just not humanly or scientifically possible. You can't all be the exact opposite of Butch. Not unless Claude Sr. just cloned Dick from Craig and then cloned you from Dick. And I don't think anybody'd discovered what DNA is all about way back then."

"We're all exact opposites, too, me and Craig and Dick," Billy insisted. "But we're still more like each other than we're like Butch."

"He's right," Jay interjected, scraping at the ground with his cleats. "I know all four of them. Billy's the only one that even had a chance of playing on the PGA Tour. When he decided he couldn't make it, he saw to it that I did."

Billy winked at him, chuckling.

"That's kind—and true."

Jay informed me that prior to meeting Billy he had learned everything he knew about golf from his uncle Bob Goalby, the 1968 Masters champion. After winning his share of junior golf and high school tournaments around his hometown of Belleville, Illinois, Jay had followed his Uncle Bob's urgings to attend Wake Forest University in the fall of 1972. Curtis Strange enrolled the following year, and their college team proceeded to win back-to-back NCAA championships in 1974 and 1975. In December of 1976, Jay had won his PGA Tour card on his first attempt at Q School.

"Billy started caddying for me in 1978," he recalled. "We were together on the Tour on and off for the next thirteen years. He became my eyes and ears. I'd say, 'Billy, give me something to get it in the hole here.' And then he'd do it, whatever it was, choosing the right club or thinking out the right strategy. At the time, he was more of a psychologist than a teacher. Then he got married, and I kind of lost my security blanket."

Over the past several years, however, Jay and Billy had forged a successful new student-teacher alliance. In 1995, Jay had racked up $822,259 in official PGA Tour earnings, ranking number sixteen on the money list, right behind Tom Lehman and Ernie Els. That boosted his career earnings to over $5.4 million. With what he'd banked already this year, he had become one of the top twenty-five lifetime money winners, just a few notches back of my buddies Bruce Lietzke and Ben Crenshaw. The only blemishes on 1995 had been losing the Ryder Cup matches under the captaincy of fellow Wake Forest alum Lanny Wadkins and, despite turning in top-ten finishes in the Masters, the U.S. Open, and the PGA, failing to win his first major championship.

"It's just my nature to play conservatively, maybe to a fault," Jay conceded. "I used to think I had the type of game that's suited for winning a U.S. Open, but I've always seemed to do a little better at the Masters. I was only one shot off the lead going into the final round last year. I'd still love to win one of the majors someday, but I won't consider myself a failure if I don't."

I told Jay that his admission reminded me of the almost identical words I'd heard from Lietzke at the Shell Houston Open a few days earlier. On the afternoon following round one, I'd met Bruce inside the clubhouse bar to talk about old times and the very different roads our lives had taken since we'd played junior golf against each other. Just as we had begun reminiscing, Crenshaw passed by on his way out of the locker room and sat down to join us.

"It was like we were all fifteen years old again," I recalled. "Ben and Bruce start talking about playing in the Texas State Junior Championship like it happened last week. I mentioned something about those old rubber mats they used to have on the tee boxes at Breckenridge Park in San Antonio, and Ben said he could still smell the sandwich stand out by number twelve. Then Bruce thanks Ben for skipping the 1968 Texas junior to play in this Jaycees tournament up north so he could win it one year for a change. Ben says, 'Aw, you woulda won it anyway.' And Bruce says, 'Like hell I would've. You were far and away the best golfer in Texas back then, no contest.'

"Well, sooner or later the subject of winning major championships comes up. Now, as we all know, Bruce Lietzke plays the lightest schedule of any of the top one hundred and twenty-five money winners on the PGA Tour. He only enters eighteen to twenty events a year because he likes being with his family, coaching Little League, and tinkering with all those muscle cars of his. He told me he owns five or six hot rods, including an '87 'Vette and a '68 Plymouth Road Runner. Anyway, Ben starts teasing him, saying that Bruce doesn't really care about the majors. And Bruce says to Ben. 'You know something, you're right.' And then he recounts this little anecdote about why that is."

Jay and Billy perked their ears as I told them that Bruce had claimed his style of goal setting was molded at the age of eight when he announced to his mother that he wanted to "play on the PGA Tour one day against Sam Snead and Gary Player." But unlike most other kids, who typically pretended that the three-footers they practiced on the putting green were to beat Jack Nicklaus or Arnold Palmer in the Masters, he had indulged in his own private brand of make-believe.

"When I was a kid my opponent was always this imaginary kid named 'Johnny,' " Bruce had confided. "Jack Nicklaus was my idol, but Johnny was the guy I had to beat. He wasn't Jack Nicklaus and he wasn't Johnny Miller. He was just Johnny. Every week, I'd pick up the newspaper and find out what city the Tour was playing in. Then I'd practice my shots around winning that tournament. If the pros were playing in, say, the Cleveland Open, I'd pretend that I had to make my three-footers to beat Johnny and win first place in the Cleveland Open. I won lots of Tour events playing against Johnny. But for some reason, I never played against Johnny to win a major championship."

I paused to light a Schimmelpennick, then finished off the saga of Bruce Lietzke and his imaginary childhood alter ego.

"Bruce says he quit competing against Johnny when he got to college, but the bottom line is still the same. He'd love to win a major, of course, particularly the PGA, so he could get a ten-year exemption. But he ain't gonna let not winning a major ruin his life.

He doesn't even enter the U.S. or British Opens anymore. And now he says he's planning to cut back his tournament schedule to only ten events per year until he's old enough to play on the Senior Tour."

Jay and Billy rolled their eyes with undisguised envy.

"Now I know where we went wrong," one of them said.

"Yeah, all this time we've been playing against Jack Nicklaus when what we should've been trying to do is beat Johnny."

a few minutes later, Dick and Lanny's group cleared off the third green, and it was time to get back in the saddle again. Jay offered to relinquish the honor of hitting first, gesturing for me to take his place.

"You lead us off on this one," he said. "Maybe it'll change our luck."

"Just make sure you stick it up there close," Billy added, "so your ball will be inside Johnny's."

I retreated to my own little world to debate club selection. The third tee gazed down on an enormous undulating green that sloped back toward it. The pin sheet showed the distance as 185 yards, with the flag crowded only eleven paces from the front edge, and the wind was following us. I didn't want to be too long because any downhill putt would be faster than Bruce Lietzke's hot rods; but I sure as hell didn't want to leave my tee shot in the front bunker and be staring a third straight bogey in the face.

My old man's spirit seemed to be whispering with the wind in my ear, "Hit the six iron." The Jay Haas side of me argued for a five iron, the ultraconservative play. I decided just this once to forsake my magic wand and listen to Daddy's advice; after all, this was his home course. My six iron shot flew toward the pin like a Grumman Hellcat fighter plane and landed at twelve o'clock high twelve feet above the hole. I took my time lining up the putt from both sides of the cup and both sides of the slope line. Then I drained it for our team's first birdie of the day.

"We havin' fun now, bro?" I asked, pumping my fist.

"Way to go, Buzz," my brother cheered.

"'I don't think Johnny can top that one," Billy Harmon said, chortling. "Let's see if we can start a run now."

Number four was not necessarily the most promising place to

try to bag our second bird. Once the best par-four on the course, the hole had been designed by the venerable Donald Ross as a 435-yard dogleg right that demanded a perfectly faded three wood off the tee and an accurate long or middle iron to a crowned green. Following the Joe Finger redesign in 1970, number four had become a 549-yard dogleg-right par five, and quite possibly the stinkiest hole on the course, often rewarding well-struck shots with crappy bounces and septic lies.

The only way to get home in two on the "new" number four was to place your tee shot in front of a fifteen-yard-wide chute that had been cut through the trees short of the corner. That was a sucker play, however, that could result in a bogey or worse if your three wood second shot failed to carry the fairway traps in front of the green or bounded right toward the bayou. The wise route was to follow a good drive with a high-arching five iron over the trees at the corner. Then you could have a standard 100-yard wedge for your third shot that might set up a makable putt.

With the rising wind pushing at my face, I made my smoothest Texas swing so far and drove the ball straight down the middle of the fairway a good ten yards past the chute. Jay had to whallop his best drive of the day just to get a couple of paces beyond me. Billy caught his tee shot flush on the screws but still couldn't touch either one of us.

"That's what you call a Wal-Mart," he joked. "There's enough room to put a superstore between my ball and yours."

As we climbed the upslope of the fairway, I saw a gaunt, pink-skinned figure emerge from the woods on the left. With his silken blond hair, hollowed eyesockets, and baggy windblown white slacks, he looked like a ghost. But I immediately recognized his swaying, big-stepping gait and his shrill voice echoing against the trees.

"Hah-ree bay-bee!"

It was John "Fat Cat" Walzel, the real-life Johnny I had competed against as a kid. When last I'd spoken to his older brother, I had been told that Johnny was battling HIV and on the verge of death.

"El Gato Gordo!" I shouted back. "Wonders never cease."

Johnny stopped in the middle of the fairway and bent over to inspect the markings on the two balls lying just beyond the chute.

"Oh, my God," he said, arching his brows in disbelief. "Is that your tee shot?"

"Yep."

"Isn't that Jay Haas's ball right next to it?"

I nodded.

"Hay-ree bay-bee!" he exclaimed again. "Give me five!"

I slapped his open palm, then hugged him with both arms.

"Where the hell have you been, Johnny? I must've called your home number half a dozen times since I got to Houston. I know I left at least three messages, but I got no call-backs. Guess you're dialing finger's broken."

"I've been kind of incommunicado the last few weeks," Johnny informed me. "As you can see, I ain't the old Fat Cat anymore. But it looks like we're on the road to recovery. We sure hope so, anyway."

From a nostalgic point of view, or any other one, the only thing that could have been better than my reunion with Crenshaw and Lietzke at the Shell Houston Open was having Johnny Walzel at my side in the Claude Harmon Memorial. I played the rest of number four and the five holes after that like a man inspired, matching Jay Haas shot for shot. But the real joy came from trading clichéd barbs with *"El Gato No Mas Gordo,"* as he called himself now, and from just seeing my boyhood friend alive and kicking up a storm of bullshit.

When someone in our fivesome complimented me for putting a "good roll" on my narrowly missed birdie putt at the fourth, Johnny and I countered in unison, "Yeah, but you can get good rolls at a bakery." After a perfectly shaped draw off the tee of the dogleg-left fifth hole, I hit a rather tentative pitching wedge twenty-five feet short of the pin. We looked at each other grinning, and simultaneously asked, "Does your husband play?" On the short sixth hole, I nailed a five iron at the pin but suffered a wicked kick that catapulted the ball over the green. When I finally sank an eight-footer for a scrambling 3, Johnny reminded me of Lee Trevino's truism: "There's two things that never go far—dogs who chase cars and pros who putt for pars."

On the par-four seventh and the par-five eighth, I pounded drives up with and a couple of paces past Jay's. My approach shots were also inside Jay's and outdid our ongoing speculation about whatever efforts Lietzke's imaginary friend Johnny might have made. Although I rimmed out my birdie putts on both holes despite bakery-quality rolls, the real-life Johnny was duly impressed with the power of my ball striking.

"You never had length off the tee like that, Hah-ree bay-bee."

"Owe it all to my new and improved Texas swing," I replied, "and about a buck-fifty of lead tape."

"Well, you ought to stock up," Johnny allowed. "I figure it's working out to about ten yards for every fifty cents worth of tape."

Ironically, my newfound length created a dilemma on the tee of the ninth hole, a 380-yard dogleg right with a gulley full of gunch and trees on the inside corner and a pond fronting the green. In a practice round two days earlier, when the hole was playing downwind, my drive had carried over the corner, taken two hard hops, and plopped into the water. Although the hole was now playing upwind, I decided to go with a three wood off the tee, only to watch in anguish as my ball stopped short of the corner in the shadow of a fifty-foot pine tree.

Moments later, I started to learn why Jay Haas was a bloody but unbowed survivor on the PGA Tour and why I still had light-years to travel before even coming close. The cut five iron I whalloped into the ninth green was in contention for being the shot of the day. It landed on the back left corner of the green, then skidded to within five feet of the pin. But Jay did me one better. Having pushed his drive into the gunch-filled gulley at the corner, he hit a recovery shot that made Seve Ballesteros look like a piker, threading his way through a three-foot gap between a privet hedge and some overhanging branches. I watched in awe as his ball cleared the pond and settled in the middle of the green.

Jay went on to make a two-putt four, finishing the front nine at even par. I had a chance to match his score by sinking my five-footer for birdie. But rather than trust my own instincts, I asked Billy and Jay to help me read the putt. Where I'd gauged it as a full ball outside the left lip, they both advised me to rap it at the left center. I missed the putt on the low side.

"Oh, Hah-ree bay-bee, that put the hurt on us." Johnny sighed, rolling his eyes at his own sophomoric pun. Then he announced, "I've got to make like Carl Lewis and run."

I gave him another long hug, promising to keep in closer touch. Then I told him he'd better be sure to keep himself healthy for my sake as well as for his.

"We all love you, and we can't do without you, *El Gato No Mas Gordo*."

"You're telling Noah about the flood," Johnny said, grinning as we bid each other good-bye. "Go get 'em on the back side."

*   *   *

On the way to number ten, I was greeted by more ghosts from the past, present, and future. An old girlfriend who had twice gotten married and divorced since our fling back in the late 1970s came out of the clubhouse wearing a pink-and-white dress tighter than number-two fairway. She kissed me on both cheeks, then offered me a sip of her daiquiri and said that I was looking more and more like the ABC News anchorman Peter Jennings these days. I told her she could give Diane Sawyer a run for the money.

"Already have," she replied with a cryptic smile.

Doc Harper caught up with us in the cart tunnel beneath the pro shop and asked after my ailing back. When I told him it wasn't like a two-by-four anymore, thanks partly to the stretching exercises he'd prescribed, my old girlfriend started giggling so hard she spilled half her daiquiri down the front of her dress.

Out in the sunshine on the other side of the tunnel, I saw a lawyer for one of Houston's biggest energy companies approaching us from the practice range. He had his suit coat draped over one arm and a copy of Butch Harmon's new book, *The Four Cornerstones of Winning Golf*, tucked under the other. He said he'd heard that I was going to write an article about his company for one of the nationally circulated business magazines.

I glanced over at my old girlfriend, who was still mopping daiquiri juice off her dress, then mimicked her earlier rejoinder.

"Already have," I fibbed, adding with a sly grin, "Read it and weep."

On the tenth tee, I gazed at the picture window of the golf shop as I took my practice waggles, reminding myself to get in the saddle and give it the old "uh-one-uh-two" tempo. The hole was a 540-yard dogleg-right par five, and I knew it presented a perfect opportunity to impress our eclectic gallery with a big drive. But I also knew I could get into some very deep doodoo if my Texas swing suddenly went south on me.

The seemingly effortless motion I put on that drive produced a whack that another old pal later claimed to have heard out on River Oaks Boulevard. My friends watched wordlessly as the ball soared 300 yards down the left side of the fairway. After they saw Jay Haas nod approvingly, then smack his own drive just to the left of mine, they gave both of us a round of applause. I responded by trying to imitate the kind of casual wave PGA Tour pros give on TV, and turned away from the gallery to watch Billy Harmon, Jim Crane, and my brother hit their tee shots.

"Someone just told me Davis Love got home on this hole with a five iron," Jay reported when we started down the fairway. "I figure he hits his five iron about one-ninety, so he must have moved his drive out there about three-fifty."

"That's incredible." I sighed. "Seems like Love and Couples and Tiger Woods are playing a different game than the rest of us."

Jay smiled, shaking his head and twirling his driver. I noticed for the first time that he was still using an old-fashioned persimmon-headed club rather than a high-tech titanium model like mine.

"A guy like Davis doesn't win every time," Jay said with a sigh, as if he were reading my mind. "We're not playing against them individually so much as we're playing against the course. Golf's not like tennis, where a guy can blow you away just by hitting great serves. There's distance and there's accuracy, and you need some of both. I tried switching to a metal driver several years ago, but it didn't seem to add much length, and I couldn't work the ball as well with it. The bottom line is that no matter how far you hit it or what kind of clubs you use, everybody's still got to get the ball in the same hole."

Jay quickly proved his point. We had hit almost identical drives, and both of us had approximately 240 yards to the tenth green. He cracked a nice-looking three wood that was sailing directly toward the back right pin until a gust of wind knocked it into the green-side bunker. I came off my three wood, and wound up short and right of the bunker.

I tried to get within birdie range by hitting a delicate flop shot, but my ball landed on the fringe and checked up fourteen feet below the hole. Jay calmly blasted his bunker shot to within three feet. I missed my putt, and he made his. When I checked on his official PGA Tour statistics after the round, I discovered that he was currently the leader in the sand saves category.

The next eight holes turned into a kind of slow-motion reenactment of the previous ten. I usually kept up with Jay off the tee, and occasionally outdrove him, but he kept outscoring me time after time. On the par-five fourteenth, he made another birdie from the green-side bunker while I had to scramble for par. On the par-four sixteenth, a gallery of anonymous golf fans gathered to observe our drives. I tried to put something extra on mine and pushed it into the right rough. Jay smoothed his drive right down the middle. He almost made another birdie there; I had to get up and down to save another par.

On number seventeen, a dogleg-left par four over water, we were greeted by the same gallery that had watched us tee off on number ten. I hit a near-perfect drive to the right edge of the fairway. Jay blew his through the short grass onto an oval of hardpan dirt surrounded by willow trees. I got a case of nerves and chunked my pitching wedge into the front bunker, transforming a potential birdie into an embarrassing bogey. Jay punched deftly off the hardpan and barely missed another bird.

When we reached the eighteenth tee, I suddenly realized that my obsession with comparing myself to Jay had caused me to ignore the overall spottiness of our team play. After contributing a couple of timely birdies on the front, Billy Harmon seemed to have put his game on automatic pilot, becoming a nonfactor on the back. Jim Crane had matched Jay's birdie on the fourteenth, contributing a net eagle with his handicap stroke. He had also birdied the seventeenth. Despite the fact that Jim was playing from the front tees, I felt a little jealous on learning that he was even par on the day, but I was also glad he was doing so much to help our team.

My brother, however, was not a happy camper, as I could tell from the McEnroe-like scowl that had clouded his formerly sunny face. Perhaps because of the double-edged pressure of having to play with pros and his own older brother, Bill had been forcing his hockey-style shots ever since the second hole. On a better-than-average day, he might have expected to shoot in the low 80s and contribute at least three or four net birdies with his fifteen handicap. On this horrific day, he had contributed only one net par to the team, and he needed to make a natural par on the last hole to shoot a 95.

As we trudged down the eighteenth fairway, I started muttering Mick Jagger's line, "You can't always get what you want, but if you try sometime, you just might find you get what you need." The Hurt-Harmon-Haas-Crane team got neither. My brother bogeyed the hole for a 96. The rest of us missed long birdie putts and had to settle for pars. Jay Haas wound up shooting a solid two-under-par 70, while I finished with a shaky two-over-par 74. Jim Crane came into the clubhouse with an impressive 72, and Billy Harmon came into the clubhouse to get a drink and tell everybody what a good time he had had playing with all of us.

Our team's low net total of 135 put us in a respectable position in the middle of the pack but kept us out of the money by six strokes. The winning fivesome, led by Bill Rogers and Bobby Wadkins, shot an astonishing eighteen-under-par 126. The low pro-pro team, to no one's surprise, was Fred Couples and Houston Country Club head pro Paul Marchand, a former assistant pro at ROCC, who combined for a seven-under-par best ball of 65. Their fivesome also tied for fourth in the low net category at 129.

at the posttournament dinner, I had to keep pinching myself to be sure that the people I was meeting and the words I was hearing weren't just part of some fantastical charade designed to fool me into believing that I really belonged among the pantheon of golfing greats in the room. Butch Harmon volunteered that he'd never heard of anyone making a comeback like mine after such a long layoff. As if to belie his sibling's rivalrous claims that he was the black sheep of the family, Butch then went out of his way to introduce me to John Schroeder, one of the early investors in Cobra Golf, who told me he was delighted that his company had supported my quest. Then Dick Harmon introduced me to Fred Couples, who congratulated me on winning my first pro tournament.

"You and I have something in common," Freddy said, twisting sideways to stretch his infamously bad back. "We've both won the same number of times this year—once."

I was too starstruck to point out that the money I had won in the 40+ Tour tournament at Heathrow was less than one-thousandth of the $630,000 he had won at the Players Championship.

"Let's go for two," I suggested meekly.

"From what I saw out there today, you've got a very good game," Jay Haas told me when I stopped by his table to say goodbye. "Are you going to spend the next five years getting ready for the Senior Tour?"

I shrugged, reminding him of the famous and probably apocryphal Harvey Penick story addressing that very question. According to the version I'd heard, a cocky low-handicapper had cornered Penick one day at Austin Country Club and informed the fabled teaching pro that he had made a great deal of money over the past twenty years and now intended to spend the next five years preparing for the Senior Tour.

"Well, you ought to meet that guy across the room then," Penick had reportedly replied. "He's also made a lot of money in the last twenty years, and he's also gonna spend the next five years getting ready for the Senior Tour. His name's Tom Kite."

I told Jay that competing against Tom Kite was actually the least of my worries.

"When I turn fifty years old, I'm gonna have to tee it up against Ben Crenshaw, Bruce Lietzke, and Johnny."

"I think you can beat Johnny right now," Jay returned, wishing me luck against the other two if I ever did decide to chase the Senior Tour.

The only damper on the Claude Harmon Memorial was the mood I found my brother in when we got back to his house. Bill looked like he wanted to kill himself. He kept wandering about the living room with a grimace on his face, clicking the TV channels from hockey game to hockey game and apologizing for his performance on the golf course. He reminded me of someone else I knew—his older brother.

"I let us down, Buzz," he lamented. "If I'd just played half decent, we would've won."

"You're too hard on yourself, bro," I said, repeating some all-too-familiar words. "Sure, you had a tough day. But Jay and Billy and I could've played a lot better, too. It wasn't just your fault that we didn't win. Besides, you're gonna get a chance to redeem yourself in the very near future."

I informed my brother that I was hereby making him an offer he could not refuse for fear of dishonoring our late father's golfing legacy. He had to play as my partner in the Sag Harbor Golf Club Member-Guest tournament at Barcelona Neck on June 1.

"The team of Hurt and Hurt is going to kick some butt. We can't let Toad have all the fun."

Bill muted the TV, staring down at the carpet for what seemed like an eternity. Then he looked up at me and smiled for the first time since the very first hole of the day.

"Okay, Buzz, you got it. I'll be there," he promised. "Bring on them frog legs."

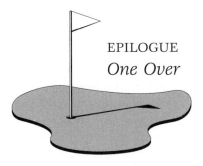

EPILOGUE
One Over

barcelona Neck welcomed me back with a flourish of green unlike any I'd ever seen there before. The Lyme tick–infested little
linksland looked like a whole new world. Thanks to the record
spring rains following the record winter snowfall, all the trees were
blooming with leaves and the same fairways that had been burned
out to a brown crisp the summer before were thick with grass. For
the first time in memory, it was actually possible to take a divot
with a sand wedge or short iron without digging up a pile of dust
or skulling your ball into the woods.

For the first time in history, it was also possible to hit your
driver off a tee without the risk of breaking your wrists. Alongside
the ball washers, there were now broom handles with nail points
on the ends for the purpose of excavating tee cavities in the all-
weather mats that served as the launch pads for each hole. All the
tee markers had been repainted, and there were separate sets for
the front and back nines and the ladies' tees. And the entire course
had been remeasured with a laser device to insure the accuracy of
the fairway yardage sticks.

In the meantime, the new board of directors of the Sag Harbor
Golf Club had succeeded in keeping the New York State bureauc-
racy at bay. Auditors from the Department of Environmental Con-

servation had examined the financial records compiled by the old board and had declared them a mess. But Marshall Garypie Jr., Jimmy Schiavoni, Paul Bailey, Bob Kiselak, and their fellow club officers had put the current books in order and had convinced the DEC that the appropriate operational changes had been made as requested.

Happily, the hard-core membership of the Sag Harbor Golf Club had not changed character. All the regulars were still their bawdy, irreverent selves. When I led my brother Bill out onto the porch on the morning of the member-guest tournament to introduce him to the gang, we were greeted by the traditional round of beery, ruffian cheers. Then Charlie Collins, the high-handicapper who looked like a white-haired Buddy Hackett, asked me to repeat his favorite punch line about the club's location.

"Say, Harry, tell us again what you said to those other touring pros when they asked you where the Sag Harbor Golf Club is."

"I said it's right between Maidstone and Shinnecock."

As laughter once again roiled the porch, I wondered if the fellows I had met during my quest for golfing fame and fortune would appreciate the humor or the uniqueness of these primeval surroundings. Ben Crenshaw, the avid historian of the game, probably would've gotten a kick out of the scene. Bruce Lietzke, who hailed from an East Texas oil refinery town, could have fit right in with or without his imaginary friend, Johnny. But I figured most of the others were too busy chasing their own dreams to care about the Sag Harbor Golf Club.

My former Q School classmate Shane Bertsch had signed on with Glenn Karp's management firm, but he been struggling just to make the cuts in the dozen PGA Tour events he'd gotten into so far. As of June 1, 1996, his total winnings were only $5,052, just a few grand more than my take on the 40+ Tour. By the end of the summer, he would rank a lowly two hundred fifteenth on the money list with $21,537. Mike Swartz, his former playing partner in the Final Stage of Q School, would be at one hundred fifty-sixth with $68,218. Allen Doyle, the forty-seven-year-old former amateur and Nike Tour phenomenon, would be right on the cusp in one hunderd thirty-fifth place with $94,259, about eighteen grand short of being among the top 125 money winners granted exemptions for the 1997 PGA Tour.

My no longer adversarial idol, Greg Norman, had also suffered a continuing run of bum luck. Although he remained at the top of the Sony World Rankings, he soon fell from first on the PGA Tour money list to number ten. One of the reasons for his drop in earnings would be attributable to a calamity in the Canon Greater Hartford Open, where the Shark voluntarily disqualified himself after discovering that some new balls he was tournament testing for Maxfli did not have the proper numerical markings.

Ironically, former Hooters Tour stars Jack O'Keefe and Brett Quigley, who failed to make the cut at Q School in December 1995, appeared to have good chances of qualifying for the PGA Tour in 1997. At summer's end, O'Keefe would rank at number seven on the Nike Tour money list with $89,507. Following a victory in the Philadelphia Classic, Quigley would jump from fourteenth to number six. Sadly, my fellow Texan and former Stage One classmate Eric Epperson would go in the opposite direction. In late March, he had ranked twenty-second on the Nike Tour list with $8,955. But by late August, he would no longer be among even the top forty money winners. Notah Begay III, the highly promising Native American and former Stanford star, would likewise be missing from the Nike rankings.

Hooters Tour veteran and bon vivant Spike McRoy would resuscitate another disappointingly mediocre season in the minors by winning a tournament at Ridgewood Lakes the week after Labor Day and rejoin the top ten money earners. Ty Armstrong, the perennial Q School repeater, would fare even better, winning over $44,000 to rank third on the Hooters list, but his performance would be overshadowed by Andrew Morse's record string of four straight victories. Javier Sanchez, the Mexican-born wonder, would qualify for his fourth U.S. Open but fail to make the cut at Oakland Hills—and fail to crack the top twenty-five on any of the minorleague circuits. I would not hear from my former Myrtle Beach playing partners Steve Jones and Jim Johnson or from my prediction-prone former caddy Johnny West.

My pals on the 40+ Tour would attempt to move on to greener pastures with varying degress of success. Eddie Pearce would get a sponsorship deal with Titleist to carry him through until he was old enough to play on the Senior Tour. In the interim, he would join Johnny Walzel's brother Bobby on the Golden Bear Tour of Florida formed by Jack Nicklaus, and tune up for another run at PGA Tour Qualifying School in the fall of 1996. Jim Hays would qualify for the U.S. Senior Open championship, appear briefly on the leaderboard in round one, then fail to make the cut. Jim Barfield and Loretta Sturgill would begin preparations for the 40+ Tour's first international tournament in Caso de Campo in October, where they would offer a record first prize of $10,000.

Most of the hotshot amateurs I'd encountered in the first competitive step of my quest way back in August 1995 would continue to tread the same fairways and water hazards as before. I would run across the names of Matthew Esposito and Matt Corrigan on the pairings sheets for U.S. Open and New York State Open qualifiers, but I would not see Bill Bartels listed among the qualifiers for the 1996 U.S. Amateur. The notable exception to every rule, of course, was Tiger Woods, who would win a record third straight U.S. Amateur in late August, then turn pro with endorsement contracts from Nike and Titleist reportedly worth over $40 million.

A couple of my fellow old fogeys would keep chasing their own dreams against all odds. Short game guru Tom Jenkins would make his first PGA Tour cut in many years at the Michelob Championship in Kingsmill, Virginia, but he would eventually finish in a tie for last place, winning only $2,313. The irrepressible Dean Sessions would keep trying, and keep failing, to make it through a Monday qualifier for a PGA Tour event.

Ivan Lendl, the former number-one-ranked tennis player in the world, would also continue his struggle to make a name for himself in pro golf. As in recent years past, he would spend most of his summer competing on the North Atlantic Tour. But he had already warned me that he intended to chase after my footsteps when he left a message on my answering machine following my victory at Heathrow Country Club back in April.

"I see from reading in the *Golfweek* newspaper that you have finally won a tournament," Ivan's recorded voice had said. "Congratulations, that's great. I understand that you made a hole-in-one, which is never bad. And I also see that you were four under after four holes and hung on. But I hope you win all you can in the next three and a half years on that tour, because then I'm coming in."

the question that perplexed me as my brother and I teed off in the Sag Harbor Golf Club member-guest tournament was whether or not I was coming in or going out again. Back in June 1995, I had set out on my golfing quest with the dual aims of becoming a better person and a better player. Alison had recently assured me that despite some occasional temperamental flare-ups, I had made some significant strides toward the first goal. My scores in the 40+ Tour tournaments at Heathrow and Deer Island suggested that I had made significant progress toward the second goal, as well.

Eden Foster had discussed my pro golfing future in some detail, and had outlined a two-phase competitive program. Phase two, which we also referred to as the "5.5 Year Plan," called for making a run at the Senior Tour shortly after I turned fifty years old in November 2001. Phase one was the "1.5 Year Plan," which called for making a second run at the PGA by repeating the same basic steps I had just completed with the goal of making it all the way through Q School in the fall of 1998. Between now and then, Eden had declared, it was time to take our teacher-pupil relationship to another level.

"You've graduated from being a rusty amateur to a real pro," he had told me. "I'll be happy to watch you hit balls and give you my critique whenever you like. But there aren't a whole lot more changes we can make. You've got to decide how you want to swing, then start to trust it and stick with it."

After hearing that, Bobby Jones's observation about the innate uncertainty of the game of golf had begun to ring truer than ever for me. I had hoped to identify the missing element I had lacked as a youth, the key ingredient for golfing success that players like Crenshaw and Lietzke had always seemed to possess. In fact, I had discovered that there was not just one essential element but many. You needed all of Allen Doyle's three *H*'s—your hands, your head, and your heart—working at full capacity. You needed an ostensibly contradictory mixture of strength and flexibility, confidence and humility, patience and boldness, sobriety of purpose and a sense of humor, as well as an unquechable capacity for wonder.

I reckoned that it was possible to summarize most if not all of these qualities in three basic rules for winnning at professional golf. Appropriately, all three rules were inspired not only by my own personal experience but by the contributuons of my wife, Eden, and everyone else who had encouraged me along the way. They were as follows:

Watch the Ground Where the Money Is: This was a revision of the old adage to keep your head down with a customized mnemonic twist suited especially to pros. It applied to every club in the bag from putter through driver, and it was a perfect dictum to supplant the mistaken notion that you were supposed to keep your head absolutely still at all times during the golf swing.

Swing the Club Like You're Making Love to Your Wife: This dictum also applied to every club in the bag, and it offered an unforgettable way to emphasize the importance of maintaining a proper tempo with every swing. As the 40+ Tour's inimitable teaching pro, Mike Thompson, might put it, "She wants it nice and slow . . . she wants you to make it last as long as possible." And as I would add, she also wants you to keep it smooth.

Love Every Hole Like All the Other Holes: If you don't, the other holes will get jealous. As my wife pointed out, this dictum was immensely superior to the old adage that you should take one hole at a time. Loving every hole in its turn gave all the *H*'s—hands, head, and heart—something active to do at all times. The corollary to this propostion was to love all your shots like all your other shots.

Although these rules sounded elegantly simple and romantic, I was already being reminded that golf demanded tough love—and a great deal of virtually nonstop practice. In the four weeks since the Claude Harmon Memorial down in Houston, I had been chained to my writing desk most of the time, and my golf game had steadily deteriorated. I had lost the tempo and timing of my Texas swing, and along with it, all the newfound length that my boyhood buddy Johnny Walzel had marveled at. My short game was so shoddy, I'd have been better off replacing my gap wedge with a garden hoe, and my putting stroke was once again afflicted with the Tom Watson yips.

I was also, for all intents and purposes, broke. It was hardly reasonable to expect to get by on $1,030, but those winnings had covered less than 3 percent of my golf-related expenses, which did not include such things as the mortgage on my house, food, and so forth. The subtotal of my out-of-pocket expenditures over the preceding twelve months was $37,931, and I had played only a limited schedule of fifteen events, many of them eighteen-holers. The categorical breakdown rounded to the nearest dollar was:

Golf lessons	$1,780
Physical trainer, Biolean	$1,983
Chiropractors, medical	$1,159

Greens fees	$2,725
Entry fees	$6,330
Clubs and equipment	$2,475
Caddies, carts	$1,150
Range balls	$1,310
Balls and gloves	$1,090
Golf clothes, shoes	$1,779
Travel, airfare, and lodging	$16,152

The real price I'd paid to pursue my golfing quest, however, was much higher than those figures indicated. In fact, my out-of-pocket expenses, or so-called hard costs, paled by comparison to the "soft" costs. I had to account for all the time I had spent re-learning golf, practicing golf, playing golf, thinking about golf, reading about golf, arranging golfing itineraries, filling out golf tournament entry forms, and traveling from golf tournament to golf tournament when I could have been otherwise gainfully engaged in a conventional business enterprise. If I applied only a modest charge of $20 per hour, the total cost of my quest was well over $100,000.

All of a sudden, I realized that Alison's admonition to "watch the ground where the money is" had a painful new meaning. My finances had effectively been driven into the ground, and my head was down in the dumps about it. Chasing the pro golf circuit was as expensive as supporting a drug addiction, and similar in form and substance. I didn't want to keep fighting a time-consuming, money-losing battle that threatened to rob my soul and murder my self-esteem if I did not come close to achieving my competitive goals.

n̄ot surprisingly, my preoccupations only compounded the difficulties of leading the team of Hurt and Hurt to victory in the member-guest. I could not decide whether it was for better or for worse that we were paired with Jack Somers and his son, Kevin, who had something of an off-day themselves. My brother kept struggling to control his hockey-style swing, only to find himself once again hacking back and forth across the fairways from rough lies to even rougher lies. I kept grousing at Jack the Rat to keep his mouth shut every time I missed another birdie putt.

But our late father was evidently watching over his golfing

prodigals. Bill finally contributed to our team score on the very last
hole of the day by making a scrambling par save at the eighteenth.
That enabled us to win the low gross team title by two strokes with
an even-par 70. I won the individual low gross with a one-over 71.
Toad's team had a best ball score in the middle 70s and never posed
a serious threat.

"How come you didn't play that good last year?" Toad chided
me at the posttournament beer fest, evidently forgetting that our
team had been two under in 1995. "I'll tell you why. It's because
you're nothin' but a goddamn polywog. Every morning from now
on, you ought to get up and look in the mirror and say to yourself,
'I ain't nothin' but a goddamn polywog.' "

Although such mindless babble attested to the fact that Toad
was still the club's number-one ball buster, I could tell by his tone
of voice that something was really bothering him, something other
than failing to win the Sag Harbor Golf Club member-guest. I eventually learned from one of our fellow members that Toad's girlfriend, Sandy, had been diagnosed with breast cancer. She now
faced a harrowing summer of surgeries and chemotherapies. I
pulled Toad aside and offered to do anything I could to help.

"There's not much any of us can do except hope that the doctors do a good job," he replied. "We've got her hooked up with the
Montefiore Hospital in New York, which is supposed to be one of
the best places there is for treating this kind of cancer. Sandy
doesn't want anybody to give her special attention or go around
feeling sorry for her. She just wants to go on living her life as
normally as possible."

Toad paused to take a sip of beer, then added, "I just hope I'm
half the man I think I am, because I really do love her and she
really does need me to stand by her now."

At first, hearing the bad news about Sandy and seeing the way
it had affected Toad made all my agonizing over whether or not to
keep playing golf seem pretty petty. But the more I thought about
it, the more I realized that my problems were not so trivial. I was
facing yet another midlife crisis that was of neither greater nor
lesser importance in the grand scheme of the universe than anyone
else's. The only difference between Sandy and me was that her
choices appeared to be limited and mine appeared to be wide open.
Sooner or later, both of us would have to tee off on the ultimate
Final Round.

"Buzz, it's strictly up to you," my brother reminded me when
I asked for his advice. "If you enjoy playing golf, keep playing. If

it's not any fun and you don't get any satisfaction out of it, then quit. Life's too short to play a game you don't really want to be playing."

Just as I was about to tell Bill to stick that kind of advice in a place where the sun didn't shine, he offered to share something about our late father's passing that he had been keeping to himself. When Dad had taken terminally ill, I had been working in Los Angeles, and my flight back to Houston had gotten in approximately sixty seconds after he died. But my brother, who had been at his bedside throughout the ordeal, told me that he had tried to keep the old man conscious by asking him a series of simple questions.

"Do you know what day it is, Daddy?"

"No."

"Do you know what year it is?"

"No."

"Do you know what hospital you're in?"

"No."

"Do you what your doctor's name is?"

"No."

Finally, Bill had asked a question that our father could answer. It concerned an experience he could not forget even while losing the battle against Parkinson's disease on his dying day.

"Daddy, do you know what you shot when you won the pro-am at Seminole?"

The old man had needed only a split second to reply.

"One over."

As Bill and I climbed into the Jeep to drive home, I took a long look around Barcelona Neck, gazing at the newly luxuriant greenery, the birds and the deer flitting about the forests, the freshly painted tee markers glistening in the sun, the blue-collar golf nuts boozing away on the clubhouse porch.

Our father's last words seemed to echo over the linksland with unspoken implications for his sons' futures. I presumed my brother would keep playing both golf and hockey until he was too old to draw a club back and too weak to stand on his skates. There was no longer any question about whether or not I would keep playing golf. I had finished the day just as our father had ended his life— one over.

I knew now that I had to come back another day to see if I could get to even par or better.

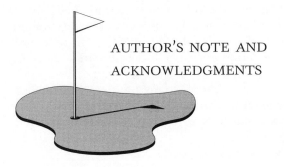

AUTHOR'S NOTE AND
ACKNOWLEDGMENTS

This book is a work of nonfiction. All the events described actually took place. All the people depicted are real with the following exceptions: the characters Artie and Buck in chapter 1 are composites based on various members of and visitors to the Sag Harbor Golf Club; the characters C. Barkley Davis II and Bill Weeds in chapter 4 are pseudonyms for real people about whom certain minor identifying details have been changed. The author kept a daily journal and compiled files containing more than one hundred interviews upon which the dialogue recounted in the book is based; in certain instances, conversations have been paraphrased or shifted slightly in time sequence to maintain narrative continuity.

The author takes full responsibility for any flaws or errors in the book, and wishes to emphasize that the editorial views expressed by the narrator are entirely his own. With those caveats, he would like to offer thanks for the encouragement, assistance, and moral support he has received from numerous individuals and golf facilities in writing this book. They include:

Alexander Auersperg, Paul Babcock, Bill Bartels, the William Becker family, Clay Brittain, John H. Brown, William Broyles Jr., Cliff Calvert, Joe Ciafolo, Cobra Golf, Theodore B. Conklin III, Gregory Curtis, Tad Dixon, Matthew Esposito, Robert Farrell, Russell Frankel, Eugene Goldberg, Marc Grossberg, Charlie Grubb, Al and Margaret Guerrina, Jim Gund, Hampton Golf, Dr. Dana Harper, Ward Haynes, Barbara Hearst, Jim Herre, Hooters Corporation, Thomas Hill, Dana Hurt, Bob Hyde, Joseph Ialacci, Ralph and Ala Isham, Doc Jardin, Alison Jenks, Robert Trent Jones Golf Club, Glenn Karp, Rik Kirkland, The Maidstone Club, Lee Moore, National Golf Links of America, Noyac Golf and Country Club, Ray Odierna, Dan Okrent, Paul Parash, Mark Parash, Dr. Will Parker, George Plimpton, Poxabogue Golf Course, River Oaks Country Club, Jimmy Roberts, Vincent Rom, Tim Rosaforte, Stan Rumbaugh, Arthur Schoen, Ed Shank, Shinnecock Hills Golf Club, Lee B. Stone, Stonebridge Ranch Country Club, Dorrance Smith, Nancy F. Smith, Mr. and Mrs. Richard W. Smith, Patrick Staveley, Loretta Sturgill, Michael M. Thomas, Jim Vincent, Kevin Wade, John Walzel, Johnny West, Earvin "Magic" Wilson, and E. Parker Yutzler Jr.

The author would like to express his thanks to the following professional golfers who gave generously of their time in interviews, on the practice tee, and/or out on the golf course: Wally Adams, Shane Bertsch, Notah Begay III, Jackson Bradley, Ren Budde, Jim Chancey, Ben Crenshaw, Allen Doyle, Gary Emmons, Eric Epperson, Charlie Gibson, Jay Haas, Butch Harmon, Craig Harmon, Billy Harmon, Jim Hays, Bob Joyce, Gary Koch, Ivan Lendl, Bruce Lietzke, Mike Long, Spike McRoy, Greg Norman, Rick Powers, Tony Sessa, Dean Sessions, Bob Walzel, and Dan Wilkins.

The author owes a boundless gratitude to certain professionals whose teaching and counseling contributed enormously to the improvement of his golf game and mental attitudes, most especially: Eden Foster, Dick Harmon, Tom Jenkins, Eddie Pearce, Jim Barfield, Mike Thompson, Barry Hamilton, Dr. Bob Rotella, and the late Jay Moore, whose invaluable friendship will be dearly missed. The author is likewise indebted to all the members of the Sag Harbor Golf Club, including but not limited to the following: Jim Schiavoni, Tom Sabloski, Billy Boeklin, Paul Bailey, Val Miller, Jack Somers, Frank Libert, Lenny Rodriguez, Whitey King, and the late Charlie Collins.

Finally, the author would like to thank Sloan Harris, his agent at International Creative Management; Lou Aronica and Stephen S. Power of Avon Books; Melanie Hauser, his erstwhile fellow writer and obliging research assistant; his friend Bart Richardson; his brother William R. Hurt; and his wife, Alison Becker Hurt, without whom this book would not have been possible.